Engaging Indonesia

Critical Dialogues on Culture and Society

Engaging Indonesia brings together current debates in social and cultural studies relating to the study of Indonesia, with the aim of giving voice to both leading and emerging Indonesianists. Critical and interdisciplinary, the books in the series contribute to knowledge formation by addressing pressing issues facing the country–cultural, social, and political–from contemporary and historical perspectives. Works may include research-based monographs, edited volumes, handbooks, and translations of both recent, and seminal/historical works. The series is particularly welcoming of topics relating to issues of urban and environmental change, to questions of identity and place, to problems of governance and conflicts, to the politics of representation, language, and performances, and to the global and postcolonial contexts in which these are addressed. Special consideration is given to studies that cover underrepresented regions and marginalized voices, as well as those that seek to recover lost archives, uncounted political events, or forgotten historical figures. Relevant to students and scholars from a broad range of disciplines in the humanities and social sciences with a particular interest in researching Indonesia, the series champions intellectual engagement with the archipelago's rapidly changing landscape - from within, and beyond.

Trina Fizzanty · Ikbal Maulana
Editors

The Digitalization of Indonesian Small and Medium Enterprises

Human Capital, Inclusivity and Platform Capitalism

Springer

Editors
Trina Fizzanty
National Research and Innovation Agency (BRIN)
Jakarta, Indonesia

Ikbal Maulana
National Research and Innovation Agency (BRIN)
Jakarta, Indonesia

ISSN 2948-2909 ISSN 2948-2917 (electronic)
Engaging Indonesia
ISBN 978-981-97-0028-8 ISBN 978-981-97-0029-5 (eBook)
https://doi.org/10.1007/978-981-97-0029-5

This Springer imprint is published by the registered company Springer Nature Singapore Pte Ltd.
The registered company address is: 152 Beach Road, #21-01/04 Gateway East, Singapore 189721, Singapore

This book is dedicated to Prof. Dr. Erman Aminullah, our mentor, for his constructive ideas and endless support to our research and publication

Preface

The book is the result of research conducted from 2020 to 2021, a period coinciding with the COVID-19 pandemic. During this challenging time, businesses, including micro, small, and medium enterprises (MSMEs), grappled with restrictions on social mobility and the closure of markets and malls. Nevertheless, the research highlights the remarkable adaptability of MSMEs as they navigated through the pandemic and embraced digital technology, which collectively accelerated the digitalization of MSMEs.

This book would not have been possible without the completion of the research. During the pandemic, the invaluable support of numerous individuals and organizations was instrumental in carrying out this study. We extend our heartfelt appreciation for the financial assistance provided by The Indonesia Endowment Funds for Education (LPDP), a unit under the Ministry of Finance of the Republic of Indonesia. This research was conducted under National Priority Research Program for the Development of Indonesia's Digital Economy No. 199/E1/PRN/2020. The idea to embark on research in this emerging field with a multidisciplinary team was proposed by Prof. Dr. Tri Nuke Pudji Astuti, the former Deputy of Social Sciences and Humanities (IPSK) at the Indonesian Institute of Sciences (LIPI). The research was facilitated and supported by Dr. Agus Eko Nugroho, who was the head of the Research Center for Economics-LIPI at the time and now holds the position as the Chairman of Research Organization of Government Governance, Economy and Society Welfare (OR TPEKM) at the National Research and Innovation Agency (BRIN). This research would not have achieved its current level of quality without the guidance of Prof. Erman Aminullah, our mentor, whose profound insights have significantly shaped this book. We extend our gratitude to the sources, including Micro, Small, and Medium Enterprises, government entities, and universities. Academics from the University of Andalas, the University of Gajah Mada, and GICI Business School generously shared their expertise in researching MSME business and entrepreneurship. They also facilitated our access to local MSME networks, which greatly facilitated this research. Central government officials from the Coordinating Ministry for Economic Affairs and the Ministry of Cooperatives and SMEs, Republic of Indonesia, along with the Ministry of Communication and Information, have generously provided their insights, aiding our understanding of central government policies concerning the digital transformation of MSMEs. Furthermore, government officials from the provinces of West Sumatra, West Java, and DI Yogyakarta have contributed valuable information about local-level policies and programs.

The research has produced both a technical report and a journal article. However, it was Prof. Dr. Ahmad Najib Burhani, the Chairman of Research Organization of Social Sciences and Humanities (OR IPSH) at the National Research and Innovation Agency (BRIN), who suggested and motivated us that we compile and publish our research work as a book. He played a pivotal role in facilitating the publication process, collaborating with Springer and RMPI BRIN. As the editors of this book, we extend our heartfelt appreciation to our fellow contributors, who are part of the same research team, for their unwavering commitment and collaborative efforts.

Jakarta, Indonesia

Trina Fizzanty
Ikbal Maulana

Contents

Editors and Contributors

About the Editors

Trina Fizzanty is Head of the Research Center for Education at Indonesia's National Research and Innovation Agency (BRIN) in Jakarta. She was the former Director of Research Center for the Development of Science and Technology, Indonesian Institute of Sciences (LIPI). She was the principal investigator for the research project "The Development of Digital Economy Ecosystem of SMEs in Indonesia" (2020–2021). She holds Ph.D. degree from The University of Queensland, Australia in Integrative System. Her research area is on management of innovation and R&D. She has published her research in international journals and books. She worked collaboratively with other scholars on several international research projects and also works as a reviewer for international journals and she was on the Editorial Board of LIPI Press. Her current publication is "Interactive Components of Digital MSMEs Ecosystem for Inclusive Digital Economy in Indonesia" in Journal of The Knowledge Economy, November 2022.

Ikbal Maulana is a researcher at the Research Center of Society and Culture, National Research and Innovation Agency (BRIN). He has a master's degree in computer engineering and worked as a programmer and system analyst before becoming a researcher and pursuing a Ph.D. degree in philosophy. His current research interests concern the impact of information technology on society and democracy, philosophy of technology, and social epistemology. His relevant publications in line with the book's topic include chapters titled "Big Brothers Are Seducing You: Consumerism, Surveillance, and the Agency of Consumers," "The Cultural and Institutional Barrier of Knowledge Exchanges in the Development of Open Source Software," and "Challenges of Developing Countries in Imitating Technological Progress." All three chapters are solely authored by the author.

Contributors

Luthfina Ariyani National Research and Innovation Agency, Jakarta, Indonesia

Nyimas Latifah Letty Aziz National Research and Innovation Agency, Jakarta, Indonesia

Aisah Putri Budiatri National Research and Innovation Agency, Jakarta, Indonesia

Trina Fizzanty National Research and Innovation Agency, Jakarta Selatan, Indonesia

Ikbal Maulana Research Center for Society and Culture, National Research and Innovation Agency (BRIN), Jakarta, Indonesia

Nawawi Research Center for Population, National Research and Innovation Agency (BRIN), Jakarta, Indonesia

Nika Pranata National Research and Innovation Agency, Jakarta, Indonesia

Ikval Suardi National Research and Innovation Agency, Jakarta, Indonesia

Joko Suryanto National Research and Innovation Agency, Jakarta, Indonesia

Adityo Wicaksono National Research and Innovation Agency, Jakarta, Indonesia

Abbreviations

AFTECH	Indonesian Fintech Association
AI	Artificial Intelligence
AOSD	ASEAN Online Sale Day
APBN	Indonesia Government State Budget
ASEAN	Association of Southeast Asian Nations
ASN	State Civil Servants
B2B	Business-to-Business
B2C	Business-to-Customer
Bappenas	National Development Planning Agency
BJB	West Java Bank
BPS	Central Agency of Statistics
BUMN	State-Owned Enterprises
COD	Cash on Delivery
CRM	Customer Relationship Management
DBE	Digital Business Ecosystems
DEA	The Digital Enterpreneurship Academy
Digitalfin	Digital Financial Inclusion
DIY	Daerah Istimewa Yogyakarta (Special Region of Yogyakarta Province)
DKI	Daerah Khusus Ibukota
DPIIT	Department of Industry Promotion and Domestic Trade
E-commerce	Electronic Commerce
EDI	Electronic Data Exchange
EE	Enterpreneurial Ecosystem
FGD	Focus Group Discussion
GDP	Gross Domestic Product
GPFI	Global Partnership for Financial Inclusion
ICT	Information and Communication Technology
IMF	International Monetary Fund
IoT	Internet of Things
IPO	Initial Public Offering

ISEI	Association of Indonesian Economic Scholars
IT	Information Technology
ITE	Electronic Information and Transaction
Jercovid	Jogja Economic Resilience for COVID-19
Kadin	Indonesian Chamber of Commerce and Industry
KUR	People's Business Credit
LIPI	Indonesian Institute of Sciences
LMS	Learning Management System
MBS-EC	Minangkabau Business School—Entrepreneurship Center
MoU	Memorandum of Understanding
MSMEs	Micro, Small, and Medium Enterprises
NFTs	Non-Fungible Tokens
NIK	National Identity Number
OECD	The Organization for Economic Cooperation and Development
OJK	Financial Services Authority (OJK)
P2P	Peer to Peer
Peradi	Indonesian Advocates Association
PMSE	Trading Through Electronic System
POS	Point of Sale
PPE	Personal Protective Equipment
PSBB	Large-Scale Social Restriction
R&D	Research and Development
RPJMN	National Medium-Term Development Plan
Setkab	Sekretaris Kabinet (The Cabinet Secretary)
SiBakul	Business Actor Development Information System
SMERU	An independent institution for research and policy studies
SMEs	Small Medium Enterprises
TDAP	Trade Development Authority of Pakistan
TFP	Total Factor Productivity
UMK	Micro and Small Enterprises
UPI	Unified Payment Interface

Chapter 1
Introduction

Trina Fizzanty and Ikbal Maulana

1.1 Background

The digital revolution has changed the way business is done. Today we are witnessing the advancement of digital technology, a society increasingly connected through the internet, the development of artificial intelligence (AI), the Internet of Things (IoT), and other emerging technologies found in agriculture, manufacturing, logistics, marketing, finance, and other sectors of the economy. The digitalization of business is enabling the generation of data at every stage of the business process, the analysis of data to evaluate performance, and increased connectivity or integration within and between organizations. This digitalization is fostering an increasingly open and integrated economic system that is connected to a vast network of local, national, and even global economic actors.

Every business monitors its operations by leveraging data and tracking metrics such as sales volume and inventory turnover. While manual methods exist, an increasing number of businesses are opting to digitize their data, allowing for efficient computer processing. Digitization involves converting analog information into a digital format, which computers can store, process, and transmit (Jason Bloomberg in Forbes, 2018). On the other hand, digitalization entails integrating digital technology into various aspects of social life, thus restructuring communication and media infrastructures (Jason Bloomberg in Forbes, 2018). Consequently, MSMEs may undergo digitalization without the necessity of digitizing their data and, as such, embrace technological advancements in their overall business operations. Many

T. Fizzanty (✉) · I. Maulana
National Research and Innovation Agency, Jakarta, Indonesia
e-mail: trin003@brin.go.id

I. Maulana
e-mail: ikba002@brin.go.id

T. Fizzanty and I. Maulana (eds.), *The Digitalization of Indonesian Small and Medium Enterprises*, Engaging Indonesia, https://doi.org/10.1007/978-981-97-0029-5_1

MSMEs utilize digital platforms to promote and sell their products without digitalizing their business operations, namely, digitizing their operational data and integrating their business and production systems. Even their transaction data are only stored in the platform's database and not integrated into their system, which is either manual or lacking altogether.

Today people, businesses, devices, data, and processes are making billions of connections, leading to the growth and expansion of the digital economy (Deloitte, nd). To take advantage of the digital economy, businesses and consumers need to have access to, and the ability to leverage, digital technologies. Achieving this necessitates a shift in policies to address technological and capability constraints faced by economic actors. Every action taken on a digital platform, including interactions and transactions within digital business platforms, generates data, which can be collected and analyzed by those who have access to the system, that is, the platform companies. This data analysis aims to enhance transparency in platform usage, and those who possess these data can leverage it to intervene in the platform to their own advantage. Besides that, digital platform businesses benefit from network effects, which means that they become more valuable as more people use them. Moreover, the competition among network companies tends to be characterized by "the winners take all", and, hence, the digital ecosystem may ultimately be dominated by a single platform (Shapiro & Varian, 1999).

The advent of the digital economy has opened up new opportunities for MSMEs to overcome traditional barriers and access to global markets. Digital technologies have provided MSMEs with cost-effective tools and platforms to increase operational efficiency, reach a larger customer base, and improve competitiveness. The proliferation of smartphones, high-speed internet connections, and the rise of e-commerce platforms have revolutionized the way MSMEs operate and interact with their stakeholders. Digital platforms enable seamless integration of the processes of MSMEs and those of other business actors, such as digital payment companies and shipping companies. Meanwhile, digital technology also enables automated production in MSMEs. However, some issues remain regarding the facilitation of inclusive economies and the generation of business opportunities for entrepreneurs in rural areas, those less educated, and female entrepreneurs. While there has been extensive research on the digitalization of MSMEs, there is limited research on the MSME digital ecosystem (Aminullah et al., 2022). The primary objective of this book is to explore the digital transformation of MSMEs as interconnected processes within an ecosystem. This implies that the transformation does not solely take place within MSMEs but involves inter-organizational processes as well.

The Indonesian economy, like most economies in other countries, is dominated by the micro- and small economy. MSMEs form the backbone of the Indonesian economy with 65.4 million enterprises or 99.9% of the total enterprises in Indonesia. These MSMEs also contribute to 97% of the labor force, 60.3% of GDP, and 14.4% of Indonesia's exports (ASEAN Investment Report, 2022). The Indonesian government supports the digital economy as a source of economic growth, incentivizes digital startups and MSMEs to embrace digitalization, and provides policies to support the emerging sector.

Amid the COVID-19 pandemic from 2020 to 2021, digitalization became essential for business survival. Several economic surveys in Indonesia demonstrated the advantages of using digital platforms such as Central Bureau of Statistic (BPS), Indonesian Institute of Sciences (LIPI), The SMERU Research Institute, and others for MSMEs to survive during the pandemic. In the post-pandemic era, with the removal of physical restrictions and businesses operating normally as before, digitalization continues to thrive. Indonesia's digital economy contributes to 40% of the total digital economy in Association of South East Asian Nations (ASEAN) countries. The digital sector is expected to grow and reach 400 billion US$ in 2030 in ASEAN. Indonesia has already been a home to 13 unicorns, i.e., start-up companies with a valuation of more than US$1 billion.

Indonesia, a vast archipelago comprising over 17,000 islands, faces ongoing disparities in access to information technology infrastructure, giving rise to a lingering digital divide. While technology has become more user-friendly, the widespread deployment of these technologies throughout the country remains a formidable task. Consequently, achieving inclusive development of the digital economy presents a complex challenge.

The digitalization of MSMEs can serve a dual purpose: enhancing connectivity through the use of social media and e-commerce platforms and automating various aspects of business and production processes, whether partially or comprehensively. Automation can be a costly endeavor, requiring businesses to invest in all the necessary technology themselves. By contrast, improving connectivity can be carried out through digital platforms. Even micro-business owners with basic smartphones can leverage social media platforms for marketing, customer interactions, and engagement in transactions with buyers from anywhere through e-commerce platforms. However, digitalization can be implemented across a spectrum of innovativeness, necessitating varying levels of knowledge and entrepreneurial acumen, which in turn result in different levels of competitiveness. While merely participating in the digital economy is accessible to any MSME with local internet access, becoming a competitive player in the digital ecosystem requires MSMEs to overcome various challenges, including technological, financial, and entrepreneurial obstacles. In Indonesia, national and global digital platforms such as Tokopedia, Lazada, and Shopee have been instrumental in facilitating the adoption of e-commerce by MSMEs. The COVID-19 pandemic further accelerated the digital transformation of MSMEs, and this transformation continues beyond the pandemic. While platform companies have a vested interest in encouraging users to increase their platform utilization, ultimately it is up to MSMEs to capitalize on these platforms and enhance their competitiveness within the digital ecosystem. Digital platforms are a type of digital ecosystem, in which various actors with different roles (coordinating, being complementary, or competing) are interconnected digitally to create a certain value. The digital ecosystem will be extensively discussed in Chap. 6.

Digital ecosystems are networks of heterogeneous entities, comprising buyers, organizations, and technological elements, which facilitate the interactions and transactions and safeguard the security of the interactions and transactions against possible fraud. To participate and flourish in the digital ecosystem, MSMEs need to have human resources with technological capabilities and the ability to implement sociotechnical adaptations and innovations (Aminullah et al., 2022). However, as argued in Chap. 3, this is the main problem faced by MSMEs; acquiring digital talents or upgrading their own skills is often too expensive for them. Hence, they require government support to overcome the various barriers to enter the digital ecosystem, ranging from providing technologies to financial support. Besides the platform companies, supporting companies, which ease the transactions, are also necessary for the success of the ecosystem. The availability of integrated digital payment and delivery systems will ease the transactions between MSMEs and their customers (Fizzanty et al., 2021).

1.2 MSMEs Digitalization, Human Capital, Inclusivity, and Platform Capitalism

In the context of the digitalization of MSMEs, human capital becomes a crucial factor, which determines the success and sustainability of these companies. Digital skills and capabilities are critical for MSMEs to effectively take advantage of digital technologies. However, many MSMEs face the challenges of acquiring and developing the necessary human capital to cope with the complexity of the digital age. In addition, digital social networking through e-commerce or social commerce has forced MSMEs as producers or intermediaries to actively respond to, and serve, consumer demands in a timely manner. As a result, MSMEs need to hire individuals for specific tasks to serve consumers. Other issues, such as the digital divide, limited access to quality education and training, and the need to upskill and retrain are significant barriers for MSMEs on their path to digital transformation.

Fostering inclusivity in the digitalization of MSMEs is imperative. While digital technologies present vast opportunities, they also carry the potential to magnify existing disparities. It is vital to guarantee that every MSME, irrespective of its size, location, or industry, enjoys equitable access to digital tools, resources, and prospects. Inclusive digitalization entails dismantling obstacles like cost, digital literacy, and connectivity, while fostering an enabling environment where MSMEs from diverse backgrounds can prosper in the digital economy.

An e-commerce platform functions similarly to a conventional market, where buyers and sellers exchange goods and services. Nevertheless, there are fundamental distinctions. In a platform, participants do not engage directly; instead, the platform acts as an intermediary, facilitating exchanges on their behalf. To ensure trust in these exchanges, platforms establish participation rules and provide infrastructure, including communication networks, verification procedures, and exchange processing capabilities (Reuver et al., 2018). Platforms achieve this by monitoring or surveilling participants' actions on the platform and making all activities transparent. While this transparency fosters trust, it also grants the platform substantial influence over participants due to its access to their behavioral data and the ability to shape the rules of interactions and transactions. This, in turn, raises concerns about platform capitalism or surveillance capitalism that unfairly exploits the low bargaining position of its users or the transparency of users' online behavior (Maulana, 2019; Vallas, 2019; Zuboff, 2015). Hence, comprehending the interactions between MSMEs and digital platforms is essential for developing policies and strategies that foster equitable competition, safeguard workers' rights, and ensure sustainable growth.

Some MSMEs are now also using digital technologies in the production process. Aminullah et al. (2022) reported problems with global competition, relocation of jobs, and importation of raw materials. Digitalization can have two conflicting effects on businesses: it can enable the development and implementation of efficient and innovative products and processes, and yet it can also lead to a reduction in the number of human resources through partial- or full-process automation, potentially requiring fewer people to perform tasks that previously demanded a larger workforce. Automation can also yield standardized products by enabling identical machinery used anywhere to produce the same standardized goods, thus, potentially erasing local uniqueness. This book will explore the essence and repercussions of digitalization on Indonesian MSMEs, along with their strategies for overcoming challenges and harnessing the expected opportunities digitalization presents. Framed within the context of the digital business ecosystem, it will also delve into the roles of other entities such as the government, platform companies, and supporting organizations.

1.3 Objectives, Approach, and Methods of the Book

This book seeks to understand the digital transformation of MSMEs within the framework of platform capitalism and digital ecosystem. While platform capitalism provides opportunities and challenges due to the possession of user data by platform companies, digital ecosystems broaden the views to consider various factors, from the role of the government to the role of supporting companies and the availability of digital talents. The chapters in this book address topics such as the status of the digitalization of Indonesian MSMEs, digital talent in Indonesian MSMEs, digital financing for MSMEs, the position of MSMEs in the discourse of platform capitalism, the dynamics of digital ecosystem of MSMEs, and governance in the digitalization of MSMEs. By exploring these key topics, this book aims to contribute to existing knowledge and understanding of MSMEs digitalization while offering practical recommendations for policymakers, entrepreneurs, researchers, and other stakeholders involved in promoting MSMEs growth and sustainability in the digital age.

The book contains research findings on the digital ecosystem of MSMEs in Indonesia in 2021 (Fizzanty et al, 2021). This research combines quantitative analytical methods (surveys) and qualitative methods (case studies, focus group discussions (FGDs), field observation workshops, and seminars) with integrated data triangulation processes at the national and local levels, as well as text analysis of business news reports. This approach enables a more comprehensive understanding of the digital transformation processes for MSMEs to identify critical points for improving the MSMEs ecosystem to enable the transition to digitally-based enterprises.

At the national level, an online survey of 601 MSMEs was conducted to explore and understand the current digitalization status of MSMEs and to identify ecosystem components that may influence the digital transformation process (Fizzanty et al, 2021). In other words, this national survey was conducted to understand the adoption of digital businesses/technologies among MSMEs that have already adopted them. Then, a digitalization survey was conducted at the regional level, both online and offline (face-to-face), using a non-probability sampling method to select MSMEs samples from three provinces in Indonesia: West Java Province, Yogyakarta Special Region Province, and West Sumatra Province, with a total of 300 respondents.

To gain a deeper understanding of the behaviors and characteristics of MSMEs in the three provinces studied, a qualitative approach was used, including case studies through interviews and site visits to selected MSMEs, both those that have implemented digitalization in their business operations and those that have not. Eight case studies were selected for the West Sumatra Province, and six case studies each for the West Java and Yogyakarta Special Region Provinces. Most of the selected case studies focused on the food, fashion, and handicraft sectors, which represent most of the characteristics of the MSMEs surveyed at the national level.

Focus group discussions were also conducted in the three selected provinces, with the participation of spokespersons from the cooperative and MSME agencies in each region. These activities aimed to obtain a comprehensive overview of the development, characteristics, and performance of MSMEs in each province, as well as to understand the programs and strategic policies implemented by local governments. In addition, field observation workshops and seminars were conducted in the selected sample provinces with the participation of stakeholders, such as government officials, entrepreneurs, MSMEs professionals, and academics. The goal was to link the findings from the field research with the implemented policies and programs to ensure the successful digital transformation of MSMEs in the future.

The authors also used current references and data to update the status of MSMEs digitalization in Indonesia and added references on digitalization issues of MSMEs in other countries to enable comparisons. One paper used text analytics from online news to present current issues of digitalization in MSMEs. With all these methods, we hope that readers will appreciate that the book is still relevant in the post-pandemic era.

1.4 Structure of This Book

Excluding the Introduction and Epilogue, this book comprises seven chapters, which explore various facets influencing the digital transformation of MSMEs in Indonesia.

The **second chapter** focuses on "Digitalization of Indonesian MSMEs: Innovation Challenges and Opportunities". It is argued that the digital economy provides a new source of economic growth through the extensive use of digital business networks and data and, thus, promotes business efficiency. What about the context of MSMEs in Indonesia? Using data from the Indonesian Digitalization Survey and updated data on the digitalization status of Indonesian MSMEs, Trina Fizzanty concludes that Indonesia's digital economy is growing and competitive in the region. Some challenges to digitalization in Indonesia remain, such as the Information and Communication Technology (ICT) infrastructure gap, digital literacy, data privacy, and other issues. Meanwhile, the emergence of digital startups offering e-commerce platforms facilitated the transformation of MSMEs into digital enterprises. Their contribution to economic inclusion, productivity, and innovation needs to be reviewed. The COVID-19 pandemic affected the performance of MSMEs in terms of revenue and profit, especially those that were not connected to the digital network. Therefore, the conversion of MSMEs to the digital economy maintained and secured the market for MSMEs during and after the COVID-19 pandemic. Most MSMEs connected through social media and market platforms, and only a small percentage of MSMEs use digital technologies to support business management and production. As in other countries, the majority of MSMEs have no access to, or limited support from, research and development. As a result, digitalization has little impact on MSME innovation and productivity, which Sollow calls the "productivity paradox". In the end, the author concludes that digital platforms are necessary for MSMEs to take advantage of the market, but that they are not sufficient to improve MSMEs productivity and innovation without research and development (R&D) and business and manufacturing support.

In the **third chapter**, titled "Unlocking Digital Talent in Indonesia's MSMEs: Issues and Challenges", Nawawi highlights that the digital capacity of MSME human resources is critical to supporting the digital economy and digital transformation of Indonesia's MSMEs. In addition, he recommends that efforts to engage more MSME entrepreneurs in the digital economy are linked to the need to develop digital talent and entrepreneurship among MSMEs stakeholders, particularly through the digitalization of product marketing via digital platforms and marketplaces. However, the author identifies at least three major challenges in developing digital talent among MSMEs in Indonesia, which can be classified into three categories, namely levels of MSME digitalization, digital literacy, and structural capital. In other words, the author argues that MSMEs do not know what capacities are needed to support their digital capabilities. As for MSMEs' digital literacy level, only 9.32% of MSMEs use digital technology to operate the business, and only a small proportion of MSMEs, 2.66%, use digital technology to support the entire digital economic process, from ordering raw materials to product design, production, and marketing. The lack of digital literacy and low educational levels of business owners is one of the difficulties in the efforts to improve the digital capabilities of MSME stakeholders in Indonesia, which are part of the challenges related to the level of digital literacy. The structural capital challenge relates to the ability to access and use the Internet for productive activities and innovation adoption. The Indonesian government made it easier for MSMEs to access education and training in digital literacy. Based on the MSMEs survey (Fizzanty et al, 2021), it was found that the digital skills in Indonesian MSMEs are mainly in the area of digital marketing and limited in the area of digital business and production capabilities of MSMEs. To ensure the effectiveness of the digitalization program for MSMEs, the author proposes to consider four categories of MSME talent capacity as evaluation criteria developed based on two parameters: the age of the entrepreneur and his/her digital literacy to show readiness to adopt digital technology. The first category is young, talented MSME entrepreneurs with high digital literacy. Second, conventional entrepreneurs with sufficient digital skills. Third, entrepreneurs who need more equipment and digital literacy. Fourth, older entrepreneurs who are not familiar with digital technology.

The fourth chapter, titled "Digital Finance for MSMEs: Issues, Challenges, and Keys to Promote Inclusive Growth" addresses the topics of digital finance for MSMEs, challenges in this area, and strategies for promoting inclusive growth. Nika Pranata, Ikval Suardi, and Joko Suryanto discuss the issue of fintech adoption and financial inclusion. Digital transformation of MSMEs requires funding that can be invested in digital technology and the digital transformation process. The problem is that MSMEs often do not know how to access funding sources and what technologies to invest in, and frequently do not meet financial institutions' requirement. This is indicated by the Financial Services Authority report, where Indonesia's financial literacy is reported at 49.8% (in 2022), even though financial inclusion is already at 85.1%. In the first section, this paper reviews the role of government institutions and various programs to support MSMEs funding, which are spread across 18 ministries. To encourage more effective and efficient program funding, the government plans to consolidate MSMEs funding from these many ministries and integrate funding policies for MSMEs from various bank and non-bank sources. Through the omnibus law (Job Creation Law), the government also provides funding facilities and fiscal incentives. The COVID-19 pandemic encouraged MSMEs digital transformation policies and access to digital financing (fintech) in Indonesia. Fintech, including digital payments, digital banking, peer-to-peer lending, and crowdfunding, continues to grow in Indonesia. The presence of financial technology or fintech plays a key role in accelerating financial access for Indonesian MSMEs, which opens up MSMEs' role in digital platforms. A number of issues and challenges in the transformation of digital financing are reviewed next, namely: (i) proper policy support in accessing digital finance; and (ii) availability of supporting infrastructure for digital financial service systems and facilities. In the next section, this paper presents the results of research on MSMEs in Indonesia when the COVID-19 pandemic occurred in 2020. A survey of 601 MSMEs showed that: (i) MSME funding sources were partly from bank loans, then family loans, and then cooperatives, while funding sources from fintech were only 23.1%; (ii) the COVID-19 pandemic encouraged MSMEs to enter digital platforms and fintech, the digital payments form the largest share of digital platforms (OVO, Gopay, and others). One of the important roles of fintech is to increase the proportion of consumers in the banking sector. The presence of fintech through online lending platforms has become an alternative for MSMEs to obtain capital, leading to easier processes despite higher interest rates. The number of MSMEs accessing online lending continues to increase after the recovery period of the COVID-19 pandemic. Also relevant is the use of emerging technology by fintech to study the characteristics of prospective borrowers. In the final section, the author uses examples from several countries to demonstrate lessons learned in digital financial inclusion, namely China, India, and Pakistan. The development of fintech in these three countries continues to increase, and it is inseparable from technological advances. China and India have developed cutting-edge technology to encourage digital financial inclusion, such as AI, big data, etc. The need for digital financial inclusion and sustainable growth of MSMEs has led to the rapid development of digital technology. This technological development is also supported by regulations that support digital financial inclusion, such as the need for credit for MSMEs in an efficient and safer manner. In the final section, the author proposes several recommendations to encourage increased access of MSMEs to digital finance services, including: (i) the promotion of cooperatives in providing digital financial services, due to their wide network support to MSMEs, through fiscal and non-fiscal incentives, credit insurance, and management training for cooperatives; (ii) the encouragement of accelerated access to IDXCoop collaboration; (iii) the acceleration of the completion of the MSME financing roadmap; (iv) the establishment of a trust fund for financing and development of MSMEs; and (v) the supervision of the implementation of the Omnibus Law related to MSME financing.

The **fifth chapter** deals with "The Position of MSMEs in the Discourse of Platform Capitalism". It begins by examining how social media platforms, by enhancing social interaction and broadening social networks, have opened up business opportunities ranging from marketing to economic transactions. However, as social media platforms were not originally designed for conducting business, there are inherent risks when engaging with strangers. Occasional news reports highlight online shopping fraud occurring on social media platforms like Facebook or Instagram. E-commerce platforms are designed to prevent fraud as well as offer consumers the convenience of easily finding desired goods and services. Furthermore, they streamline transactions by incorporating online payment systems and ensuring the smooth shipment of goods through seamless integration with delivery service companies. These platforms act as intermediaries and data aggregators, necessitating efficient and comprehensive user data collection and analysis to effectively fulfill their role as intermediaries. Ultimately, digital platform companies gain a crucial advantage by understanding the behavior of producers, merchants, and consumers, therefore allowing them to shape the rules of the digital platform game, a form of exploitation according to the author. In Indonesia, a number of e-commerce platforms are actively competing to serve users, including businesses and consumers, thus contributing significantly to the digital transformation of MSMEs. However, the primary objectives of these platform companies revolve around increasing user counts and transaction volumes, with less regard for the source of goods, be they imported or locally produced. While platform capitalism in Indonesia enhances connectivity, particularly between MSMEs and consumers, it also presents a potential threat to domestic production sectors, as it becomes easier for competitive imported products to enter the local market.

The **sixth chapter** focuses on the regional aspects of the MSMEs digital ecosystem. Adityo Wicaksono and Lutfina Ariyani chose the title "The Dynamics of Economy in the Regional Digital Ecosystem of MSMEs". The authors highlight the dynamics of the digital economy in Indonesia before and after the COVID-19 pandemic and examine three key ecosystem views, namely the business ecosystem, the entrepreneurial ecosystem, and the digital ecosystem, which provide an essential framework for understanding the dynamics of digital transformation. The authors apply the digital ecosystem to present the actors involved in digital transformation in the three regions of Indonesia as case studies and the challenges they faced during the COVID-19 pandemic. Some hurdles faced by MSMEs were a broken supply chain, financial and limited capabilities, and adoption of the digital business model. The authors raise the phenomenon of the dynamics of MSMEs' responses to the development of digital technology, especially e-commerce. The use of e-commerce platforms by MSMEs had begun to gain popularity before COVID-19 and increased rapidly with the emergence of the COVID-19 pandemic. The digital platform was developed by digital industry novices in Indonesia and other countries and experienced a boom when the COVID-19 pandemic broke out. This context encouraged more and more businessmen to enter either as manufacturers or resellers. This led to increasingly fierce competition between businesspeople who are members of the digital platform. How does the digital ecosystem actually emerge and function? This chapter provides a systematic overview of the three forms of ecosystems: Enterprise, Entrepreneurship, and Digital Ecosystems. In each of these ecosystems, there are actors and their respective roles, which interact and constantly adapt. Understanding the digital ecosystem and how it operates at the macro level provides the basis for examining the digital ecosystem of MSMEs in the three Indonesian provinces, which are the focus of this study: MSMEs in West Sumatra, West Java, and Yogyakarta. The authors show that some MSMEs became role models for other enterprises in the ecosystems, and that other MSMEs took on coordinating roles for joint marketing, collaborating with academia and government to improve product quality. MSMEs also play a role as distributors or resellers of digital platforms, whose function is to provide product information to consumers while providing feedback to manufacturers on product quality. The third type of MSMEs are followers or passives, which are usually micro-enterprises or households, which do not yet have digital skills. The role of these MSMEs determines how value creation can be created or sustained. This study identified supporting actors in the digital ecosystem, e.g., to support the digital ecosystem, such as associations, universities, distributors, and other actors. The authors then compare the challenges faced by MSMEs before the pandemic, in the early stages of the pandemic, and during the pandemic. Some of the challenges they faced during the pandemic were: a disorganized supply chain, limited financial capital and access to skills, and the need for business model adaptation. Prior to the pandemic, there were few central government agencies and well-known e-commerce companies that actively engaged in the digital ecosystem and became the dominant players, prompting several MSMEs and large retailers to participate in the ecosystem. During the pandemic, the central government became less important and was replaced by local governments, which were aware of the situation of MSMEs in their regions. In the beginning, the central government and prominent e-commerce were dominant in the development of the regional digital ecosystem. In the later phase of the pandemic, local governments became more dominant than the central government in supporting MSMEs' digital transformation. Prominent e-commerce platforms consistently acted as dominant players, sustaining the ecosystem by providing their services. MSME champions emerged during this transition, becoming role models to attract other MSMEs to enter the digital ecosystem. The authors successfully illustrate the dynamics of the digital ecosystem before, in the early stages and during the COVID-19 pandemic. In the early stage of the COVID-19 pandemic, there were some challenges, such as a disorganized supply chain, MSME financial constraints, limited access and capabilities, and the need for business model adjustments. In the end, the authors conclude that the digital ecosystem of MSMEs in the regions changed dynamically in the period before, during, and after the COVID-19 pandemic. The ecosystem became crowded and less organized during the early phase of the pandemic to survive this unexpected event. The more crowded the digital ecosystem was, the more competition there was among MSMEs, thus forcing them to return to offline mode, which reduced the number of players in the ecosystem.

The **seventh chapter** focuses on the governance of the digitalization of MSME in Indonesia. Nyimas Latifah Letty Azis and Aisah Putri Budiarti discuss "The Role of Government in Facilitating Digital Economy for MSMEs". This chapter delves into the government's pivotal role in supporting MSMEs, particularly in promoting digitalization for their sustained growth. It discusses challenges, government policies at various levels, and incorporates insights from field studies in three Indonesian provinces: West Java, West Sumatra, and Yogyakarta. This chapter highlights how the digitalization of MSMEs in the three provinces gained strength through collaborations between local governments and private digital platforms. However, despite the government's commitment to digitalizing MSMEs, the programs have not achieved their full potential due to three primary issues: uneven access to government programs for business actors, lack of integration of national MSME data, and suboptimal coordination between central and regional governments regarding MSME digitalization efforts. Consequently, it is imperative for the governments to establish comprehensive plans and improved coordination mechanisms to address these challenges effectively.

The lessons drawn from Indonesia's experience with the digitalization of MSMEs will be summarized in the Epilogue, which concludes the book. Additionally, it will provide insights into future research directions and policy recommendations.

References

Aminullah, E., Fizzanty, T., & Nawawi, N. et al. (2022). Interactive components of digital MSMEs ecosystem for inclusive digital economy in Indonesia. *Journal of Knowledge Economy.*

de Reuver, M., Sørensen, C., & Basole, R. C. (2018). The digital platform: A research agenda. *Journal of Information Technology, 33*(2), 124–135. https://doi.org/10.1057/s41265-016-0033-3

Fizzanty,T., Aminullah, E., Nawawi, Maulana, I., Suryanto, J. Aziz, N.L.., Pranata, N., Budiatri, A.P., Suardi, I., Ariyani, L., and A. Wicaksono (2021) Pengembangan Ekosistem Ekonomi Digital UKM Indonesia. Prioritas Riset Nasional Pengembangan Ekonomi Digital Indonesia Tahun 2020. Laporan Akhir Kegiatan (No. 199/E1/PRN/2020) Organisasi Riset Ilmu Pengetahuan Sosial Humaniora. Badan Riset dan Inovasi Nasional (Indonesia).

Maulana, I. (2019). Big brothers are seducing you: Consumerism, surveillance, and the agency of consumers. In O. Ozgen (Ed.), *Handbook of research on consumption, media, and popular culture in the global age*. IGI Global.

Shapiro, C., & Varian, H. R. (1999). *Information rules: A strategic guide to the network economy*. Harvard Business School Press.

Vallas, S. P. (2019). Platform capitalism: What's at stake for workers? *New Labor Forum, 28*(1), 48–59. https://doi.org/10.1177/1095796018817059

Zuboff, S. (2015). Big other: Surveillance capitalism and the prospects of an information civilization. *Journal of Information Technology*, 30(1), 75–89.

Trina Fizzanty is Head of the Research Center for Education at National Research and Innovation Agency (BRIN), Indonesia. She was the former Director of Research Center for Science and Technology Development, Indonesian Institute of Sciences (LIPI). Her research area is on management of innovation and R&D. She was the principal investigator for the research project "The Development of Digital Economy Ecosystem of SMEs in Indonesia" (2020-2021). She holds PhD degree from The University of Queensland, Australia in Integrative System. She has published her research in international journal and books. She worked collaboratively with other scholars in several international research projects and also works as a reviewer for international journals and she was as the Editorial Board of LIPI Press. Her current publication in international journal with a title "Interactive Components of Digital MSMEs Ecosystem for Inclusive Digital Economy in Indonesia" in Journal of The Knowledge Economy, November 2022.

Ikbal Maulana is a researcher at the Research Center for Society and Culture, National Research and Innovation Agency (BRIN), Indonesia. He has master degree in computer engineering and worked as programmer and system analyst before becoming a researcher and pursuing PhD degree in philosophy. His current research interests concern the impact of information technology on society and democracy, philosophy of technology, and social epistemology. His relevant publications in line with the book's topic include chapters titled "Big Brothers Are Seducing You: Consumerism, Surveillance, and the Agency of Consumers," "The Cultural and Institutional Barrier of Knowledge Exchanges in the Development of Open Source Software," and "Challenges of Developing Countries in Imitating Technological Progress." All three chapters are solely authored by the author.

Chapter 2
Digitalization of Indonesian MSMEs: Innovation Challenges and Opportunities

Trina Fizzanty

Abstract This chapter aims to present the performance of the digital economy in Indonesia and the opportunities for MSMEs for digitalization, especially the use of digital platforms. Using data from the Indonesian digitalization survey (2021), Three provinces (West Sumatera, West Java and DI Yogyakarta) as case studies, and secondary data on the digitalization status of Indonesian MSMEs, it was found that the conversion of MSMEs to the digital economy was maintained and secured the market for MSMEs during and after the COVID-19 pandemic. Most MSMEs are connected through social media and market platforms, and only a small percentage of MSMEs use digital technologies to support business management and production. Digitalization facilitated MSMEs to take advantage of the market; however, it had little impact on MSME innovation and productivity. Meanwhile, digitalization of MSMEs in the production sector will open a new business model, despite some challenges such as job displacement and global competition. The entrepreneurship capacity of MSMEs is a key to transforming digitalization into innovation.

Keywords Micro · Small and medium enterprise · Digitalization · Innovation · Entrepreneurship · Indonesia

2.1 Introduction

Digital technologies, such as the Internet, IoT, AI, and many other types of technologies, are exponentially growing and today are being utilized in various sectors, such as the economy, healthcare, education, and many other sectors. Digital technology, unlike other forms of technology, is a general-purpose technology, which is highly adaptable to suit various applications and purposes, thus continually fostering innovation. The vast opportunity for the emergence of various digital innovations is inseparable from how people imagine and shape the future.

T. Fizzanty (✉)
National Research and Innovation Agency, Jakarta Selatan, Indonesia
e-mail: trin003@brin.go.id

T. Fizzanty and I. Maulana (eds.), *The Digitalization of Indonesian Small and Medium Enterprises*, Engaging Indonesia, https://doi.org/10.1007/978-981-97-0029-5_2

Digitalization refers to information technology (IT) utilization. It has been discussed widely by Beniger (1986) in his book "The Control Revolution". Digitalization is a minimum requirement to survive in a modern industry and to compete in today's digital age. The terms of digitalization and digitization are sometimes used interchangeably. Digitization is the conversion of analog information and encoding it into digital information that computers can store, process, and transmit (Forbes). Meanwhile, digitalization refers to the use of digital technology within social life by restructuring digital communication and media infrastructures (Jason Bloomberg in Forbes).[1] This concept is also different from digital transformation, which not only refers to digital technology but also the reorientation of the organization to achieve customer-driven objectives, which are needed to transform businesses and their relevant strategies.

The use of digital technologies in the economic sector can be found in supporting production, logistics, marketing, finance, and other economic activities. Digitalization promotes an increasingly open and integrated economic system, connected to a vast network of local, national, and even global economic actors. The development of digitalization in the economic sector has given rise to a new form of economy called the digital economy.

The digital economy is a new source of economic growth. Economic activity results in billions of everyday online connections between people, businesses, devices, data, and processes (Deloitte, n.d). The opening of accessibility toward digital technology and the Internet has enabled the growth of the digital economy, which has transformed current business and market governance. Indonesia continues to develop the digital economy, which is expected to overcome the middle-income trap, create new jobs, and promote inclusiveness and economic efficiency. This expectation is well-founded, as Indonesia's digital economy grew fourfold between 2015 and 2019, with a total transaction value reaching US$41 billion in 2019. The latest study by Google Temasek, Bain and Company (2022) found that the value of Indonesia's digital economy will reach USD 77 billion in 2022 or a growth of 22% (yoy). By 2025, the value of the digital economy is expected to increase to USD 130 billion and triple by 2030. Among the digital economy sectors, e-commerce is the largest contributor with a value of USD 59 billion in 2022, growing at a rate of 22% (yoy). This is followed by other digital sectors, which are food delivery and transportation at USD 8 billion and online media and travel.

Indonesia's competitiveness in the digital economy is high among Southeast Asian countries. The value of Indonesia's digital economy is the largest. In 2022, Indonesia's digital economy was valued at US$77 billion, followed by Thailand (US$35 billion) and Vietnam (US$22 billion). Indonesia's contribution to the digital economy is expected to remain the largest among Southeast Asian countries in 2025 (Google, Temasek, and Bain and Company 2022).

[1] https://www.forbes.com/sites/jasonbloomberg/2018/04/29/digitization-digitalization-and-digital-transformation-confuse-them-at-your-peril/?sh=7ac05172f2c7 (access date: June 25th 2023).

2.2 Digital Economy and Inclusivity

The digital economy has been considered as a means for economic growth, but in this economy, who is involved and benefits? This is a crucial issue for Indonesia, which is diverse in terms of the population's socioeconomic backgrounds, educational levels, gender, regions, financial capacity, and other factors. Some studies found that Indonesia faces some challenges to ensure the inclusiveness of the digital economy, such as bridging the digital gap in infrastructure associated with disadvantage, particularly at the frontiers and in the outermost regions, and addressing the lack of digital literacy, the cost of digital access, social and data security, and the less productive use of internet access (Bachtiar et al., 2020).

There are many ways in which the digital economy supports inclusiveness and technological innovation. The digital economy has opened up access for business entrepreneurs to access the banking system through digital finance and digital payment systems. Lessons learned from other countries assist with understanding how the digital economy supports inclusiveness. In China, the digital economy has opened the opportunity to integrate rural and urban development, reduce the digital divide between urban and rural development (Wang et al., 2023) and enabled elderly people to upgrade their consumption (Yuan He et al., 2022). Digitalization has also opened opportunity for MSMEs in Germany to improve technological innovation (product and process innovation) through R&D. How does digitalization impact technological innovation? The new product or process is derived from new skills, competencies, knowledge development, and acquisition (Nambisan et al., 2020). Digitalization has limited impact on new products and processes, especially in non-R&D MSMEs. MSMEs with R&D capacity impact on innovation rather than digitalization (Radicic and Petkovic, 2023). Following this study, this chapter, using data from the Indonesia Digitalization Survey (Fizzanty et al., 2021), aims to outline research findings of digitalization and its impact on innovation challenges of MSMEs.

2.3 Digital Economy and Sustainable Development

The development of the digital economy is expected to make a positive contribution to sustainable development and innovation. For example, in China, based on data from between 2013 and 2019, the digital economy has contributed to high-quality development, reduction of regional inequality, development of innovation, and green development (Yang et al., 2022). On the other hand, according to Pangestu and Dewi (2017), the role of the digital economy in Indonesia in 2017 has not had a real impact on productivity, efficiency, and innovation, as indicated by the total factor productivity (TFP) from the use of digital technology, which has not been significant. There are several reasons thought to be underlying this (Pangestu & Dewi, 2017): (i) the low access of the population to the Internet in Indonesia (78%), such that the conditions of "hyperconnectivity" have not been sufficiently met to be able to transform markets, transactions, and the economic organization; (ii) the economic value from the use of the Internet has not been optimally utilized, as it is primarily used to access social media and search for information; and (iii) limited availability of digital talent in Indonesia. This is what Solow (1987) described as the "productivity paradox", meaning the rise of using Information and Communication Technology (ICT) in the economic sector resulted in a small increase in productivity. The phenomenon of the productivity paradox also occurred in developed countries such as the USA, UK, Germany, and Japan (Dewan and Kramer, 1998; Van Ark, 2016; Stanley et al., 2018). In these countries, digital technology has not been fully utilized yet.

Currently, the digital economy in Indonesia is growing rapidly as technology develops, and digital access begins to increase, but in absolute terms it is relatively low and uneven. A number of reports show that internet access in Indonesia is increasing, especially the use of mobile phones with internet access. However, the internet network and infrastructure are unequal, such that access to digital information is still limited. Currently, less than 30% of Indonesia's population has access to the Internet. On Java, Indonesia's most populous island, only 52.5% of the population has access to the Internet, while outside Java, the population with Internet access ranges from 26% in Papua to 48% of the population in Kalimantan (ERIA, 2023; Lurong Chen et al., 2023).

The inequality of digital access between regions is the first challenge, the other is the less productive use of the Internet. People in the western regions of Indonesia access the Internet more than the eastern regions of Indonesia (Fig. 2.1). Indonesians spend an average of 7.4 h per day accessing the Internet, and on average, half of that time, or 3 h, is spent on social media (Statista, 2022). The digital behavior of Indonesian society has created a thriving market for businesses. While tangible product sales can be safeguarded from foreign competitors, information-based products and services, including social media, gaming, music, and film, are primarily controlled by international providers. Hence, those who can better appropriate the development of IT infrastructure are companies such as Google, Netflix, Zoom, and others.

In addition to social media, marketing through digital platforms or e-commerce occupies the second largest share, which is used as a means for consumers and producers to transact. With the increasing use of e-commerce in Indonesia, several issues have arisen, including data protection, quality assurance, and protection of local industries from unbalanced competition from imported products (Negara and Soesilowati, 2021). The serious challenges facing e-commerce in Indonesia are policy and regulatory uncertainties, relatively low internet penetration, poor logistics infrastructure, low quality of human resources, and low penetration of digital payments. Similar findings were also reported by DS Innovate & Tiktok 2023), who stated that the two main challenges for MSMEs in adopting digital technology are low digital literacy (human resource capacity) and limited access to financial institutions.

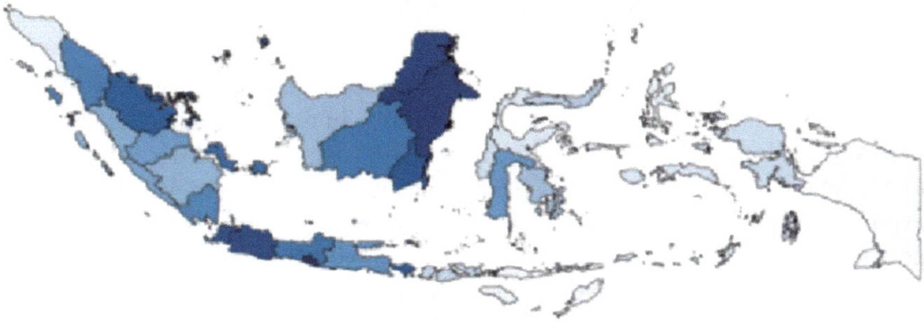

Fig. 2.1 The number of population that accessed the Internet within three months (end of 2022) in Indonesia. *Source* The Central Bureau of Statistics-Indonesia. (https://www.bps.go.id/indicator/2/70/1/persentase-penduduk-usia-5-tahun-ke-atas-yang-pernah-mengakses-internet-dalam-3-bulan-terakhir-menurut-provinsi-dan-jenis-kelamin.html; access date: 21 November 2023; the map is produced using QGIS application)

2.4 Digital Startups in Indonesia

The rise of digitalization of MSMEs in Indonesia has emerged due to a growing number of MSMEs that are aware of the availability of digital startups to support their business. A study conducted by DS Innovate and TikTok found that most MSMEs (87%) were already aware of local startups or technology companies that could help them with digital solutions. Indonesia is a paradise for the startups' ecosystem. According to Startup Ranking, the number of startups in Indonesia reached 2,390 in 2022, ranking second in Asia; most of these are digital startups. The high ranking of Indonesian startups is due to their appropriation of the vast Indonesian market, which is one of the largest markets in Asia. The Indonesian startups' characteristics, however, are different from the startups in developed economies such as in the Silicon Valley in the USA, which have high development capability. Indonesian startups have to recruit overseas IT engineers from Bengaluru—India and Singapore (Maulana & Hardiyanti, 2021). The startups produce various digital platforms to support MSME businesses, such as commerce, logistics, finance, business management, and many others.

MSMEs' digitalization priorities are payment, product innovation, business operations, funding, logistics, and increasing digital competency (DS Innovate & TikTok, 2023). Most commonly, MSMEs adopt digital marketing as the area chosen to start with (DS Innovate & Tiktok, 2023). They use various digital channels, including social media, to increase their online business presence. Social media is the most popular digital medium for MSMEs as a marketing medium, followed by e-commerce as a medium for consumers' interaction. The growth of the digital economy has contributed to digital startups in e-commerce platforms. Several of these have reached unicorn status, with a total value of a minimum of one billion US$, for example, Gojek, Tokopedia, and Bukalapak.

2.5 Indonesia MSMEs and the Digital Economy

Indonesia's economy, like most economies in the world, is dominated by MSMEs. MSMEs, with 65.4 million business units or 99.9% of the total number of businesses in Indonesia, form the backbone of the Indonesian economy. MSMEs also contribute to 97% of the workforce, 60.3% of gross domestic product, and 14.4% of Indonesia's exports (ASEAN & UNCTAD, 2022). The government's target is that by 2024, i.e., post-pandemic, the export contribution of these MSMEs will increase to 17% of Indonesia's total export value (Indonesian Ministry of Cooperatives and SMEs).

As discussed above, the rise of MSMEs in the digital economy is inextricably linked to the role of technology companies or local startups. To address several challenges faced by MSMEs, technology companies need to develop digital solutions for MSMEs. What are the conditions of MSMEs that need to be addressed by technology developers? To answer this question, an overview of MSMEs in Indonesia is needed as will be provided in the following (DS Innovate & TikTok, 2023). First, the distribution of MSMEs between regions in Indonesia is uneven. More than 60% of MSMEs are located on Java Island, with a small portion outside of it. Second, most MSMEs (75%) are engaged in trade and service activities, including accommodation and food services, with only 14.5% engaged in manufacturing. Third, MSME economic actors experience limitations in managing digital businesses, because there are still many people from Generation X who are mostly lacking in digital literacy, even though there are currently other generations who are digitally literate, namely the Millennials (37.71%) and Generation Z (1.63%).

Despite the challenges faced by MSMEs in terms of digital access, based on a DS Innovate and TikTok survey conducted of 1,305 MSMEs, 83.8% use digital technology to support their business operations (DS Innovate and TikTok, 2022: 41). This fact demonstrates that the COVID-19 pandemic encouraged the digitalization of MSMEs. Almost all MSMEs reported that the use of digital technology, including the use of digital payment, shopping (e-commerce), shipping, and delivery services, had secured and increased their business productivity during the pandemic. The highest priority use of digital services for MSMEs is product/digital marketing, followed by consumer transaction payments, and innovative product/service creation or development (Fig. 2.2).

2.6 Impact of the COVID-19 Pandemic on the Performance of MSMEs

Before the COVID-19 Pandemic, the Indonesian Economic Census reported that in 2016, only 3% of MSMEs had digital access. Three years later, the digital access of MSMEs continued to increase and amounted to around 8.06 million companies (13%) of a total of 62 million MSMEs. When the COVID-19 pandemic spread globally, most of the MSMEs were affected by the pandemic, resulting in a decline of business

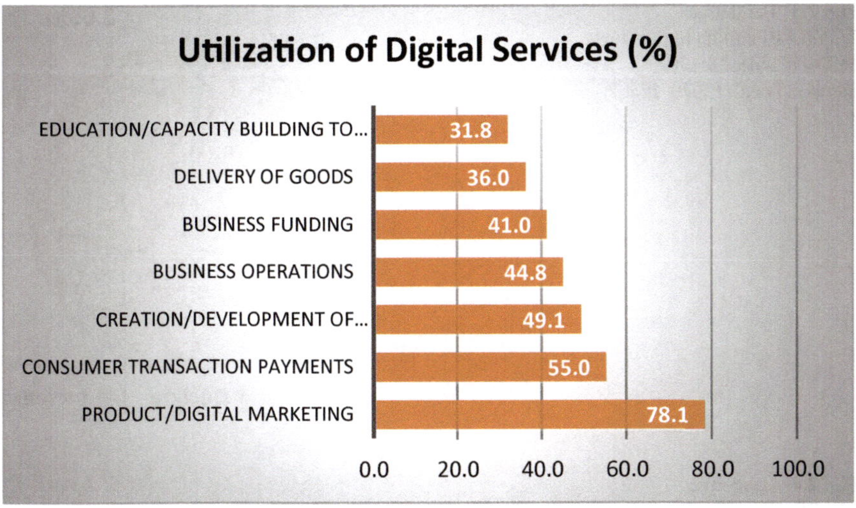

Fig. 2.2 Level of priority of the utilization of digital services within MSMEs. *Source* Modified from Fig. 49 (DS Innovate & TikTok., 2023. *MSME Empowerment Report, 2022: 42)*

performance. To comply with health protocols, almost all physical business activities and production were restricted. As a result, MSMEs faced problems such as cash flow shortage and supply chain disruption. Reports from China and Indonesia confirmed the situation. In China, the decline in performance caused by logistics or supply chain constraints postponed the resumption of work and led to marketing problems (Sun et al., 2022). In Indonesia, MSMEs faced similar problems in that they struggled to meet suppliers of raw materials and marketing products, and consumers' purchasing capacity declined.

The state of MSMEs at the beginning of the pandemic in Indonesia was captured by several survey results. First, a survey conducted by the Central Bureau of Statistics in 2020 showed that out of 35,992 businesses, there were 28,923 affected MSMEs. Due to physical contact restrictions, 67.22% of MSMEs were unable to operate (March–July 2020), and then gradually recovered, as shown by 19.26% of MSMEs operating in August 2020. A survey by the Research Center for Economics, Indonesian Institute of Sciences (LIPI), in May 2020 (Sambodo et al., 2020) confirmed these findings. Their online survey of 679 MSMEs in 24 provinces in Indonesia showed that 94.69% of MSMEs experienced a decline in sales (Fig. 2.3) and 58.76% a decline in product price (Fig. 2.4).

The MSMEs most affected were in the manufacturing, accommodation, hospitality, and trading sectors. Restrictions on physical interactions put pressure on the production side due to supply chain disruptions, a decline in consumers' purchasing power, and an increase in raw material costs, while MSME entrepreneurs continued to maintain workers at the same wage level.

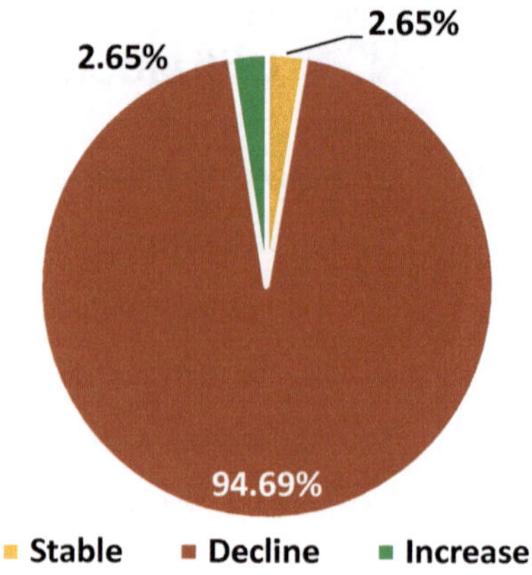

Fig. 2.3 Pandemic COVID-19 and its impact on MSMEs' sales. *Source* Sambodo et al. (2020, *Fig. 7, p.13)*

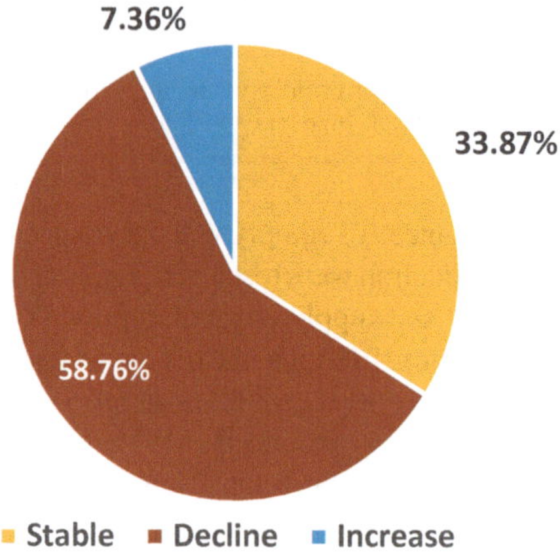

Fig. 2.4 Pandemic COVID-19 and its impact on MSMEs' product prices. *Source* Sambodo et al. (2020, Fig. 7, p.13)

This condition affected the level of confidence in the future of the business, with almost 72.02% of MSMEs stating that they would not be able to maintain their business until October 2020. The COVID-19 pandemic has had a significant impact on the performance of MSMEs in many countries, including Indonesia. Compared to pre-pandemic conditions, sales and profits declined by more than half. The results of the Research Center for Economics Indonesian Institute of Sciences (LIPI)'s survey in 2020 showed that some MSMEs experienced a decrease in profits of more than 50%. MSMEs that rely exclusively on physical marketing were the most affected by the COVID-19 pandemic, as shown by the very significant decline in sales of more than 75% (Fig. 2.5). This reality has driven and accelerated the digital transformation process of MSMEs. This survey demonstrates that the incorporation of digital technology offers enhanced prospects for MSMEs to uphold their sales, in contrast to relying exclusively on conventional physical marketing strategies. Approximately 40% of digitally active MSMEs encountered a sales decline exceeding 75%, while

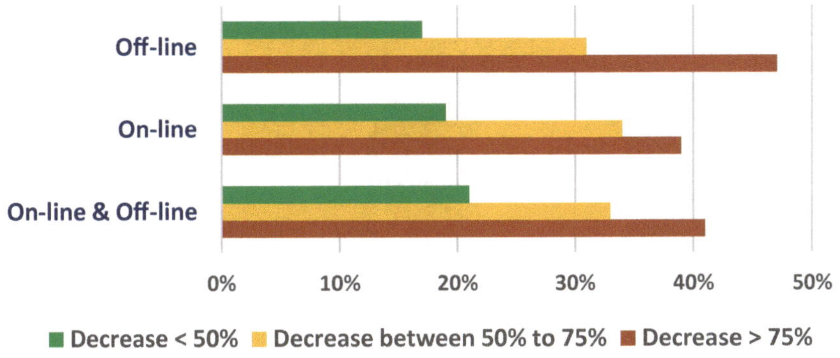

Fig. 2.5 The digital market and its impact on MSME sales during the COVID-19 pandemic. *Source* Sambodo et al. (2020, Fig. 7, p.13)

almost 50% of those primarily dependent on physical marketing experienced a comparable sales reduction of over 75% (Sambodo et al. 2020).

Despite MSMEs experiencing crises due to the pandemic, the pandemic has also accelerated the digitalization of MSMEs to make their businesses survive. MSMEs that can use digital platforms in digital marketing and innovation achieved success and profitability (Hossain et al., 2022). According to the Indonesian E-commerce Association (IDEA), the growth of MSMEs going digital is increasing year by year. Before the COVID-19 pandemic, around 12.8 million people entered the e-commerce platform, and in 2022, the number of digital MSMEs reached up to around 21.9 million. On the other hand, the digital economy revenue in 2022 reached US$77 billion or an increase of 22% from 2021, with a total digital economy revenue of US$63 billion. A similar finding was also confirmed by LIPI's survey of 601 MSMEs in Indonesia in 2021 (Fizzanty et al., 2021). This study confirmed that the COVID-19 pandemic forced MSMEs to adopt digital technology, especially in marketing their products or services, in that nearly 70% of MSMEs utilized digital marketing (Fig. 2.6).

Interestingly, the pandemic crisis encouraged close cooperation between the government and digital entrepreneurs (platform companies) to facilitate the digital transformation process of MSMEs. For example, the Ministry of Communication and Information formed a partnership with Tokopedia, a unicorn digital company in Indonesia, which supported the market for MSMEs during the COVID-19 pandemic, and the Government of Surabaya cooperated with GoTo, one of the biggest platform companies in Indonesia, to support the market for MSMEs' products and similar partnerships in other regions. During the pandemic, there was a rapid increase in the number of MSMEs going digital, especially in support of trade transactions. According to the Coordinating Ministry of Economic Affairs, 15.9 million MSMEs had gone digital as of October 2021, an increase of about 8 million business units in the two years of the pandemic. In 2022 there was a fairly rapid increase in the

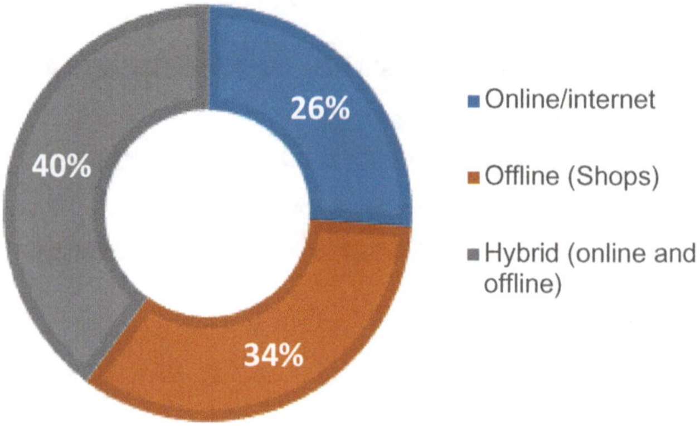

Fig. 2.6 MSMEs' marketing strategy during the COVID-19 pandemic. *Source* Fizzanty et al. (2021)

number of MSMEs that have gone digital, namely 20.76 MSMEs out of a total of 62 million MSMEs.

The presence of digital technology provides MSMEs with greater opportunities to sustain their sales compared to using physical marketing alone. The LIPI's survey (Fizzanty et al., 2021) showed that regardless of whether MSMEs were using digital technology or not, they experienced a decline in sales of more than 75%. The decline in sales was experienced by around 40% of MSMEs (using e-commerce) and almost 50% of MSMEs (employing physical marketing).

In the post COVID-19 era, there was an increase in digital access among MSMEs. This year (2023) marks the revival of MSMEs in Indonesia with a contribution to the gross domestic product of 61% and the national income of 16.65%. Moreover, it occupies 97% of the total workforce in Indonesia. Interestingly, a study conducted by DailySocial and TikTok in 2022 among 1.500 MSMEs in several cities in Indonesia showed that 62.3% of businesses were already using digital technology for business operations by implementing digital solutions, and 37.7% were just beginning to utilize it. Generally, these MSMEs are led by age groups using the Internet proficiently, especially the Millennials, who are more accustomed to digital technology (so-called "digital natives"). Small-scale businesses with a maximum business operation of one to six years are fast adopters of digital business practices.

Some factors affect MSMEs' decisions to adopt digital technology (Fizzanty et al., (2021). The predominant factor is user and business competition, where more users or competitors are involved in digital technology, and there is more pressure for MSMEs to get involved in the digital market. The interactions with technology providers and government have less of an impact on MSMEs in adopting digital technology. The role of the government is to increase MSMEs' capacity going digital.

How advanced are MSMEs in Indonesia in the context of digital transformation? Digital usage by MSMEs in Indonesia is still in the early stages as seen in Fig. 2.7. A survey of 611 MSMEs conducted by Fizzanty et al. (2021) found that most MSMEs were only at the stage of using the Internet for communication purposes (48%),

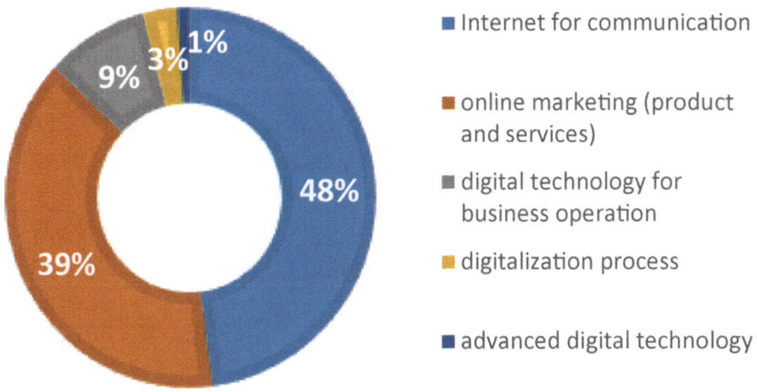

Fig. 2.7 Digital application of MSMEs in Indonesia. *Source* Fizzanty et al. (2021)

followed by marketing of products (39%). Meanwhile, other activities such as using the digital realm to streamline business operations and production were still minimal, let alone using advanced digital technology. This gradual use of digital technology is a form of digital transformation, which requires MSMEs not only to use it but also to adopt a management system that is different from the traditional one.

MSMEs in Indonesia are still in the early stages of digitalization using the Internet for communication and product marketing. LIPI's survey (Fizzanty et al. 2021) found that MSMEs were more inclined to utilize the Internet for communication purposes (48%) and products/services marketing (39%). Meanwhile, the use of digital technology for other purposes was relatively limited, such as business operations (9%), running digital processes (3%), and using advanced digital technology (1%).

The sociotechnical components include external actors who influence MSMEs to adopt digital technology, funding sources to implement digital technology, digital interconnectedness to business partners, and the benefits of being digitally connected. Who are the most influential actors for MSMEs to adopt digital technology? Based on the survey of MSMEs' digitalization in Indonesia (Fizzanty et al. 2021), the buyer is the most influential actor for MSMEs to adopt digital technology (44.93%), followed by business competitors (26.6%), MSMEs' own decisions (14.6%), and technology vendors (8.32%). The larger the number of buyers and competitors who are interconnected on the digital platform, the higher the pressure for small businesses to adopt digital technology. Adopting digital platforms in the context of the COVID-19 pandemic is a survival strategy for the MSMEs. Meanwhile, in the post-pandemic COVID-19 era, new habits started to grow; however, the role of the digital market for customers and businesses in this new era needs further research.

Digitalization is a strategy for MSMEs to widen their business network and create close links to the market. Due to digitalization, MSMEs are most interconnected to buyers (69.3%), followed by suppliers of raw materials (42.26%) and transportation, logistics, and suppliers of equipment (Table 2.1). Digitalization facilitates various actors in the digital ecosystem to interlink with, and support, the market.

Table 2.1 Digital connection with business partner

No	Option	Percent (%)
1	Buyer	69.38
2	Supplier of raw material	42.26
03	TransportaLogistic tion	28.12
4		26.79
5	Supplier of equipment	24.63
6	Other options	2.00
TOTAL		193.18

*Source*Fizzanty et al. (2021)

The digital ecosystem consists of many actors who are involved and interact, particularly with customers along the supply chain. The digital ecosystem of trading platforms also creates opportunity for MSMEs to connect with business actors other than customers, such as suppliers of raw materials and equipment, delivery and logistics companies, and financial institutions. Digitalization of production systems or automation, however, supports MSMEs to customize their products or to produce standard products with a greater market scope (Fizzanty et al., 2021).

2.7 Digital Technology and Innovation

We are now in the era of post-pandemic COVID-19. To support MSMEs' survival in this era and during the pandemic, the essential tool for MSMEs is innovation and adopting digital technology to link to networks (Caballero-Morales, 2021). MSMEs adopt digital technology while considering four factors: (i) external actors, (ii) funding for technology adoption, (iii) connectedness to business actors, and (iv) the benefits of digital adoption (Fizzanty et al., 2021). The most influential actors for MSMEs to adopt digital technology are customers (44.9%), business competitors (26.6%), self-initiatives (14.6%), and technology providers (8.3%). Most MSMEs use digital technology to reach or expand their market through social media, market-places, or websites, and a very small number of MSMEs apply digital business application and digital production. Using digital technology led to around 5–10% greater cost-efficiency and an increase in sales of 5–10%.

The main benefit of MSMEs going digital is the speed of access to information and connection to actors in the network. For a producer or a trader, information about consumer feedback and market opportunities is essential to develop a business. The other benefits include online information or data management capabilities (21.8%), where the digital applications to manage business and data analytics are available. Other benefits are the availability of data that facilitates the development of new products or new processes (16.47%) and allows for quick changes in production or

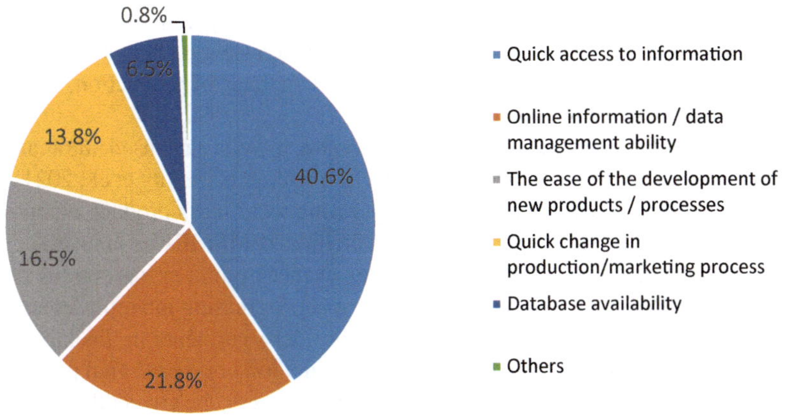

Fig. 2.8 Digital access and innovation for MSMEs in Indonesia. *Source* Fizzanty et al. (2021)

marketing processes (13.81%). Limited databases remain a challenge for MSMEs (Fig. 2.8). The use of digital technology has encouraged some MSMEs to innovate in terms of business, product, or process innovation (Aminullah et al., 2022), such as creating a variety of products. However, if MSMEs only use the marketplace or social media, digital technology's impact on innovation would be less significant, except for cost-efficiency and market feedback.

The use of digital platforms has increased competition among MSMEs entrepreneurs. The openness of information about products and prices in the digital market has encouraged some MSME entrepreneurs to innovate their business. Through the digital platform, MSMEs obtain abundant information about the competitors' products and prices and also about customers' behaviors and preferences. According to case studies in three regions in Indonesia, data analytics is one advantage of using digital platforms (Fizzanty et al., 2021). Digital platforms sometimes also provide services to support MSMEs in market research. The capacity of MSME entrepreneurs to analyze the data and use their knowledge to create a new product/process or new business model is essential. The use of digital technology is one condition for MSMEs to expand their business network; however, it is not sufficient to make them competitive. The entrepreneurs' capacity of transforming digital-based business into a new product, process, or business model is essential.

The use of digital technology, such as automation in production systems, increased MSMEs' production capacity and flexibility. Case studies of MSMEs in three regions in Indonesia (Fizzanty et al., 2021) found that the use of digital technology or automation in a fashion company in West Java supported the company to produce customized fashion garments to serve local customers. Digital technology facilitated a company to co-create garment design and produce unique fashion for the customer. The use of digital technology supports MSME entrepreneurs to come up with a new product, process, or business model, i.e., digital innovations (Ramdani et al., 2021). Digital technology of MSMEs involved in catering promotes a new business model.

Currently, a growing number of businesses in Indonesia operate as cloud kitchens. Cloud kitchen refers to a business that has no physical restaurant but only offers take-away food. This business concept creates higher efficiency of production, decreased production costs, and lower investment.

On the other hand, a study of a fashion company in West Java used automation to upgrade its capacity to serve the mass production market (Fizzanty et al., 2021). The automation replaced handmade embroidery garments to mass produce embroidery garments. To some extent, automation has facilitated MSMEs to innovate, create a new product, or utilize a new process. However, automation has serious consequences for MSMEs, such as reducing job creation, increasing job replacement, and exposing MSMEs to global competitors. Embroidery garments in Tasikmalaya is an example of unanticipated consequence of automation or using digital production. The more standardized the product and production process, the greater the possibility of MSMEs being exposed in a highly competitive domestic market. Without a unique product that differentiates them from competitors, it is easier for competitors to copy products at a more competitive price. Digital technology will facilitate MSMEs to innovate, in terms of product, process, or business model. However, the entrepreneur plays a strategic role in examining and applying a new way of doing business or producing a new product (Bessant and Tidd 2020). MSME entrepreneurs face limitations of resources and capabilities. Due to this limitation, transforming MSMEs into digital businesses is challenging, and failure to do so will hamper MSMEs to perform well. Cennamor et al. (2019) found that digital platforms can improve MSMEs' entrepreneurial performance indirectly through network capability. Digitalization will open up opportunities for MSMEs to perform and innovate if the MSME entrepreneur has the capability to maintain and utilize the network to achieve higher performance.

2.8 Conclusion

The digital economy in Indonesia appears to be a promising source of growth. The digital economy, including digital startups, is growing in Indonesia, and the country is recognized as having leading startups in the region. Startups promote digital platforms to help MSMEs to expand their networks and provide business management solutions. MSMEs' digitalization contributes to cost-efficiency and increased sales, ensuring their survival during the pandemic COVID-19. In the post-pandemic era, MSMEs' digitalization must be linked to innovation as a strategy for MSMEs to improve performance. According to a survey of MSMEs' digitalization in Indonesia and case studies in three regions, digitalization has made it easier for MSMEs to access information and data about market behavior and trends. The use of digital technology in manufacturing has accelerated MSMEs' ability to serve markets, but some challenges remain. MSMEs rely on information and networks to buyers and competitors to develop new products and processes. Entrepreneurs' ability to manage networks is critical to the successful digitalization of MSMEs.

References

Aminullah, E., Fizzanty, T., Nawawi, N., Suryanto, J., Pranata, N., Maulana, I., Ariyani, L., Wicaksono, A., Suardi, I., Azis, N. L. L., & Budiatri, A. P. (2022). Interactive components of digital MSMEs ecosystem for inclusive digital economy in Indonesia. *Journal of the Knowledge Economy*. https://doi.org/10.1007/s13132-022-01086-8

ASEAN and UNCTAD. (2022). ASEAN investment report 2022. Retrieved June 23, 2023, from https://asean.org/wp-cotent/uploads/2022/10/AIR2022-Web-Online-Final-211022.pdf

Aslam, A., Naveed, A., & G. Shabbir. (2021). Is it an institution, digital or social inclusion that matters for inclusive growth? A panel data analysis. *Quality & Quantity, 55*, 333–355.

Bachtiar, P., Diningrat, R.A., Kusuma, A. Z. D., Al Izzati, R. & A. Diandra (2020) Ekonomi digital untuk siapa? Menuju ekonomi digital yang inklusif di Indonesia. Research Report. Jakarta: The SMERU Research Institute. December 2020. https://smeru.or.id/id/publication-id/ekonomi-digital-untuk-siapa-menuju-ekonomi-digital-yang-inklusif-di-indonesia. Access date: 2 December 2023.

Beniger, J. R. (1986). *The control revolution: Technological and economic origins of the information society*. Harvard University Press.

Bessant, J., & Tidd, J. (2020). *Managing innovation: Integrating technological, market, and organization change* (7th ed.). John Wiley.

Caballero-Morales, S. O. (2021). Innovation as a recovery strategy for SMEs in emerging economies during the COVID-19 pandemic. *Research in International Business and Finance*, *57*(October 2021), Article 101396. https://doi.org/10.1016/j.ribaf.2021.101396.

Cenamor, J., Parida, V., & Wincent, J. (2019). How entrepreneurial SMEs compete through digital platforms: The roles of digital platform capability, network capability, and ambidexterity. *Journal of Business Research, 100*(July 2019), 196–206. https://doi.org/10.1016/j.jbusres.2019.03.035.

Chen, L. (2023). Chapter 1 Introduction - Lurong Chen Kalamullah Ramli Muhammad Suryanegara, Economic Research Institute for ASEAN & East Asia, Indonesia. Retrieved from https://policycommons.net/artifacts/3525073/chapter-1-introduction/4325778/ on 30 Jan 2024. CID: 20.500.12592/4vz4gq.

Deloitte. nd. What is digital economy? Unicorns, transformation and the internet of things. https://www2.deloitte.com/mt/en/pages/technology/articles/mt-what-is-digital-economy.html

Dewan, S., & Kraemer, K. L. (1998). International dimensions of the productivity paradox. *Communications of the ACM, 41*(8), 56–62. https://doi.org/10.1145/280324.280333

DS Innovate and TikTok. (2023). MSMEs empowerment report 2022. Retrieved June 25, 2023, from https://drive.google.com/file/d/1lNIqPUo5FADJUkUfqcMKjfdAck_juAt1/view

Fizzanty, T., Aminullah, E., Nawawi, Maulana, I., Suryanto, J., Aziz, N. L., Pranata, N., Budiatri, A. P., Suardi, I., Ariyani, L., & Wicaksono, A. (2021). Pengembangan Ekosistem Ekonomi Digital UKM Indonesia. Prioritas Riset Nasional Pengembangan Ekonomi Digital Indonesia Tahun 2020. Laporan Akhir Kegiatan (No.199/E1/PRN/2020). Organisasi Riset Ilmu Pengetahuan Sosial Humaniora, Badan Riset dan Inovasi Nasional (Indonesia).

Google, Temasek, Bain and Company. (2022). *E-conomy SEA 2022 report*. Retrieved June 17, 2023, from https://services.google.com/fh/files/misc/e_conomy_sea_2022_report.pdf.

He, Y., Li, K., & Wang, Y. (2022). Crossing the digital divide: The impact of the digital economy on elderly individuals' consumption upgrade in China. *Technology in Society, 71,* 102141. https://doi.org/10.1016/j.techsoc.2022.102141

Hossain, M. A., Akhter, F, & Sultana, M. M. (2022). SMEs in COVID-19 crisis and combating strategies: A systematic literature review (SLR) and a case from emerging economy. *Operations Research Perspectives*. *9*(2022), Article 100222. https://doi.org/10.1016/j.orp.2022.100222.

Maulana, A., & Hardiyanti, R. (2021). The absorption of HRST from technology-based companies of Indonesia. *Journal of STI Policy and Management, 6*(1), 67–75. https://doi.org/10.14203/STPM.2021.300.

Nambisan, S., Lyytinen, K., & Yoo, Y. (2020). Digital innovation: towards a transdisciplinary perspective. *Handbook of digital innovation*, 2–12.

Negara, S.D., & Soesilowati, E.S. (2021). E-commerce in Indonesia: impressive growth but facing serious challenges. Perspective. *ISEAS Yusof Ishak Institute, 2* Agustus 2021, 102.

Pangestu, M., & Dewi, G. (2017). Indonesia and digital economy. In E. Jurriëns & R. Tapsell (Eds.), *Digital Indonesia: Connectivity and Divergence* (pp. 227–255). ISEAS Publishing.

Radicic, D., & Petković, S. (2023). Impact of digitalization on technological innovations in small and medium-sized enterprises (SMEs). *Technological Forecasting and Social Change, 191,* 122474.

Ramdani, B., Raja, S., & Kayumova, M. (2021). Digital innovation in SMEs: A systematic review, synthesis and research agenda. *Information Technology for Development, 28*(2), 58–60. https://doi.org/10.1080/02681102.2021.1893148

Sambodo, M. T., Nugroho, A. E., Fizzanty, T., Hidayat, A. S., Endah, N., Cahyono, B. D., Handoyo, F. E., Novandra, R., Farandy, A. R., Adityawati, S. P., & Febiyansah, P. T. (2020). Kertas Kebijakan: Dampak Pandemi COVID-19 terhadap Kinerja Makroekonomi dan UKM: Mitigasi dan Langkah Pemulihan. Pusat Penelitian Ekonomi, Lembaga Ilmu Pengetahuan Indonesia (Indonesia).

Stanley, T. D., Doucouliagos, H., & Steel, P. (2018). Does ICT generate economic growth? a meta-regression analysis. *Journal of Economic Surveys, 32*(3), 705–726. https://doi.org/10.1111/joes.12211

Statista. (2023). *Average daily time spent using various media and devices in Indonesia in 3rd quarter 2022, by activity.* Retrieved June 23, 2023, from https://www.statista.com/statistics/803524/daily-time-spent-using-online-media-by-activity-indonesia/.

Sun, Y., Wu, M., Zeng, X., & Peng, Z. (2022). The impact pf COVID-19 on the Chinese stock market: Sentimental or substantial?. *Finance Research Letters, 38*(January 2021), Article 1011838. https://doi.org/10.1016/j.frl.2020.101838.

Van Ark, B. (2016). The Impact of digitalization on technological innovations in small and medium-sized enterprises (SMEs). *Technological Forecasting and Social Change, 191,* 122474.

Wang, Y., Peng, Q., Jin, C., Ren, J., Fu, Y., & Yue, X. (2023). Whether the digital economy will successfully encourage the integration of urban and rural development: A case study in China. *Chinese Journal of Population, Resources and Environment, 21,* 13–25.

Yang, Q., Ma, H., Wang, Y., & Yang, L. L. Q. (2022). Regional on the influence mechanism of the digital economy on regional sustainable development. *Procedia Computer Science., 202,* 178–183. https://doi.org/10.1016/j.procs.2022.04.025

Yuan, H., Li, K., & Y. Wang. (2022). Crossing the digital divide: The impact of the digital economy on elderly individuals' consumption upgrade in China. *Technology in Society, 71,* 102141

Trina Fizzanty is Head of the Research Center for Education at Indonesia's National Research and Innovation Agency (BRIN) in Jakarta. She was the former Director of Research Center for the Development of Science and Technology, Indonesian Institute of Sciences (LIPI). Her research area is on management of innovation and R&D. She was the principal investigator for the research project "The Development of Digital Economy Ecosystem of SMEs in Indonesia" (2020–2021). She holds PhD degree from The University of Queensland, Australia in Integrative System. She has published her research in international journal and books. She worked collaboratively with other scholars in several international research projects and also works as a reviewer for international journals and she was as the Editoral Board of LIPI Press. Her current publication in international journal with a title "Interactive Components of Digital MSMEs Ecosystem for Inclusive Digital Economy in Indonesia" in Journal of The Knowledge Economy, November 2022

Chapter 3
Unlocking Digital Talent in Indonesia's Micro, Small, and Medium Enterprises: Issues and Challenges

Nawawi

Abstract This paper examines the opportunity and challenge of efforts to increase digital talent among MSME actors in Indonesia. The main idea of this paper departs from the general understanding that having digital talent is a key part of digital transformation for MSME actors in Indonesia. It is also a strategic step in supporting efforts to increase MSME's business capacity and economic contribution to the economy. However, business owners need more digital literacy and adequate educational background, which explains the complexity of efforts to increase digital talent capabilities among MSME actors in Indonesia. Most MSME actors utilize business digitalization to expand their online marketing process. They also still rely on conventional transactions in their business, so digital-based activities are usually carried out as an alternative to expand the market and obtain additional income. This paper pointed out that the process of digitalizing MSMEs is influenced by the ability of business owners to understand the benefits of the digital economy. Efforts to digitalize MSMEs should be carried out according to the needs, readiness, demographic, and business characteristics of MSME actors.

Keywords Digital talent · MSME actors · Digital characteristics

3.1 Introduction

The digital economy is transforming economic activities and human life worldwide, including in contemporary Indonesia. It has also generated unprecedented opportunities for the involvement of businesses in micro, small, and medium enterprises (MSMEs) with new forms of digital activities and offering new business opportunities, efficiency gains, economic empowerment, and better access to increased welfare (Sevrul and Saner, 2014). Efforts to bring more MSME entrepreneurs into the digital

Nawawi (✉)
Research Center for Population, National Research and Innovation Agency (BRIN), Jakarta, Indonesia
e-mail: Nawa003@brin.go.id

T. Fizzanty and I. Maulana (eds.), *The Digitalization of Indonesian Small and Medium Enterprises*, Engaging Indonesia, https://doi.org/10.1007/978-981-97-0029-5_3

economy have also been linked to the need to develop digital talent and entrepreneurship among MSME players, particularly via digitalizing product marketing through digital platforms and marketplaces (Udacity and Ipsos, 2022). Consequently, governments are trying to implement programs to accelerate inclusive digitalization by expanding the digital ecosystem to MSMEs (Kominfo, 2019).

Indonesia has great potential for a digital economy (Edwin & Ross, 2017). This economic potential is highly correlated with a large population of up to 250 million and is dominated by a productive age, with a medium age of 28. It is also supported by rapidly growing urban areas and internet use within societies. In Indonesia today, over half of Indonesians, or about 150 million people, are living in cities and towns. By 2045, more than 70 percent of the population or about 220 million people, will live in urban areas. As Indonesia becomes urbanized, so has it increased the use of the Internet. In this context, the more internet use increases among societies, the higher the opportunity for developing an internet-based digital economy.

The digital economy can be defined as incorporating data and the Internet into production processes and products, new household and government consumption forms, fixed-capital formation, cross-border flows, and finance (IMF, 2018). In addition to having an economic impact, the digitalization of MSMEs can have a cascading and transformative impact on the labor market, economy, environment, education, health, and governance (Pangestu & Grace, 2017). According to Setkab (2021), the growth of the digital economy in Indonesia will reach eightfold in 2030, from Rp 632 trillion to Rp 4,531 trillion. MSMEs from many sectors will play a crucial role in this growth. Based on data issued by the Ministry of Finance in March 2021, MSMEs in Indonesia totaled 64.2 million units, contributing more than 61 percent of gross domestic product (GDP) with a value of Rp 8,573.89 trillion. In addition, MSMEs absorbed 97 percent of the total labor force and attracted up to 60 percent of total investment in Indonesia. Meanwhile, MSMEs also contributed 14.37 percent of total non-oil and gas exports from Indonesia, worth Rp293.84 trillion by 2021.

While Indonesia has a large population, the digitalization of MSMEs continues to face various constraints. Research conducted by the Center for Digital Society (2019) and Hermawan (2022) found that the most binding digitalization of Indonesian MSMEs affecting effectiveness lies in four aspects. The first constraint is the connection between the use of information technology and the educational background. With the educational background of MSME actors generally dominated by middle to lower education (many have only finished elementary and middle school), most MSMEs need better-prepared human resources to utilize information technology effectively. Consequently, increasing digital literacy among MSMEs in Indonesia is a fundamental issue that must be overcome immediately.

The second constraint is related to access to information technology. In this case, the desire of MSME players to digitalize their business will only succeed with the support and availability of internet access and other supporting digital infrastructures. In contemporary Indonesia, not all MSMEs have the requisite infrastructure for digitalization because of capital limitations and sporadic distribution of digital infrastructure, including internet access, even on the island of Java (Supriyanto, 2016). The third obstacle concerns the organizational management capability of MSMEs in

Indonesia. This issue is strongly related to the fact that only some MSMEs can take advantage of existing networks, with few realizing the importance of networking with other entrepreneurs, professional associations, the government, and financial services. The fourth constraint relates to internet access, which does not support the digitalization of the MSME business. Most MSMEs in Indonesia already have access to internet facilities, yet only some take advantage of the information available for business growth and advancement (Yanti and Yusnaini, 2018). Most internet use in Indonesia focuses on entertainment, thus needing more digital opportunities offered by the digital economy (Pangestu and Dewi, 2017).

Based on the above issues, this study examines efforts to increase digital talent among MSME actors in Indonesia. To what extent do MSMEs in Indonesia understand the process of digitalizing their business, and how can government implementation programs support them effectively to increase digital talent for MSMEs themselves? These issues serve as the main research questions to explore. The data used in this study comes from the results of a combination of qualitative and quantitative studies conducted in the provinces of West Sumatra, West Java, and Yogyakarta in 2020–2021. These three research locations were chosen considering MSMEs' business level and readiness to implement digitalization. This condition means that the level of achievement and development of MSME digitalization in these three provinces can generally represent what is occurring in Indonesia. However, at a specific level, there needs to be restrictions according to the characteristics of MSME actors in each region.

3.2 Digital Talent and Its Significance for MSMEs

The current and future world economy is expected to be increasingly dominated by activities related to digital technology (Scahwab, 2016; OECD, 2020). Various innovations in digital technology have provided many significant benefits for economic actors, both on a large scale and for MSME players. A study by the OECD (2020) concluded that digital technology reduces transactions and costs by providing better and faster access to market information. It also provides effective communication between buyers and sellers, making it easier to bring together suppliers and networks in a business chain (OECD, 2020). In the business world, this process is known as digital transformation, where companies adapt their operations to new technology (Udacity and Ipsos, 2022).

Pangestu and Dewi (2017) and Edwin and Ross (2017) found that using digital technology by MSMEs has provided them benefits to enter a wider market, including the global market. They have greater access to various opportunities and resources, including access to financial credit, training, and new customers, which are increasingly being made available online. It also supports innovation, greater access to innovation assets, and the potential to generate data and analyze their operations in new ways to drive improved performance (OECD, 2020). Business players that fail to transform digitally cannot keep up with more competitors because they cannot iterate as quickly, automate processes, or analyze data when making business decisions (Katsonis & Botros, 2015). Therefore, having digital talent is a key part of digital transformation for MSMEs.

What exactly is digital talent? Why is it important to support the digitalization of MSMEs in Indonesia? A report published by Udacity and Ipsos (2021) defines *digital talent* as any ability, competence, or skill a person possesses to optimize their role in developing the digital economy. These abilities and skills vary greatly depending on the level of readiness of each digital business being developed. In the Indonesian context, developing digital talent for MSME actors is crucial, considering that not all MSME actors in Indonesia understand the process and skills needed for digital-based business development (Arifin, 2011; Ariyansah, 2018). In many cases, the development of digital talent for MSME actors in Indonesia is carried out in a learning-by-doing process according to how well they understand the benefits of digital promotion and the ability to manage transactions online (Arifin, 2011; Ariyansah, 2018).

The Learning Management System (LMS) is an example of an institution in Indonesia that focuses on efforts to develop digital talent. This program is carried out under the coordination of the Ministry of Communication and Information Technology through the digital talent scholarship program. The program is open to the public, including vocational graduates, MSMEs, professionals, and state civil servants. Based on the curriculum developed, the digital training offered varies greatly, from basic intermediate to advanced levels.

One of the programs, namely the Digital Entrepreneurship Academy (DEA) Program, is a training scholarship aimed at the general public aspiring Small and Medium Enterprises, as well as MSME business actors who want to move up in terms of utilizing digital technology to improve their business. DEA training aims to encourage the improvement of digital skills from basic to intermediate for prospective MSME entrepreneurs. This academy targets participants from the general public who want to start a business and MSME players. They learn about the formation of a digital entrepreneurship mindset and introduction to digital entrepreneurs by explaining concepts and practices. This training is specifically for participants who do not have a business yet but have an interest in starting a business, or already have a business but do not yet utilize digital technology, preferably do not have a social media account, or experience selling on marketplaces/social media.

Digital talent training that adapts to the needs of participants certainly needs to be developed. A roadmap for the development of digital talent in Indonesia needs to be developed according to the needs of the type of training and the characteristics of potential users. This condition is important considering that the success of developing digital talent for MSMEs is not only seen from the programs provided but also the extent to which the training provided is useful and can be directly applied to support the development of digital-based MSME businesses.

Each country has different needs regarding digital talent development. The process depends on the stages of the digital economy itself and its development in each country. In the Indonesian context, digital talent development is more about introducing basic knowledge related to the digital economy, how to start digital promotion, and the ability to manage online transactions. Meanwhile, in countries where the digital economy has become a common need (society, state, and private), the need for digital talent is adjusted to consider existing deficiencies, as with the results of the study reported by Udacity and Ipsos (2022), countries such as France and Germany are focused on innovation, while the United States aims attention at agility and adaptability. The United Kingdom, on the other hand, cares most about financial performance pressures. These concerns directly correlate with the need for talent transformation and how the country prepares to optimize the benefits of the digital economy.

3.3 Challenges of Digital Talent Development

Data in Table 3.1 below shows that the stages of achieving business digitalization by MSMEs in Indonesia are still dominated by efforts to market products online (see Table 3.1). Only 9.32 percent of MSMEs use digital technology for the company's operations. As many as 2.66 percent use digital technology to support the entire digital economy process, from ordering raw materials, product design, and production to marketing.

This data indicates that most MSME actors in Indonesia still utilize business digitalization to expand their online marketing process. Thus, the process of digitalizing MSMEs is influenced by the ability of business owners to understand the benefits of the digital economy. Basic training related to the benefits and strategies of online promotion for MSMEs is urgently needed at this level. This category includes creating attractive digital consumer advertisements, good communication skills to respond to online buyers, and understanding the online transaction process.

MSME actors in this category also still need business assistance, considering that often, if losses occur due to transaction errors, this will result in a loss of demand for MSME actors to utilize online platforms consistently. They also still rely on conventional transactions in their business, so digital-based activities are usually carried out as an alternative to expand the market and obtain additional income.

3.3.1 Level of MSMEs Digitalization

In practice, MSME actors not connected to digitalization still exist. However, the number varies depending on the region and the needs of each MSME actor. Based on the results of an interview with a small-scale business actor in Jogjakarta who operates a local food business, she said that her resistance to digitalizing her business was more about practicality. She claims that without digitalization, her business is quite profitable. Another reason is that selling online requires special time and certain skills that she still needs to gain, so if he tries, he worries that he will disappoint his customers. In this case, practical business reasons are often the main deciding factor for MSMEs in Indonesia to become involved in digital promotions or not. Usually,

Table 3.1 Level of digitalization of MSMEs

Aspect	Category	Not connected	Digitally connected	Promote via online	Use digitalization for marketing and operational	Almost digitalized	Fully digitalized
Total		77	190	255	56	16	7
	%	12.81	31.61	42.43	9.32	2.66	1.16
Gender	Male	59	132	137	43	12	3
	%	76.62	69.47	53.73	76.79	75.00	42.86
	Female	18	58	118	13	4	4
	%	23.38	30.53	46.27	23.21	25.00	57.14
Education	Elementary	7	2	8	3	2	0
	Secondary	9	17	16	3	2	0
	High school	41	95	117	25	8	4
	Diploma 1	1	6	3	0	0	0
	Diploma 3	5	13	20	3	1	0
	Undergraduate	13	56	86	20	3	3
	Postgraduate	0	1	4	2	0	0
	Others	1	0	1	0	0	0
	Jumlah	77	190	255	56	16	7
Number of workers	Self-employed	57	111	125	21	6	2
	2–5 workers	19	63	101	17	2	2
	6–19 workers	0	8	17	10	4	0
	20–29 workers	1	4	3	5	2	0
	30–99 workers	0	2	4	2	1	2
	> 99 workers	0	2	5	1	1	1
	Total	77	190	255	56	16	7

Source Fizzanty et al. (2021)

they will start and try digital businesses if conditions require them to use digital applications. For example, the use of purchase transactions is increasingly leaving the use of cash and product marketing through social media.

3.3.2 Level of Digital Literacy

The lack of digital literacy and inadequate educational background of business owners can illustrate the complexity of efforts to increase the digital talent capabilities of MSME actors in Indonesia (Kartika, 2019). This problem is one of the biggest challenges in the digitalization of MSMEs in Indonesia. The increased use of digital technology in modern business has made digital literacy skills more essential.

Over the past decade, computers, mobile telephones, tablets, and the Internet have become prominent in any business. Since it offers a structured way of getting familiar with the digital world, MSME actors with digital literacy skills become comfortable and confident in navigating online platforms. In contrast, those who lack this skill may struggle. Furthermore, since most financial transactions are now administered online, MSME actors must be confident in using the digital economy as their alternative way of developing business.

As Schwab mentioned in his book (2016), digital business is not just using digital applications but also building business networks digitally, innovating through various digital services, and adopting various digital devices that continue to develop rapidly and dynamically. Further, Jordana and Suwarto (2017) also explained that digital literacy is not just the ability to use new technologies, learn to use a new device, or even apply the devices and technologies to the learning process. On the contrary, digital literacy is the ability to adapt highly, which allows people to harness technical skills and navigate the diverse information in the digital world. Technical ability to access technology can now be changed later in the day. However, digital literacy makes a person ready in the present and the foreseeable future for any form of technology that will exist later.

Rahayu and Day (2017) argue that digital literacy can support the development of digital talent in several ways. It can enhance communication skills by allowing individuals to express themselves effectively online and teach them about collaboration using digital tools. Digital literacy can also improve critical thinking skills by enabling individuals to evaluate the credibility and reliability of online information. It can support the development of problem-solving skills and creativity by allowing individuals to navigate digital technology tools, troubleshoot technical issues, and use digital tools to create and share multimedia content. Therefore, an effort to understand the positive and negative aspects of digital business activities is significant for MSMEs in Indonesia. In addition to avoiding the negative impacts of online transactions, this effort also provides a basic understanding of the digital economy, where everyone can make online transactions depending on the motives and goals they want to achieve.

3.3.3 *Level of Structural Capital*

Another challenge to developing digital talent among MSMEs in Indonesia is accessing and using the Internet for productive activities and introducing innovations. According to Deloitte (2015), intensive use of digital technologies (including the Internet for social media and e-commerce promotion) would help MSMEs increase their revenues by up to 80 percent, become 17 times more likely to introduce innovations and become one-and-a-half times more likely to create jobs. According to these findings, digitalization strategies via the Internet in MSMEs can help MSMEs scale up their business and be more productive in company revenue.

As Ariska and Lienggar (2020) explained, MSMEs are predominantly in the household business format with the support of the operational business, which mostly involves unpaid family members. When they use the Internet to support their business, it gives the advantage to household welfare directly and indirectly effects. Direct effects come from the supply side, while indirect effects emerge from internet use (Kpodar & Andrianaivo, 2011). It provides economic opportunities to bridge networks, access information, promote the product, and even support business transactions and expansion (Ariska & Lienggar, 2020). Using the Internet indirectly will boost the economy by improving productivity gains, reducing transaction costs, and creating financial inclusion among MSMEs (OECD, 2020).

Welfens (2008) argues that the Internet improves product innovation and trade and facilitates faster diffusion and distribution of knowledge. Internet use can also affect productivity due to its ability to provide alternative solutions. A study by Gilch and Jost (2020) concluded that an employee searching for ideas online had altered motivation to a more positive one. Further, this will increase the quality of work and shorten the time required to finish the job. This impact can finally increase company revenue and labor income. Greenberg (2005) found that the appropriate use of information and communication technology (ICT) helps households collect commodity market price information. This condition will eliminate intermediaries and increase household revenue. Internet use also creates an opportunity to expand sales by enabling people to engage in online transactions (Ariansyah, 2018). In the case of Indonesia, the promotion of internet coverage has a positive impact on the monthly MSMEs income. This finding provides evidence of a new pathway to escape poverty in rural areas.

3.4 Implementing Digital Talent Programs

As mentioned above, developing digital talent among MSMEs should consider the needs of MSMEs, including categorizing MSMEs based on readiness to digitalize their business. Based on the findings of this study, four categories of MSMEs can be mapped according to their readiness to adopt digital technology. The first is young, talented MSME entrepreneurs with high digital literacy. Second is conventional

Table 3.2 Digital literacy based on respondent's age classification

Level of digital literacy	Age group classification	
	Young	Senior
Low	Group 3	Group 4
High	Group 1	Group 2

Source Fizzanty et al (2021)

entrepreneurs with adequate digital literacy. Third, entrepreneurs need more devices and digital literacy. Fourth are senior entrepreneurs who need to be more literate about digital technology. The characteristics of these four types of entrepreneurs greatly influence the effectiveness of the MSME digitalization program carried out by the government and various other interested parties in advancing digital talent capacity among MSME players in contemporary Indonesia (Table 3.2).

Young, talented MSME entrepreneurs with high digital literacy are primarily located in urban areas and are adept at leveraging digital tools for their businesses. From the outset, they leverage digital platforms to expand their sources of income, enhance marketing efforts, and grow their business networks. Even though they are still doing a business combination between digital and conventional, generally, the main target is digital-based development. In developing their digital business, those in this category prioritize modern management based on the required abilities or skills. For example, marketing management uses a creative team, while customer satisfaction is handled by a separate team with good communication skills. The development of business transactions is continuously monitored and evaluated, including the design and appearance of the products offered. Young entrepreneurs in this category usually rely heavily on digital-based creative ideas to develop the MSME business that is being developed. Additionally, young MSME entrepreneurs with high digital literacy can independently acquire the technology, knowledge, and skills needed to operate online businesses. They are naturally familiar with social media and e-commerce, so all it takes is trial and error or learning by doing. With this capability, digitalization programs such as online training with advanced materials can run effectively. Efforts to improve certainly need to be encouraged by presenting success stories and tips from practitioners or digital marketers who have succeeded.

The second category is conventional MSME entrepreneurs with adequate digital literacy. MSME actors who fall into this category have been in the digital world for less than five years, have a good understanding of the use of digital devices to support business development, and have an adequate formal educational background. They are interested in developing digital businesses but still rely on high levels of conventional transactions. In developing digital talent, those in this category usually look for digital business opportunities that can be utilized to support their business development manually. Included in this category are those who have conducted business transactions online because they are driven by an urgent need to serve consumer needs and satisfaction. In developing a digital business, MSMEs that fall into this category usually need assistance and successful examples that can be used as models. They generally do not easily immediately believe in the offers that will be obtained from digital opportunities before these things are lived and felt firsthand. In this case, it is necessary for business assistance from professionals for a certain period or until they are ready to enter the digital world. Through training that can provide a basic understanding of digital business and efforts to improve promotion using digital platforms, those who fall into this category can likely develop their digital business toward more advanced development.

The third category consists of MSME actors who lack access to digital devices and have low digital literacy. Entrepreneurs with inadequate digital devices and literacy find it challenging to carry out digital-based business transformation. Training programs alone will not be effective for this type of entrepreneur. They lack interest in engaging in digital business activities. However, conducive business support, such as supporting family members with better digital knowledge, allows for the developing of digital-based businesses. Some examples of interventions that have successfully encouraged these entrepreneurs' digital transformation are gradually increasing digital capabilities carried out by several actors supporting MSMEs (local government, consultants, telecommunications companies, and marketplace platforms). This process must be preceded by assessing the condition of the entrepreneur's digital devices and capabilities. After the assessment, assistance is needed regarding internet network equipment and infrastructure. Subsequently, basic digital knowledge is imparted through training and supervision provided by MSME supervisors.

The fourth category comprises technologically illiterate senior entrepreneurs who require special attention. Training and supervision alone will not effectively encourage digital transformation in this type of entrepreneur. Senior entrepreneurs require direct assistance from professionals to set up accounts, channels, and digital content for their businesses. An example of a case running in West Java is the professional support provided by the Food MSME association at a relatively affordable cost. Senior entrepreneurs also cannot be forced to be involved in digital transformation because most of these entrepreneurs tend to be less innovative in business development (in the case of Yogyakarta, there is a very strong '*nrimo*' culture). They can often benefit from assistance in digitalization from relatives or family members, particularly children, who can help operate the business digitally.

The findings with the characteristics of respondents are important in determining the focus of targets and efforts to increase digital talent and digitalization capacity of MSME actors in Indonesia. This note is crucial for regional governments, central government/relevant ministries, and business associations that often carry out training programs on digital talent. This condition is because efforts to digitalize the businesses of MSMEs in Indonesia can only be forced by looking at the interest (need) and readiness for the digitalization process of MSMEs. In this case, the availability of data related to aspects of interest and readiness for the need to adopt digital technology in the development of Indonesian MSMEs is important, especially to support the success of the talent development process and digital transformation of Indonesian MSMEs.

The needs and readiness of MSME actors in building their digital capacity can also be seen from the methods and strategies adopted in acquiring digital-based skills. Based on the data in Table 3.3, most MSMEs in Indonesia develop their digital skills independently. Further, they refer to the government's role in providing digital training facilities. This finding indicates that the digital talent development process has not touched many MSMEs. They still rely on natural processes through a trial-and-error approach. On the one hand, this condition is positive as efforts to digitalize MSME businesses are built based on direct interest and initiative from MSME actors. On the other hand, the skills acquired need to be completed and practical.

Government agencies, both central and regional, are institutions expected to contribute to developing digital talent for MSMEs in Indonesia. The government's capacity is more qualified, considering the process requires consistent financing and adequate teaching staff and facilities. At the regional level, digital talent training activities usually involve agencies directly related to developing the digital economy, such as MSMEs and employment agencies. They are expected to become leaders in developing digital talent in the regions by implementing programs that prioritize output and directly impact the digital capacity of MSMEs. However, many digital MSME capacity development programs by local government agencies are implemented without good cross-institutional planning and coordination. For instance, the training material is often mismatched and overlapping, training participants are not recruited based on need and readiness, and there is often no follow-up program after the training is completed.

The types of training most needed by MSME actors are digital marketing, promotions, and e-commerce. This finding aligns with the characteristics of MSME actors in Indonesia, which are generally dominated by actors who are still looking for appropriate forms to digitalize their businesses. This condition is also supported by the expansion of various digital and e-commerce platforms in Indonesia, which provide various conveniences in promoting products and the benefits of digital business. Moreover, the Indonesian people are listed as one of the third largest social media users in Asia—including using e-commerce media for activities related to the digital economy.

In addition to supporting access to education and digital skills tailored to the needs and digital readiness of MSMEs, the success of transforming and developing the capacity of digital talent for MSMEs in Indonesia is also largely determined by an ongoing mentoring process. This process must be carried out by involving credible (professional) MSME assistants equipped with case resolution/consultation targets in the field as part of the supervision process of the mentoring process.

In the case of Yogyakarta, for example, reports on the mentoring process by assistants in the field were recorded systematically (digitally) so that policymakers could evaluate the effectiveness of their work directly in the field. Continuous assistance is important in supporting the success of the MSME digitalization process in Indonesia. In addition, not all MSME actors immediately apply the knowledge and skills they gain from the education and skills training process.

MSMEs generally need assistants who can be used as a place to ask questions if they encounter various difficulties in digitizing their business. Digitalizing MSME businesses involves more than marketing issues and various internet-based digital applications. Creating attractive visual content, communicating with potential customers, packing and shipping goods, and responding to consumer feedback are

Table 3.3 Reference of digital learning and type of training needed among MSMEs

Aspect	Category	Not connected	Digitally connected	Promote via online platform	Use digitalization for marketing and operational	Almost digitalized	Fully digitalized
Reference of digital learning	Central government	7	26	26	8	3	2
	Local government	14	40	39	6	2	0
	Private/ BUMN/ BUMD	3	19	26	9	1	2
	Association/ community	4	24	25	3	1	1
	Business network	7	23	31	7	2	1
	University	1	0	3	3	0	0
	Professional	2	10	18	5	3	0
	Manual	24	40	82	10	3	1
	None	15	8	5	5	1	0
	Other	0	0	0	0	0	0
	Total	77	190	255	56	16	7
Type of training needed	The use of internet and smartphone	20	63	70	14	7	4
	E-commerce	20	107	137	26	9	2
	Fintech	12	55	79	18	6	1
	Operational application	16	56	78	28	10	4
	Design	12	72	105	28	6	3
	Marketing digital	28	115	162	33	10	3
	Ekspor-impor	8	38	55	19	7	2
	Foreign language	7	44	58	15	8	2
	Software & hardware	7	60	59	25	7	2
	Not necessary	10	6	13	2	1	0
	Other	1	0	1	1	1	0
	Toal	141	616	817	209	72	23

*Source*Fizzanty et al. (2021)

some skills that also need to be understood by MSME actors going into business digitally. Many MSME players just starting a digital business consider this process 'complicated'. Therefore, the existence of assistants is important and strategic, especially to continue to motivate and provide direct solutions for MSMEs who experience various difficulties related to the business digitalization process.

Another important aspect related to MSME digitalization is strengthening the human resource capacity of MSME actors based on organizations' and local governments' creativity through various innovative programs and strategies. Group-based platforms can be an entry point for various parties to get involved in increasing the digital capacity of MSME players. This fact includes bridging information related to digitalization constraints, exhibition opportunities, opening digital business networks, and production cooperation to fulfill large orders. All of this is usually facilitated by local governments who are considered to understand better the problems MSMEs face at the local level.

Interviews with MSME actors also found that the use of 'language' that was easily understood and directly accepted by fellow group members was considered more effective in facilitating the information needs of MSME actors. Group-based forums are also able to reduce disparities between digitally trained and untrained MSME actors through a process of sharing experiences. In this context, who is speaking and who is known greatly influences the decisions of MSME actors to follow up on information about problems in the digitalization process. Institutional associations, professional organizations, or associations are recognized as closer and more trusted to bridge the need for information about the digital transformation of MSMEs. Meanwhile, the creativity or innovation of the local government through the implementation of various digitalization programs and strategies directly shows the seriousness of supporting the development of MSMEs in digitalizing their business. Therefore, good cooperation between professional associations and local government agencies in building a digital talent development ecosystem in the regions is a priority requirement. With good cooperation, the program will be more effective. The subsequent impact of efforts to increase digital talent capacity will require more work in achieving the expected output targets and impacts.

3.5 Conclusion

Having digital talent is a key part of digital transformation for MSME actors in Indonesia. Using digital technology, MSMEs can enter a wider market to expand their business, including the global market. They have greater access to various opportunities and resources, including access to financial credit, training, and new customers, which are increasingly being made available online. Therefore, developing digital talent is a strategic step in supporting efforts to increase MSME's business capacity and economic contribution to the economy.

In the Indonesian context, however, business owners' need for digital literacy and adequate educational background can illustrate the complexity of efforts to increase digital talent capabilities. For example, in digital training, the material and achievement targets must consider the characteristics of MSME actors. Those just starting a digital business need basic training, including an understanding of the ins and outs of effective digital promotion and the use of online transactions that can support business efficiency. Meanwhile, understanding digital strategies and utilizing network and business expansion is important for those with advanced digital skills and literacy. In this way, efforts to digitalize MSMEs can be carried out according to the needs, readiness, demographic, and business characteristics of MSME actors.

References

Ariansyah, K. (2018). The importance of the internet on improving economic welfare: An empirical evidence from Indonesian rural household. In *2018 International Conference on ICT for Rural Development (IC-ICTRuDev)* (pp. 118–123), Badung Regency

Arifin, Z. (2011). *The impact of mobile phones on household welfare in Indonesia: Evidence and implications* [Doctoral dissertation, University of Pittsburgh]. https://core.ac.uk/download/pdf/12210477.pdf.

Ariska, N., & Lienggar, R. (2020). The role of internet utilization among SMEs on household welfare in Indonesia. *Jurnal Ekonomi Indonesia, 9*(2), 25–37.

Center for Digital Society. (2019). Adaptability Indonesian small and medium enterprises with digital economy. Case study#47. March 2019. https://cfds.fisipol.ugm.ac.id/wp-content/uploads/sites/1423/2021/01/47-CfDS-Case-Study-Adaptability-Indonesian-Small-Medium-Enterprises-SMEs-with-Digital-Economy.pdf.

Deloitte. (2015). The Deloitte consumer review: digital predictions in 2015. The Deloitte Report. https://www2.deloitte.com/content/dam/Deloitte/uk/Documents/consumer-business/deloitte-uk-consumer-reviewdigital-predictions-2015.pdf

Edwin, J., & Ross, T. (Eds.). (2017). *Digital Indonesia: Connectivity and divergence.* ISEAS Publishing.

Fizzanty, T., Aminullah, E., Nawawi, Maulana, I., Suryanto, J., Aziz, N. L., Pranata, N., Budiatri, A. P., Suardi, I., Ariyani, L., & Wicaksono, A. (2021). Pengembangan Ekosistem Ekonomi Digital UKM Indonesia. Prioritas Riset Nasional Pengembangan Ekonomi Digital Indonesia Tahun 2020. Laporan Akhir Kegiatan (No.199/E1/PRN/2020). Organisasi Riset Ilmu Pengetahuan Sosial Humaniora, Badan Riset dan Inovasi Nasional (Indonesia).

Gilch, P., & Jost, S. (2020). Recruiting digital talent: The strategic role of recruitment in organizations' digital transformation. *German Journal of Human Resources, 35*(1), 53–82. https://doi.org/10.1177/23970022209527

Greenberg, A. (2005). ICTs for poverty alleviation: Basic tool and enabling sector. In *ICT for Development Secretariat, Department for Infrastructure and Economic Cooperation.* Sida. https://www.sida.se/contentassets/e2425616ca0542e0a55270d5087e0c3a/icts-for-poverty-alleviation1080.pdf.

Hermawan, D. (2022). *Challenges of culture-based SMEs digitalization.* Bank Indonesia Institute.

IMF. (2018). Measuring digital economy. IMF Policy Paper. https://www.imf.org/en/Publications/Policy-Papers/Issues/2018/04/03/022818-measuring-the-digital-economy

Jordana, T. A, Suwarto, D. H. (2017). Pemetaan Gerakan Literasi Digital di Lingkup Universitas Negeri Yogyakarta. *Informasi, 47*(2), 167–180. https://doi.org/10.21831/informasi.v47i2.15735

Kartika, M. (2019). Public service and micro-small enterprise developments in Indonesia. *Integrated Journal of Business and Economics, 3*(1), 108–115. https://doi.org/10.33019/ijbe.v3i1.103.

Katsonis, M., & Botros, A. (2015). Digital government: A primer and professional perspectives. *Australian Journal of Public Administration, 74*(1), 42–52. https://doi.org/10.1111/1467-8500.12144

Kominfo.go.id. (2019). *UMKM Go Online, Upaya Wujudkan Visi "Digital Energy of Asia"*. Retrieved March 7, 2023, from https://www.kominfo.go.id/content/detail/9514/umkm-go-onlineupayawujudkan-visi-digital-energyof-asia/0/berita_satker.

Kpodar, K., & Andrianaivo, M. (2011). *ICT, Financial inclusion, and growth: Evidence from African countries*. IMF Working Paper, WP/11/73. International Monetary Fund. https://www.imf.org/en/Publications/WP/Issues/2016/12/31/ICT-Financial-Inclusion-and-Growth-Evidence-from-African-Countries-24771.

OECD. (2020). *OECD Digital Economy Outlook 2020*. https://www.oecd.org/sti/ieconomy/oecd-digital-economyoutlook-2020-bb167041-en.htm

Pangestu, M., Grace, W. (2017). Indonesia and the digital economy: Creative destruction, opportunities and challenges. In J. Edwin & T. Ross (Eds.), *Digital Indonesia: Connectivity and divergence*. ISEAS Publishing.

Rahayu, R., & Day, J. (2017). E-commerce adoption by MSMEs in developing countries: Evidence from Indonesia. *Eurasian Business Review, 7*(1), 25–41.

Savrul, M., & Sener, S. (2014). The potential of e-commerce for SMEs in a globalizing business environment. *Procedia-Social and Behavioral Sciences, 150*(2), 35–45. https://doi.org/10.1016/j.sbspro.2014.09.005

Schawab, K. (2016). The fourth industial revolution. *World Economic Forum*. https://www.weforum.org/about/thefourth-industrial-revolution-by-klaus-schwab/

Schawab, K. (2016). *The fourth industial revolution*. World Economic Forum. https://www.weforum.org/about/thefourth-industrial-revolution-by-klaus-schwab/

Setkab. (2021). *Trade minister: Indonesian digital economy to grow eightfold by 2030*. https://setkab.go.id/en/trade-minister-indonesian-digital-economy-to-grow-eightfold-by-2030

Supriyanto, S. (2016). Pemberdayaan usaha mikro, kecil dan menengah (UMKM) sebagai salah satu upaya penanggulangan kemiskinan. *Jurnal Informasi, 49*(2), 23–38. https://doi.org/10.21831/jep.v3i1.627.

Udacity & Ipsos. (2022). Talent transformation global impact report - enterprise and employee insights on talent transformation in a digital—first world. https://www.ipsos.com/sites/default/files/ct/news/documents/2022-01/Talent-transformation.pdf

Welfens, P. J. (2008). ICT–productivity and economic growth in Europe. In P.J.J. Welfens & E. Walther-Klaus (Eds.), *Digital Excellence* (pp. 13–39). Springer.

Yanti, M., & Yusnaini, Y. (2018). The narration of digital literacy movement in Indonesia. *Informasi, 48*(2), 243–255. https://doi.org/10.21831/informasi.v48i2.21148.

Nawawi is currently working as Head of the Research Center for Population, National Research and Innovation Agency (BRIN). His research focus on the issues related to human resources and employment development in Indonesia. Currently he is working with two research projects related to the challenges of education and trainings in the fisheries sectors and talent development of SMEs in the digital era. Nawawi has published books and articles both as national and international publications. He obtained his PhD from the School of Politics and International Studies University of Leeds in January 2020.

Chapter 4
Digital Finance for MSMEs: Issues, Challenges, and Keys to Promote Inclusive Growth

Nika Pranata, Ikval Suardi, and Joko Suryanto

Abstract This chapter discusses the dynamics of digital financial services development and penetration particularly for MSMEs. It elaborates on its key issues, challenges, and how it accelerates inclusive growth. In doing so, it mainly utilizes national-scale survey data that has been conducted by the team toward MSMEs across sectors. It is found that digital financial services have become alternative sources of financial services needs for MSMEs, especially for those who cannot access mainstream services such as banks. In terms of service type, digital payment is the most widely used among them followed by lending services. The chapter also provides lessons learned from other countries that have been successfully developing digital financial services for MSMEs. Finally, it proposes several recommendations based on the findings.

Keywords Digital Financial Services · Digital Payment · Financial Technology

4.1 Introduction

MSMEs are essential to the Indonesian economy and have long been considered the nation's backbone. In Indonesia, there were a total of 65.4 million micro, small, and medium enterprises (MSMEs), accounting for 99.9% of all businesses in the nation. These MSMEs employed approximately 114.7 million individuals, equivalent to roughly 56% of the total workforce. The significance of MSMEs in Indonesia's economy cannot be overstated, as they contribute over 60% to the country's Gross Domestic Product (GDP) (Daily Social Indonesia, 2023). MSMEs are essential to

N. Pranata (✉) · I. Suardi · J. Suryanto
National Research and Innovation Agency, Jakarta, Indonesia
e-mail: nika002@brin.go.id

I. Suardi
e-mail: Ikva001@brin.go.id

J. Suryanto
e-mail: joko021@brin.go.id

T. Fizzanty and I. Maulana (eds.), *The Digitalization of Indonesian Small and Medium Enterprises*, Engaging Indonesia, https://doi.org/10.1007/978-981-97-0029-5_4

the Indonesian economy as elaborated in Chap. 1. However, some key challenges are hindering the acceleration of MSME development in Indonesia, including digital transformation and financial aspects.

The process of digital transformation encompasses more than just automation and information processing; it also entails systemic alterations to business processes and models (Aminullah et al., 2022a, 2022b). To make this happen, certain prerequisites are required, such as technological supporting infrastructure (technological devices, internet networks, etc.), as well as the expertise and qualifications of certain human resources (EU4Digital, 2020). Therefore, the digital transformation process, including micro, small, and medium enterprises (MSMEs), requires special funding and investment. The problem is that the majority of MSMEs do not know how to get funding to carry out the digital transformation process and what technology they should invest in. In a study conducted by the European Commission (2020) entitled "Financing the digitalization of small and medium-sized enterprises", in terms of digital transformation they divided MSMEs into two, namely digital adopters and digital natives.

Digital adopters are MSMEs that have been around for a long time before the digital era in Indonesia, particularly before the widespread application of digital technology in business-to-customer (B2C) and business-to-business (B2B) commerce several decades ago, which do not use technology as the main reference in running a business. The majority of digital adopters are still in the early stages of their digital transformation journey. They are still thinking about what technology is right for them to apply in their business. Digital adopters may focus on one or two technologies but they may choose not to implement them at all. Generally, they use a conservative approach in digitalization, namely slowly and targeting areas that can generate direct profits or in the area of optimizing operations (digital optimization). In terms of external funding, they still depend on banks to fund their digital transformation process so the digital transformation funding process is no different than funding for other purposes.

On the other hand, digital natives are MSMEs that have emerged in the digital economy era. Since their founding, they have been closely associated with technology platforms. This group is generally in the form of startups or startup companies that utilize a variety of digital technologies in running their business. They use an experimental approach and have realized the benefits of combining different technologies for business purposes. In terms of funding, they tend to seek financing to scale up their business operations through digital transformation, not to fund the digital transformation process from scratch. Unlike digital adopters who already have a network with banks, they generally still don't have much network with funding institutions, therefore, they have more varied funding source options and tend to seek funding from innovative alternative sources such as hybrid financing and online lending, crowdfunding, and others. Elaboration on this will further be discussed in the next section.

4.2 Policy and Regulation Regarding MSME Financing

The Indonesian government has made major efforts to improve small, medium, and enterprise players' access to financing. Growing financial access is anticipated to be a solution to issues that micro, small, and medium business players frequently encounter. Because these businesses are a dynamic type that can survive economic volatility and absorb a sizable staff, the government's commitment to boosting access to credit for them is seen as crucial. National Medium-Term Development Plan (RPJMN) 2020–2024 incorporates the government's support for the growth of micro, small, and medium firms based on these several factors. The RPJMN 2020–2024 states that the government's goal is to increase access to financing through the development of dedicated banking institutions for small and medium-sized businesses.

A stimulus to encourage more entrepreneurs and economic added value is expected to boost access to finance, which will influence the absorption of the workforce on a national level. Since Presidential Regulation No. 82 of 2016 about the National Strategy for Financial Inclusion, the government has committed to promoting MSMEs' access to financing. The Coordinating Minister for the Economy serves as the coordinator of programs to promote financial inclusion, which are carried out by the Presidential Regulation.

Inclusive financial policies in this case facilitate micro, small, and medium enterprises to have easy access to finance by carrying out digital financial transformation. Experience in several countries shows that digital financial transformation has a positive and significant impact on helping micro, small, and medium enterprises, especially in finding sources of business financing. The strategy to encourage inclusive financial transformation can be done in 3 (three) ways, namely providing appropriate service facilities, providing suitable products, and responsible finance through financial education and consumer protection. Implementation of policies to increase financial inclusion involves several government institutions. The challenges faced in encouraging the use of digitalization by MSMEs are increasing the use of digital facilities built by the government (especially financing) through literacy for business actors. Access to financing is considered strategic because most MSMEs do not have easy access to financing from financial institutions. In encouraging and protecting the community, especially micro, small, and medium enterprises, the role of the Financial Services Authority is very important. Various products and/or financial services in formal financial institutions must refer to the Financial Services Authority Regulation No. 76/POJK.07/2016 concerning Increasing Financial Literacy and Inclusion in the Financial Services Sector for Consumers and/or the Public.

The regulation emphasizes that Financial Service Providers are required to carry out financial literacy by providing various service products related to achieving financial inclusion. The condition of financial literacy and financial inclusion in Indonesia, according to OJK's explanation, has increased. Indonesia's financial literacy in 2019 was at the level of 38.03%, increasing to 49.68% in 2022. An increase also occurred in financial inclusion from 76.19% in 2019 to 85.10% in 2022. There has been an increase in both financial literacy and financial inclusion due to the existence of a government assistance program for the community and the increasingly widespread coverage of telecommunications services, especially cellular in Indonesia.

Moreover, MSMEs are vital contributors to the Indonesian economy. Therefore, even though the primarily responsible government agencies are the Ministry of Cooperatives and MSMEs, most ministries/agencies have MSME empowerment programs, including aspects of MSME financing. According to the Ministry of Cooperatives and Small and Medium Enterprises, currently, there are around 18 Ministries/Institutions that have MSME financing programs (Sitorus, 2019). The Ministry of Cooperatives and Small and Medium Enterprises realizes that the spread of similar programs in various government agencies results in inefficiencies and the effectiveness of these programs is not optimal.

Therefore, currently, the Ministry of MSMEs and Cooperatives is preparing a strategic plan and roadmap related to MSME development in terms of financing by consolidating MSME financing budgets spread across various government agencies. In addition, there are also plans for integrated financing policy schemes for MSMEs from various sources including banking, non-bank financial institutions including leasing, insurance, pawnshops, guarantee or insurance companies, and various other financing institutions.

Furthermore, through the omnibus law, the government also provides several facilities and conveniences for MSMEs regarding financing. For example, MSMEs get facilitation of financing and fiscal incentives by Law Number 11 of 2020 concerning Job Creation in article 92 where micro and small enterprises are given facilities/ simplification of tax administration to apply for financing facilities from the central government by statutory provisions. in the field of taxation.

Then, the law also strengthens MSME funding sources where in the third part of the criteria for micro, small, and medium enterprises regarding the provisions of article 21 which was amended to become the central government and local governments provide financing for micro and small enterprises. State-owned enterprises also provide financing from the provision for the annual profit share allocated to micro and small enterprises in the form of loans, guarantees, grants, and other financing. The law also accommodates one of the major obstacles for MSMEs to access bank financing, namely the absence or insufficiency of collateral. Through the Job Creation Law, business activities can now be used as MSME assets. These various supportive policies are aimed at increasing MSMEs' access to financing, where currently only around 11% of MSMEs access financing from banks (Media Indonesia, 2020).

Furthermore, the expansion and ease of access to financing is also an important factor in the digital transformation of MSMEs. Currently digitalizing MSMEs is one of the goals set out in the 2021–2024 Indonesia digital transformation roadmap. The government is targeting MSMEs with digital access to reach 10 million MSMEs by 2021. The availability of digital financial service systems and facilities is expected to open opportunities for MSMEs to expand their market reach. Thus, proper policy support is needed for Indonesian MSMEs, especially in accessing digital finance, so that the development of the digital financial sector can contribute to the progress of Indonesian MSMEs.

4.3 Issues and Challenges for MSMEs in Accessing Digital Finance

The Central Bureau of Statistics survey in July 2020 on the impact of COVID-19 on business owners revealed a decline in the total sales revenue of MSMEs and corporations (Badan Pusat Statistik Republik Indonesia, 2022). Around 84% of MSMEs, which accounted for 80% of 34,559 respondents, experienced a decrease in total sales revenue. The survey also indicated that 58.9% of businesses were still operating, 24% reduced their production capacity, 8.76% stopped their operational activities, and 5.4% required some employees to work from home. Meanwhile, 0.5% of businesses that produced jamu (Indonesian traditional medicine), face masks, bicycles, and internet providers exceeded their production capacity.

In this crisis, information technology utilization has become a key to MSMEs' survival as the Large-scale Social Restrictions policy has severely impacted and limited face-to-face interactions, including marketing and sales activities of MSMEs. Meanwhile, based on data from the Ministry of Communication and Informatics, out of 64.2 million MSME business actors, only 17.1% are selling online. At the same time, the rest still rely on offline services for buying and selling activities. In this regard, MSMEs could use FinTech to expand their product market, gain more accessible access to financial services products (e.g. credits, financing, payments), and reduce operational costs, including lease, utilities, and bookkeeping.

The utilization of technology also contributes to the economic recovery process. Information technology has been gaining importance from changes in how businesses operate and people's expectations of the speed of financial services during the pandemic. In this regard, FinTech is essential as it serves people who need financing and caters to the newly emerged marketing and consumption pattern in the new average era. The role is further strengthened as FinTech can also assist in the distribution of aid in cash transfers or other types of social assistance from the government.

Furthermore, the expansion and ease of access to financing are also essential in the digital transformation of MSMEs. Digitalizing MSMEs is one of the goals set out in the 2021–2024 Indonesia digital transformation roadmap. The government is targeting MSMEs with digital access to reach 10 million MSMEs by 2021. The availability of digital financial service systems and facilities will open opportunities for MSMEs to expand their market reach. Thus, proper policy support is needed for Indonesian MSMEs, especially in accessing digital finance, so that the development of the digital financial sector can contribute to the progress of Indonesian MSMEs.

The development of fintech is in line with the growth in internet access, cellphone penetration, and digital financial services, such as e-banking and other online platforms. Digital financial innovation in Indonesia is categorized into four major clusters: digital payments, digital banking, peer-to-peer lending, and crowdfunding. As a regulator, the Financial Services Authority (OJK) has carried out several strategies to accelerate the development of fintech in Indonesia, namely establishing research, policies, and regulations, creating business models and examples of business governance, and expanding cooperation between regulators, fintech hubs, and international organizations (OJK, 2020).

The fact that the transaction value of phone banking, mobile banking, internet banking, electronic money, and online loans such as peer-to-peer lending during the COVID-19 pandemic is a financial transaction that does not have a direct impact (Sugandi, 2021) means that this industry has the potential to support Indonesia in national economic recovery. For example, it has contributed to the pre-employment card program to distribute non-cash social assistance to people affected by COVID-19 (Sugandi, 2021).

In addition, the development of innovation is fundamental to creating a stable, contributing, inclusive, and sustainable digital financial environment. The synergy between fintech companies, financial institutions, microfinance, cooperatives, and community agents is an important aspect that must be carried out. Nonetheless, an inclusive and sustainable financial sector must be supported by a shared vision and clear strategy from stakeholders (Batunanggar, 2019).

4.3.1 MSME Funding Sources

Regarding sources of financing, most MSMEs 60.4% still fully use personal funds for business purposes, while 39.6% use external funds (Fig. 4.1). This aligns with several surveys conducted by BPS and other parties (Central Statistics Agency, 2019) of the 39.6% who accessed external funding, it was found that most respondents used loans from banks and family/family as their source of external financing, with the respective proportions of 56.72 and 51.26%. This is because people can still run a business using personal funds first rather than increasing business capital by borrowing from financial institutions, which will be burdensome later in paying installments.

Table 4.1 The exciting thing is that cooperatives are one of the leading choices for external financing sources, with a percentage of 38.66%. Then there are 25.63% of respondents who access financing from pawnshops. Meanwhile, for fully digital funding services (online/fintech loans), around 23.11% of them access these services for their business needs. In addition, quite a lot of them still use moneylenders for access to business financing (13.87%). Another important role of Fintech is that it can increase customer ratios in the banking sector, such as peer-to-peer (P2P) lending service facilities. Many micro-entrepreneurs do not have bank accounts. However, after their business grew thanks to capital funding from Fintech startups, they now have bank accounts and become debtors of banking institutions. The use of digital financing by MSMEs is a transitional stage from the initial phase of developing their business before using bank loan funds. This is because many micro-entrepreneurs need bank accounts, making it challenging to apply for loans from banks; if micro businesses use digital financing, they must have a bank account so that it can be said to be a transitional stage toward the banking system.

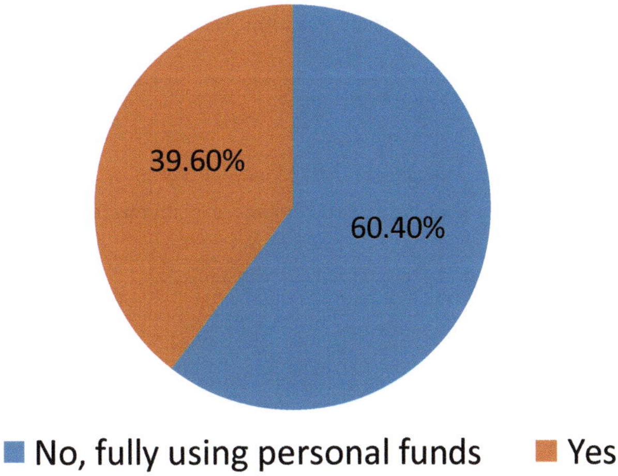

Fig. 4.1 MSME use of external funds for business purposes (banks, cooperatives, fintech, etc.). *Source* Fizzanty et al. (2021)

Table 4.1 MSME external funding sources

No	Variable	Percentage
1	Loans from banks	56.72
2	Loans from relatives/family	51.26
3	Cooperative	38.66
4	Pegadaian	25.63
5	Fintech	23.11
6	Non-relative/family informal loans	13.87
7	Others	0.84

Source Fizzanty et al. (2021)

4.3.2 MSMEs Access to Digital Finance

An online survey of 601 MSMEs in Indonesia conducted by the LIPI Research Team for the MSME Digital Economic Ecosystem in 2020 regarding digital finance revealed two aspects, namely: (1) Access to digital finance, which includes the types of services, and (2) Access to external financing, including the origin of the financing source. Digital finance is an activity of payment and financial services that uses digital technology facilities such as cellular or web through third parties. On the other hand, external financing is business financing originating from outside the MSMEs.

In the first aspect, when COVID-19 was still endemic in Indonesia, it was found that most MSMEs accessed digital financial services. Most of the most used services are online payments (71.21%), followed by online loan services 13.98%, market provisioning 11.15%, online insurance 9.15%, and others 0.17% (Table 4.2). The

Table 4.2 MSME access to digital financial services in 2020

No	Variable	Percentage
1	Online payments (OVO, Gopay, Funds, etc.)	71.21
2	Not accessing digital financial services	23.63
3	Online loans (Amartha, Modalku, Friends Money, etc.)	13.98
4	Market provisioning or financial service comparison platforms (CekAja, Cermati, etc.)	11.15
5	Online insurance (PasarPolis, RajaPremi, Asuransi88, etc.)	9.15
6	Others	0.17

Source Fizzanty et al. (2021)

description above shows that Indonesian MSMEs have well-utilized and widely used online payments. This indicates that digital transactions are increasingly crucial for MSMEs. Meanwhile, to accelerate access to and utilization of other types of financial services, such as online loans and market provisioning, policies are still needed that can support the digital economic transformation process for MSMEs. One approach that needs attention is for digital financial companies to collaborate with regional financial institutions with access to knowledge related to MSMEs and local wisdom from the area. Research conducted by P2E-LIPI in 2017–2019 found that this was able to increase MSMEs' access to digital financial services. Fintech is here to provide solutions to fill the gap in financing in the financial services industry sector, especially by serving microfinance to the MSMEs sector. Even though MSMEs dominate businesses in Indonesia, the amount of loans disbursed to this MSMEs group is still far from sufficient, especially when compared to loans provided by financial service providers, namely banks, to large companies. Over the years, most of the MSMEs segment did not have access to financing either from banks, capital markets, or non-bank financial institutions, despite making a significant contribution to the national economy.

4.4 MSMEs Digital Finance Toward COVID-19 Pandemic

The COVID-19 Pandemic has double-sided effects on MSMEs. In terms of business development, it impacts MSMEs negatively. To reduce the transmission of the virus, the government has imposed a strict mobility restriction policy called *Pembatasan Sosial Berskala Besar* (PSBB or large-scale social restriction). This reduces demand for MSME goods and products as people work and school from home, places are closed, etc. As a result, based on Indonesia Statistics data, it hit more MSME businesses compared to large enterprises. More than 84% of MSMEs experienced an earnings drop compared to 82% of large enterprises. The largest impact was experienced by the accommodation and food and beverages sector (92%), followed by other services (91%), transport and warehouse (90%), water and waste processing

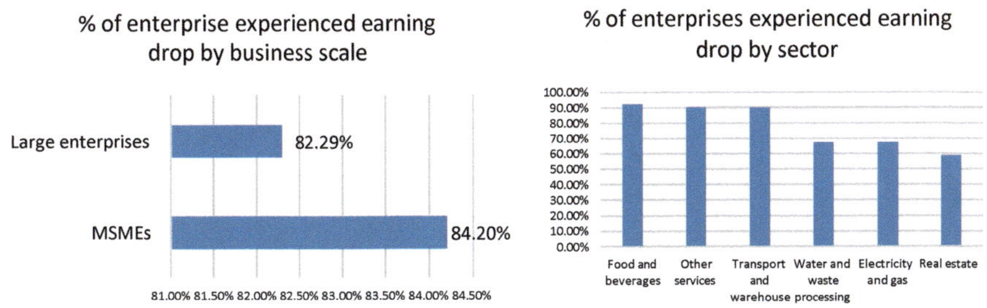

Fig. 4.2 MSMEs impacted by COVID-19 by scale and sector. Sailendra and Djaddang (2022). *Source* based on Indonesia Statistics

(68%), electricity and gas (68%), and real estate (59%) (Sailendra and Djaddang, 2022) (Fig. 4.2).

Similarly, this condition was also revealed by an Indonesian Institute of Science (LIPI) survey. In terms of sales decline, almost 95% of Indonesian MSMEs were negatively impacted by the pandemic (Rahim, 2021). The impact varied among sizes and business sectors. The largest decline was experienced by ultra-micro (49% of sales decline), followed by medium (46%), micro (43%), and small (40%).

On the other hand, the pandemic has boosted the number of MSMEs onboard to digital ecosystems. Data from the Ministry of MSMEs and Cooperative show that the number of MSMEs joining digital platforms has increased almost tripled from approximately 8 million digitally onboarding MSMEs in 2019 (13.5% of total MSMEs) to 21 million digitally onboarding MSMEs in 2022 (32% of total MSMEs). The Government of Indonesia aims to have 30 million MSMEs onboarded by 2024 (Ministry of Communication & Informatics, 2022).

4.4.1 Digital Payment

Furthermore, in terms of digital finance, the pandemic has also accelerated digital payment use. Based on Bank Indonesia statistics, both the number of digital payment transactions and the value of digital payment transactions significantly increased. Regarding the number of transactions, it has increased by almost 50% since the beginning of the pandemic (February 2020: 431 million transactions) to 642 million transactions in December 2022. The same trend also happens in terms of digital payments value which increased by 55% during the same period from IDR 3.1 trillion to IDR 4.8 trillion. The nominal amount per transaction was also increased by 66% in that period from IDR 35,179 per transaction to 58,527 per transaction (Fig. 4.3). These increases are above inflation and Indonesia's economic growth. Therefore, this shows that people and MSMEs are getting used to paying transactions digitally and feel more secure about it. To note, although there was a decrease in transactions at

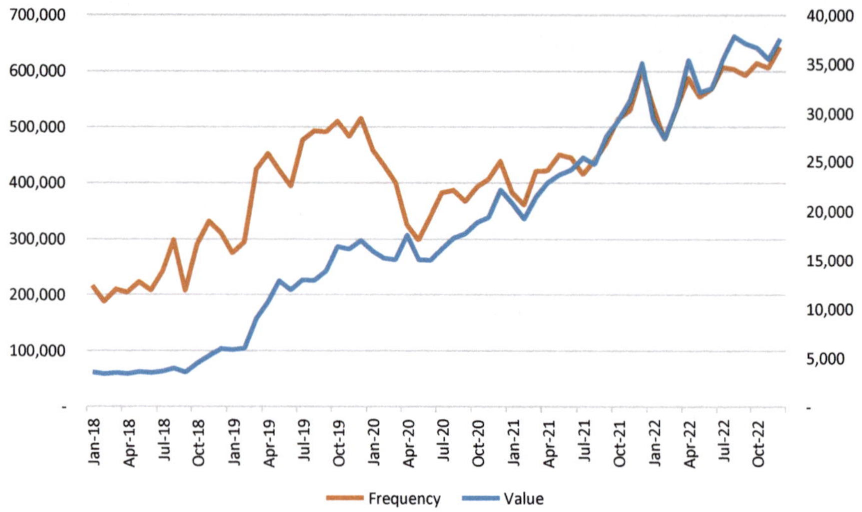

Fig. 4.3 Frequency and value of digital payments transactions January 2018–December 2022. *Source* Bank Indonesia (2023)

the beginning of the pandemic, it was likely caused by a drop in aggregate demand, not due to reluctance to do digital payment transactions.

4.4.2 *Online Lending*

Based on the Daily Social Indonesia (2023) survey, access to capital is the second largest challenge faced by local MSMEs. It is also supported by the Bank Indonesia survey found that 69.5% of MSMEs haven't received credit (Kristianus, 2022). The challenges come from both borrowers and lenders. From the borrower's side, one of the challenges is low financial literacy and lack of collateral. From the lender side, particularly banks, it is hard for them to find creditworthy MSMEs to maintain their prudential level, with the current evaluation method, most MSMEs are considered unbankable.

The emergence of financial technology through online lending has become an alternative source of financing for MSMEs. They offer simpler processes and requirements with a consequence of higher interest rates. Fintech lending platforms utilize advanced technologies like big data analytics, machine learning, and artificial intelligence to assess loan applications and evaluate the creditworthiness of borrowers. This enables them to make lending decisions more quickly compared to traditional banks while gaining a more thorough understanding of the borrower's creditworthiness. Furthermore, fintech lending platforms frequently provide smaller loan amounts and more flexible repayment terms, catering to the specific requirements of MSMEs.

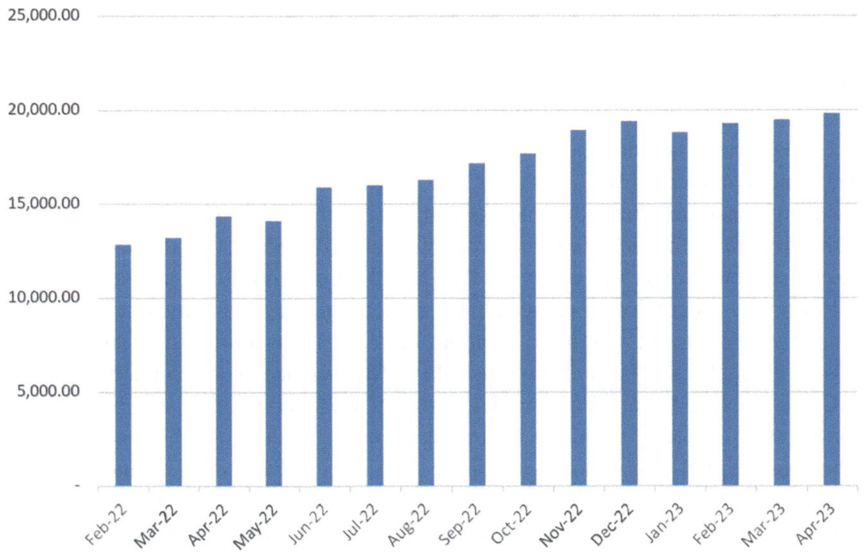

Fig. 4.4 Total amount of MSMEs online lending Feb 2022–April 2023 (in IDR 1000 billion). *Source* Authors calculation based on OJK Statistics

Based on OJK non-bank financial institutions statistics, as of April 2023, the fintech lending disbursement is about IDR 50 thousand trillion, about 39% of which is channeled to MSMEs. This proportion of MSMEs borrowing amount is higher than banks. Similar to digital payments, online lending for MSMEs has also shown an increasing trend during the recovery period from the pandemic as can be seen in Fig. 4.4.

4.5 Learning from Other Countries' Experiences

Since 2014, China's economic development has entered a new normal stage with medium–high growth speed as its essential characteristic and comprehensive and sustainable social development as its orientation. As a new powerhouse of China's economy and social development, small and micro enterprises are vital for achieving sustainable economic growth and promoting inclusive economic development. Most studies studying the drivers of sustainable growth of companies from the perspective of the macro environment, corporate social responsibility, research and development (R&D) investments, and management characteristics seek to find alternatives for sustainable growth in a combination of internal and external factors. The resource-based theory states that a firm is a collection of resources that determine its speed, mode, and growth limits. Under this average economy, China's small and micro enterprises must accept development opportunities, achieve sustainable growth, and overcome risks and challenges, given the changing complex macroeconomic environment and the continuous adjustment of industrial structure. Today, the inherent laws and operating mechanisms of sustainable growth of companies remain a significant problem (Escribá-Esteve et al., 2009).

Chinese small and micro enterprises receive their primary resources from several traditional commercial banks, and the fundamental dilemma of complex and costly financing constrains their continued growth. This natural dilemma can be overcome with digital financial inclusion, which benefits financial services for the real economy and vulnerable groups. According to the Global Partnership for Financial Inclusion (GPFI) white paper released at the G20 Hangzhou Summit, digital financial inclusion generally refers to all actions to promote financial inclusion through digital technology. Digital financial inclusion also drives the science and technology strength of China's digital financial market development, cloud computing, and block to the dominant distributed computing technology, internet technology, biological recognition and digital encryption technology, security, and big data technology, and emerging technologies such as artificial intelligence. The development of digital financial inclusion in China has made it possible for various types of financial institutions to obtain more information about borrowers through cutting-edge digital technology (Buchak et al., 2018).

The development of digital financial inclusion in China has gone through four stages. (1) Non-profit microcredit in the 1990s: The primary source of funds at this stage were donations or concessional loans from individuals or international organizations that were used to alleviate rural poverty. (2) Development of microfinance from 2000 to 2005: Formal financial institutions are the primary source of funds to promote re-employment, entrepreneurship, and improving people's livelihoods. (3) Comprehensive and inclusive finance from 2006 to 2010: At this stage, the primary funding sources are village banks and microcredit institutions. Small and micro enterprises are incorporated into the service system to provide financial services such as payments, remittances, loans, and pawning services. (4) Digital financial inclusion from 2011 to present: Since financial inclusion was first introduced at the Third Plenary Session of the 18th CPC Central Committee, the Chinese government has emphasized it in its work reports for three consecutive years. In July 2017, Secretary General Xi Jinping put forward the directive to build a financial inclusion system and digital development of financial inclusion for the first time (Yang & Zhang, 2020).

China's digital financial inclusion has gradually risen to become a national strategy. Recently, Chinese technology and financial services companies such as Alibaba Group, Tencent Holdings Ltd., and JD Group have used their technological advances to provide financial services such as mobile payments, consumer financing, and online loans to billions of individuals and tens of millions of businesses, including small and micro enterprises, thereby promoting the development of China's network and digital economy. The financial resources provided by digital financial inclusion for small and micro enterprises in China mainly include peer-to-peer (P2P) lending, online microcredit, internet banking, and internet equity crowdfunding.

According to (Yang & Zhang, 2020), digital financial inclusion and the sustainable growth of small and micro enterprises (MSMEs) have led to the rapid development of digital technology, which has driven the integration of finance and technology and has given rise to a series of new forms of finance, and brought about significant life changes—human social. Promoting inclusive and sustainable economic growth and encouraging micro, small, and medium enterprises to formalize and grow through access to financial services align with the United Nations 2030 Agenda for Sustainable Development. Therefore, our research investigates the impact of digital financial inclusion in China on the sustainable growth of small and micro enterprises. This study uses data on companies listed on the New Third Board Market of China from 2011 to 2018 and Peking University's digital financial inclusion index to empirically examine the impact of digital financial inclusion developments and mechanisms in various provinces in China. This study found that: (1) developing digital financial inclusion helps promote sustainable growth of small and micro businesses.

(2) On the other hand, developing digital financial inclusion can effectively promote the sustainable growth of small and micro enterprises in the private sector, high-tech industries, and competitive markets. (3) The mechanism for the impact of developing digital financial inclusion to encourage sustainable growth of small and micro businesses lies in reducing business financing constraints. This prevents financial crises caused by imbalances in the capital structure and liquidity, promoting sustainable growth of small and micro enterprises. The results show that, under the backdrop of high-quality economic development in China, digital financial inclusion and the reshaping of the ecological pattern of the financial industry can provide a steady flow of financial support for the sustainable growth of small and micro enterprises. In addition, micro enterprises can realize healthy macroeconomic development.

Figure 4.5 exhibits the trend of digital financial inclusion (Digitalfin) in China by year and region. With the cross-border integration of digital technology and financial services and the popularization of mobile internet technology in China, the development level of digital financial inclusion in the country is rising yearly. Despite this rapid growth of digital financial inclusion, the degree of its development varies from one region to the other. In the sample period 2011–2018, the level of digital financial inclusion in Eastern China is higher than that in Western China, owing to the developed economy, the rapid progress of internet technology, and widespread awareness of mobile payment, and there is still more room to catch up in the development of digital financial inclusion in western China (Yang & Zhang, 2020).

According to (Singapore, 2023), India, a world leader in digital payments and fintech innovation, is entering the next phase of its digital finance transformation, now eyeing digital banking prospects to address the credit focus faced by micro, small, and medium enterprises (MSMEs). It said the government was preparing a framework to allow MSMEs to get digital credit more efficiently and safely. Government officials previously activated new rules enabling digital banks to provide business loans digitally. They note that because these players can leverage cutting-edge technology and real-time data, they can introduce new credit products to the market, enhancing customer experience. And reach them so far have been excluded from the formal banking system.

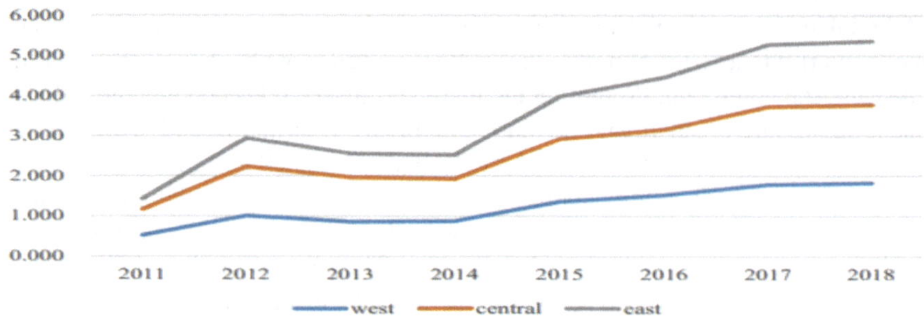

Fig. 4.5 Trends in China's digital financial inclusion by year and year. *Source* Digital financial inclusion index of Peking University (phase II) (2011–2018)

India has one of the fastest-growing fintech industries in the world. According to the Department of Industry Promotion and Domestic Trade (DPIIT), India is home to over 2,000 fintech startups, among them more than a dozen fintech unicorns, data from CB Insights shows. India Stack, a digital infrastructure project introduced over a decade ago, is an essential backer of this growth. India Stack aims to create integrated platform software for governments, businesses, startups, and developers and seeks to promote financial inclusion, improve public services and benefits, and enhance competition in India's financial sector. Several APIs currently comprise the India Stack, including the Unified Payment Interface (UPI), a national real-time payment system; the Aadhaar digital help system; and eSign, an online electronic signature service.

Having laid the groundwork for financial innovation, India must now look to the next steps of its digital finance transformation journey and focus on enabling the entry of full-stack digital banks. The report, entitled Digital Banks: A Proposal for Licensing and Regulatory Regime for India, makes a case for digital bank licensing regimes and regulatory frameworks, the potential emphasis of fully licensed and functional digital banks on financial inclusion and access to credit.

The report notes that lacking a formal regulatory framework for digital banking, India has instead witnessed the emergence of so-called new banks over the past few years. This fintech startup works with banking incumbents to offer "over-the-top" services to consumers, relying on bank balances to lend and issue deposits. Neo-banks often specialize in retail banking or MSME banking. Consumer-facing neo-banks will typically offer digital checking accounts with debit cards and savings accounts and personal financial management tools such as spending and budgeting analytics. Several platforms also provide investment products, credit facilities, and foreign exchange services. Popular neo-banks serving Indian consumers include Niyo, which claims four million customers; Freo, which has 1.5 million subscribers; and Fi Money, a neo-banking platform designed for working professionals counting one million customers.

Meanwhile, neo-banks dealing with MSMEs usually offer cost management products such as employee prepaid cards, payroll management, accounts receivable management, and business loans through banking partners. Popular neo-banking platforms catering to Indian MSMEs include RazorPayX, the business banking platform from Playtech company Razorpay, and Open, a neo-banking platform for MSMEs and startups serving more than 2.3 million businesses.

In Pakistan, more evidence is needed to analyze the impact of digitalization on MSMEs' growth and development. However, a study in India has estimated that GDP can be raised by 10% through technology adoption until 2020. In addition, the study revealed that MSMEs shifting toward digitalization achieve double growth compared to those still using traditional systems. MSMEs with leveraged digital technologies are showing. In Pakistan, more evidence is needed to analyze the impact of digitalization on MSMEs' growth and development. However, a study in India has estimated that GDP can be raised by 10 percent through technology adoption until 2020 (Rasheed et al., 2019).

Furthermore, the study revealed that MSMEs shifting toward digitalization achieve double growth compared to those still using traditional systems. MSMEs leveraging digital technologies are showing promising results. Therefore, the efficient implementation of technology in the MSME sector is a prerequisite for industry and economic growth because digitalization can resolve various MSME issues, such as firms bearing higher costs for cash management and cash flows and increased risk of theft and leakages. However, MSMEs can play securely and freely in the financial market by employing digital payment systems and undertaking digital transactions. Modern systems can significantly reduce leakages and better manage their cash flows. In addition, these MSMEs will automatically be included in the formal financial economy. In addition to aiding the financial inclusion target of 50 percent financially by 2020, it will enable MSMEs to access credit from traditional financial institutions. Furthermore, it will help reduce the credit demand gap of around Rs. 277 billion (Blancher et al., 2019).

Although digitalization can bring tremendous change in the MSME sector and boost Pakistan's economy at the expected level, various challenges hinder the growth and development of the MSME sector and economy. For example, in Pakistan, the literacy level of MSME owner-managers is shallow as they need more financial knowledge and technology. Thus, the adoption level of digital financial services could be more appreciable within their processes and payments. Similarly, MSMEs must also gain technology-related skills as they cannot adopt and work through digital systems (Rasheed et al., 2019).

In addition, the cost of digital techniques is also a significant hurdle toward adopting the need for more supporting infrastructure and technology, which are also significant deterrents to keeping MSMEs online (Rasheed et al., 2019). However, despite these challenges, the Trade Development Authority of Pakistan (TDAP), a government institute, and the Ministry of Information Technology (IT) have undertaken initiatives to digitalize MSMEs in Pakistan. For example, TDAP recently signed a Memorandum of Understanding (MoU) with a global giant in e-commerce, Alibaba. The initiative has been taken to promote exports by MSMEs in Pakistan through e-commerce channels like Alibaba. Moreover, as part of the MoU, Alibaba will take responsibility for online and offline training programs for MSMEs in Pakistan, which help MSMEs learn the skills to adopt and use digitalization. Besides, the Ministry of IT emphasized in its Digital Pakistan Policy 2017 the creation of an infrastructure enabling MSMEs to easily use and adopt digital financial services (Rasheed et al., 2019).

India is considered to be one of the world's fastest and most developing economies in the world. Over the years, the country's payments and settlement system has witnessed drastic changes with the establishment of umbrella organizations like the National Payments Corporation of India, which acts as an intermediary in channelizing all of the country's payment and settlement systems into one mainstream. In the years to come National Payments Corporation of India could perform much better in terms of quality and service by adopting advanced innovative techniques, which are being adopted by other developed countries, like fully automating the cash-based economy into a cashless economy in the upcoming future course of action. But, there are still many issues that require immediate attention like the proper availability of advanced technology, the right amount of skilled manpower, and an adequate amount of infrastructure facilities which directly or indirectly affect the development of India's payments and settlement system in the long run future course of action (Kesavan & Development, 2016).

To date, evidence from reliable empirical studies on the effect of MSME exchange markets on MSMEs is still lacking. A study by (Aggarwal & Thomas, 2017) about MSMEs in the Indian stock exchange has flaws, most importantly a very small sample of 54 listed firms, so the results have to be read with caution. The findings suggest that three years after the listing, asset size and capital structure improve, but firm performance and access to debt finance at formal financial institutions do not differ from that of similar unlisted firms. Further studies are needed to be able to assess the impact of MSME stock exchanges and which of the above benefits materialize (Sommer & Disse, 2020).

India is considered to be one of the world's fastest-growing economies. Over the years, the country's payments and settlement system has witnessed drastic changes through the establishment of an umbrella organization like the National Payments Corporation of India, which acts as an intermediary in channeling the country's payments and settlements system into one mainstream. In the years to come, the National Payments Corporation of India can perform much better in terms of quality and service by adopting advanced innovative techniques, which are being adopted by other developed countries, like fully automating the cash-based economy into a cashless economy in the upcoming future course of action. However, many issues still require immediate attention, like the proper availability of advanced technology, the right amount of skilled workforce, and an adequate amount of infrastructure facilities which directly or indirectly affect the development of India's payments and settlement system in the long run future course of action (Kesavan & Development, 2016).

To date, evidence from reliable empirical studies on the effect of MSME exchange markets on MSMEs still needs to be provided. A study by Aggarwal and Thomas (2017) about MSMEs in the Indian stock exchange has flaws, most notably a tiny sample of 54 listed firms, so the results must be read cautiously. The findings suggest that asset size and capital structure improve three years after the listing. However, firm performance and access to debt finance at formal financial institutions do not differ from that of similar unlisted firms. Further studies are needed to be able to assess the impact of MSME stock exchanges and which of the above benefits materialize (Sommer & Disse, 2020).

From the above, it can be learned that China's economic growth can be bolstered by digital financial inclusion that benefits financial services for the real economy and vulnerable groups. Digital financial inclusion is driving the scientific and technological capabilities of China's digital financial market developers, allowing various financial institutions to access more information about offerings through digital technology. India is entering the next phase of its digital finance transformation, now eyeing digital banking prospects to address the credit focus faced by micro, small, and medium enterprises (MSMEs). Digitalization has enabled MSMEs to achieve double growth compared to those still using traditional systems. Efficient application of technology in the MSME sector is a prerequisite for industrial and economic growth because digitalization can solve various problems of MSMEs, such as companies bearing higher costs for cash management and cash flow and increased risks of theft and leakage.

In Indonesia, financial technology is developing quite rapidly. In 2016, the Indonesian Fintech Association (AFTECH) was established as a forum for financial technology. Currently, according to the official website, there are 352 members of Fintech Companies, 11 financial institutions, and seven technology partners associated with the association. Fintech in Indonesia focuses on digital payments, peer-to-peer (P2P) lending, and investment. Many digital payment platforms, such as Gopay, OVO, and Dana, are widely used. P2P lending has been licensed by the Financial Services Authority (OJK) and has performed quite well so far. Additionally, it has developed a reasonably well-developed investment platform widely used in Indonesia.

Fintech has an essential role in increasing financial movement and helping to establish micro, small, and medium enterprises (MSMEs); through fintech, payments are made faster and easier, financial transactions can be accessed anywhere through applications, and investments can be monitored at any time. Fintech is an efficient, fast, and affordable financial solution. With this innovation, the public and business actors can easily access financial products and services, such as digital payments, online loans, and investments, and manage finances effectively and efficiently. Fintech also has a vital role in increasing financial inclusion, whereby individuals and businesses that traditional financial institutions have not reached can now access safe and affordable financial services. It can help reduce the attraction of financial services between people and enable more people to participate in economic activities. However, along with the development of fintech in Indonesia, some obstacles must be faced, such as data security which has become the biggest challenge for all users, and consumer protection must also have clear regulations. So it is necessary to work together with the government and private sectors to ensure the sustainable growth of the fintech industry.

4.6 Policy Recommendations

Based on the above discussions, the interesting aspect is that cooperatives are still one of the main pillars as a source of funding for MSMEs. However, among other financial institutions (banking, pawnshops, and fintech), cooperatives are lagging in terms of digitalization. Fintech almost entirely uses digital technology, while banks have also massively digitalized financial services such as opening accounts and making loans without physical access. Likewise, pawnshops have also begun to explore digital financial services. Therefore, a policy is needed that can encourage the implementation of digital financial services for cooperatives. One of the main considerations is the spread of cooperatives which are very wide and able to reach remote villages. Based on data from the Ministry of Cooperatives and MSMEs, to date, there are 123,000 active cooperatives, but only 900 cooperatives or 0.73% of them are digitally literate (Endarwati, 2020).

To move toward the digital transformation of cooperatives, currently, the Ministry of Cooperatives and MSMEs has built a Cooperative Digital Innovation and Transformation Portal (IDXCoop) which was released on 19 November 2020, where 582 cooperatives have been registered in it (Sari, 2021). According to IDXCoop, there are at least three benefits of digitalizing cooperatives, namely improving the quality of service for its members (speed, efficiency, and not being limited by space and time), more accountable governance, fee-based income, and being able to connect with ecosystems such as fintech, e-commerce, logistics, and other actors in ecosystems. In addition, digitalization will also be able to expand the market and compete with other financial institutions that have transformed earlier.

Furthermore, apart from the current digital transformation problem, there are several problems related to the supervision and legality of cooperatives. By regulation, all cooperatives are required to be registered with the Ministry of Cooperatives and MSMEs. Especially for cooperatives that collect and distribute loans, although it is not mandatory, they are encouraged to register with the OJK. Based on the findings of the P2 Economy—LIPI research, the majority of cooperatives are reluctant to register with the OJK, they are worried that they will be closely monitored. As of January 2021, only 35 cooperatives were registered with OJK from all regions in Indonesia. The majority of cooperatives have savings and loan businesses. In addition, OJK has also taken action against 50 cooperatives whose applications were registered on the Google Play Store (Franedya, 2019). This is because, according to the OJK, they are not allowed to withdraw funds from outside their members. This had become a debate in the DPR because it hindered cooperatives from developing. Therefore, a policy is needed that can encourage the digital transformation of cooperatives but with the principles of good governance (prudence) and does not violate regulations.

In this regard, we propose several policy recommendations to encourage increased access to digital financial services by MSMEs, including:

a. Optimize the role of cooperatives as financial institutions providing digital financial services for MSMEs in Indonesia considering the wide reach and distribution of cooperatives
b. Encourage accelerated access to IDXCoop through collaboration with business incubators, fintech, OJK, and Bank Indonesia.
c. Provide incentives to cooperatives that implement digital financial services. Incentives can be in the form of fiscal (subsidies, tax breaks, etc.) and non-fiscal (ease of licensing, assistance, etc.).
d. Collaborate with credit insurance to provide a credit guarantee scheme for cooperatives that conduct digital financing to MSMEs. This needs to be done considering that financial performance data shows that digital financing that has been carried out by fintech is more risky than conventional financing distributed by other financial institutions. In addition, credit guarantees have also been carried out by the People's Business Credit (KUR) where the majority of debtors are MSMEs.
e. Provide training to improve the digital capabilities of management and cooperative members.
f. Accelerate the completion of the MSME financing roadmap which is currently being prepared by the Ministry of Cooperatives and MSMEs together with the Ministry of National Development Planning/National Development Planning Agency (Bappenas) and the Coordinating Ministry for Economic Affairs. This is vital because the roadmap consolidates MSME empowerment financing from various sources including the MSME financing budget spread across 18 ministries. 2
g. Establish a trust fund for the financing and development of MSMEs from the consolidated results with the consideration that the APBN budgeting scheme has many limitations and rigidities so that it does not suit the needs, characteristics, and business dynamics of MSMEs.
h. Oversee the implementation of the omnibus law related to MSME financing, especially through the Job Creation Law.

References

Aggarwal, N., & Thomas, S. (2017). *Response of firms to the listing: Evidence from SME exchanges.* Indira Gandhi Institute of Development Research, Mumbai, November.

Aminullah, E., Fizzanty, T., & Nawawi, N. et al. (2022a). Interactive components of digital MSMEs ecosystem for inclusive digital economy in Indonesia. *Journal of Knowledge Economy.*

Aminullah, E., Fizzanty, T., Nawawi, N., Suryanto, J., Pranata, N., Maulana, I., Ariyani, L., Wicaksono, A., Suardi, I., Azis, N. L. L., & Budiatri, A. P. (2022b). Interactive components of digital MSMEs ecosystem for inclusive digital economy in Indonesia. *Journal of the Knowledge Economy* (Issue 0123456789). https://doi.org/10.1007/s13132-022-01086-8

Badan Pusat Statistik Republik Indonesia. (2022). Perilaku masyarakat pada masa pandemi covid-19; Hasil survei perilaku masyarakat pada masa pandemi covid-19 periode 16–25 Februari

2022. In *Badan Pusat Statistik Republik Indonesia.* https://www.bps.go.id/publication/2022/03/15/5026d1ebbb39697c4d2f280a/perilaku-masyarakat-pada-masa-pandemi-covid-19-hasil-survei-perilaku-masyarakat-pada-masa-pandemi-covid-19.html

Bank Indonesia. (2023). *Statistik Sistem Pembayaran dan Infrastruktur Pasar Keuangan (SPIP).*

Batunanggar, S. (2019). *Fintech development and regulatory frameworks in Indonesia.* Asian Development Bank Institute.

Blancher, N., Appendino, M., Bibolov, A., Fouejieu, A., Li, J., Ndoye, A., Panagiotakopoulou, A., Shi, W., & Sydorenko, T. (2019). Financial inclusion of small and medium-sized enterprises in the Middle East and Central Asia. In *Departmental papers/policy papers* (Vol. 19, Issue 02). https://doi.org/10.5089/9781484383124.087

Buchak, G., Matvos, G., Piskorski, T., & Seru, A. (2018). Fintech, regulatory arbitrage, and the rise of shadow banks. *Journal of Financial Economics, 130*(3), 453–483. https://doi.org/10.1016/j.jfineco.2018.03.011

Central Statistics Agency. (2019). Statistik Kesejahteraan Rakyat 2019. In *Badan Pusat Statistik Republik Indonesia.*

Daily Social Indonesia. (2023). *MSME empowerement report 2022.*

Endarwati, O. (2020). Baru 0.73% Koperasi yang Melek Digital : Okezone Economy. Retrieved May 27, 2021, from Okezone.com. website: https://economy.okezone.com/read/2020/10/08/455/2290426/baru-0-73-koperasi-yang-melek-digital

Escribá-Esteve, A., Sánchez-Peinado, L., & Sánchez-Peinado, E. (2009). The influence of top management teams in the strategic orientation and performance of small and medium-sized enterprises. *British Journal of Management, 20*(4), 581–597. https://doi.org/10.1111/j.1467-8551.2008.00606.x

EU4Digital. (2020). Digitising industry: Best practices to promote the digital transformation of SMEs in traditional sectors of the economy I EU4Digital. Retrieved July 14, 2020, from https://eufordigital.eu/digitising-industry-best-practices-to-promote-the-digital-transformation-of-smes-in-traditional-sectors-of-the-economy/

European Commission. (2020). *Financing the digitalisation of small and medium-sized enterprises: The enabling role of digital innovation hubs.*

Fizzanty, T., Aminullah, E., Nawawi, Maulana, I., Suryanto, J., Aziz, N. L., Pranata, N., Budiatri, A. P., Suardi, I., Ariyani, L., & Wicaksono, A. (2021). Pengembangan Ekosistem Ekonomi Digital UKM Indonesia. Prioritas Riset Nasional Pengembangan Ekonomi Digital Indonesia Tahun 2020. Laporan Akhir Kegiatan (No.199/E1/PRN/2020). Organisasi Riset Ilmu Pengetahuan Sosial Humaniora, Badan Riset dan Inovasi Nasional (Indonesia).

Franedya, R. (2019). Gali Lubang Tutup Lubang, Orang Ini Ngutang ke 141 Fintech! Retrieved August 30, 2019, from CNBC Indonesia website: https://www.cnbcindonesia.com/tech/20190808062416-37-90569/gali-lubang-tutup-lubang-orang-ini-ngutang-ke-141-fintech

Kesavan, V., & Development, E. (2016). A study on the overview of national payments corporation of abstract as we know that over the years India's has witnessed a significant and drastic change in the payment and settlement system , by tr. *IJRDO-Journal of Business Management, 10,* 33–46. ISSN: 2455–6661.

Kristianus, A. (2022). *Rasio Kredit Perbankan untuk UMKM Dinilai Masih Rendah.* Beritasatu.Com.

Media Indonesia. (2020). Omnibus Law Berikan Kemudahan bagi Sektor Koperasi dan UMKM. Retrieved May 27, 2021, from https://mediaindonesia.com/politik-dan-hukum/352895/omnibus-law-berikan-kemudahan-bagi-sektor-koperasi-dan-umkm

Ministry of Communication and Informatics. (2022). *21 Juta Pelaku UMKM Sudah Onboarding Digital Didorong Gernas BBI.*

Otoritas Jasa Keuangan. (2020). *Digital finance innovation road map and action plan 2020–2024.*

Rahim, A. (2021). *Digitalization shows Indonesian MSMEs the way to recovery—opinion—the Jakarta Post.* The Jakarta Post.

Rasheed, R., Siddiqui, S. H., Mahmood, I., & Khan, S. N. (2019). Financial inclusion for SMEs: Role of digital micro-financial services. *Review of Economics and Development Studies, 5*(3), 429–439. https://doi.org/10.26710/reads.v5i3.686

Sailendra, & Djaddang, S. (2022). Inklusi Keuangan Digital Pada Masa Pandemi Covid-19 Dan Normal Baru Untuk Meningkatkan Ketahanan Umkm. *CAPACITAREA: Jurnal Pengabdian Kepada Masyarakat Universitas Pancasila, 2*, 79–89.

Sari, F. L. (2021). *Peran Perbankan Dalam Adaptasi UMKM Di Masa Pandemi*. Retrieved from https://aji.or.id/upload/article_doc/AJI_BankingEditorMasterclass2020.pdf

Singapore, F. N. (2023). *India bets on digital banking to improve MSME access to finance*. Fintech News. https://fintechnews.sg/69657/fintech-india/india-bets-on-digital-banking-to-improve-msme-access-to-finance/

Sitorus, R. (2019). Tersebar di 18 Kementerian, Anggaran Pembiayaan UMKM Segera Dikonsolidasikan - Ekonomi Bisnis.com. Retrieved May 27, 2021, from Bisnis.com website: https://ekonomi.bisnis.com/read/20191112/12/1169298/tersebar-di-18-kementerian-anggaran-pembiayaan-umkm-segera-dikonsolidasikan

Sommer, C., & Disse, S. (2020). Digitalisation and its impact on SME finance in Sub-Saharan Africa: Reviewing the hype and actual developments (Issue February 2020). https://www.die-gdi.de/discussion-paper/article/digitalisation-and-its-impact-on-sme-finance-in-sub-saharan-africa-reviewing-the-hype-and-actual-developments/%0A. http://hdl.handle.net/10419/215546

Sugandi, E. A. (2021). *The COVID-19 pandemic and Indonesia's fintech markets*. Asian Development Bank Institute.

Yang, L., & Zhang, Y. (2020). Digital financial inclusion and sustainable growth of small and micro enterprises-evidence based on China's new third board market listed companies. *Sustainability (Switzerland), 12*(9). https://doi.org/10.3390/su12093733

Nika Pranata is a Researcher in the Research Center for Economic, National Research and Innovation Agency (BRIN). He was also a Research Fellow in the OJK Institute. He holds two Master's Degrees: Public Policy and Applied Economics, earned from National Graduate Institute for Policy Studies (GRIPS) - Japan and Universitas Padjajaran - Indonesia. He is a recipient of the 2014 Dean's Award for Distinguished Academic Achievement from GRIPS in Japan. He has participated in several conferences and has published various research papers on both the international and national scales. His research interests include financial technology, financial inclusion, the MSMEs digital transformation, e-commerce and the digital economy. In recent years, he has been conducting research on financial technology as well as MSMEs digital transformation and currently active in utilizing big data to solve economic problems.

Ikval Suardi is a researcher in the Research Center for Behavioral and Circular Economics, National Research and Innovation Agency (BRIN). He holds Master's degree in Management from School of Business, the IPB University, Indonesia. His research interests are in microfinance, finance, risk financing, the agricultural economy and business management. He has participated in several conferences and has published various research papers on both the international and national scales. In recent years, he has been conducting research on financing, including disaster risk financing, and currently active in utilizing quantitative and qualitative data to solve economic problems.

Joko Suryanto is a researcher from the Research Center for Economic, The National Research and Innovation Agency (BRIN). His research interests cover the fields of public economics and small and medium enterprises. He completed a master's degree from the University of Indonesia in the field of public policy. Research activities in the field of small and medium enterprises businesses become one of his areas of interest, particularly topic dealing with increase of value-added from government and other related aspects that affect the output of small and medium enterprises business activities. Currently, he is involved in research on the digital transformation of small medium enterprises.

Chapter 5
The Position of MSME in the Discourse of Platform Capitalism

Ikbal Maulana

Abstract This chapter examines how MSMEs are portrayed in the context of platform capitalism discourse, focusing on how they are perceived and treated by government and platform companies. Analyzing news articles from Kontan.co.id, a prominent Indonesian online business media outlet, reveals a narrative that positions MSMEs as the primary beneficiaries of e-commerce platforms and government policies. Notably, this portrayal is largely shaped by government and platform companies, with MSMEs themselves playing a passive role in the discourse. Therefore, having representatives who can advocate for the needs of MSMEs is crucial, influencing decision-making processes to their advantage.

Keywords Social media · Platform capitalism · E-Commerce platform · MSME · Platform companies · Imported product

5.1 Introduction

Digital platforms have disrupted various industrial sectors (Grabher & Koenig, 2020), particularly transportation, accommodation, and the retail industry. Platform economy businesses empower small-scale business actors to connect and engage with their customers and each other without the need for in-person meetings. These businesses serve as intermediaries, enabling virtual interactions and transactions between providers of goods and services, such as drivers and landlords, and users seeking those goods and services, such as passengers and renters (Leong & Belzer, 2017). The success of digital platforms, exemplified by the likes of AirBnB and Uber, has been replicated across various sectors and countries, resulting in the digital economy becoming an increasingly ubiquitous infrastructure within the modern economy (Srnicek, 2016).

I. Maulana (✉)
Research Center for Society and Culture, National Research and Innovation Agency (BRIN), Jakarta, Indonesia
e-mail: ikba002@brin.go.id

T. Fizzanty and I. Maulana (eds.), *The Digitalization of Indonesian Small and Medium Enterprises*, Engaging Indonesia, https://doi.org/10.1007/978-981-97-0029-5_5

The platform economy has been pioneered by platforms that cater not only to economic interactions but also to non-economic interactions, such as Google, Facebook, and YouTube. These platforms can monetize their large user base by exposing them to targeted advertisements that align with their specific viewing preferences. Before the emergence of Airbnb or Uber, electronic marketplaces had been introduced many years ago. However, their adoption by small businesses was limited due to the high cost and complexity of the technologies involved, which often exceeded the affordability of small enterprises. In the present day, with the rapid advancement of technology, the platform economy is revolutionizing numerous aspects of human activities, fundamentally altering how individuals work, socialize, generate value, and compete for profits (Kenney & Zysman, 2016, 2020).

The captivating aspect of the platform economy is its ability to effortlessly involve a vast number of individuals in work or business activities, utilizing the technological devices they already use, such as personal computers and even smartphones. Social media, particularly those accessible from smartphones, are widely used platforms that were initially complementary to the social sphere but have now become the primary communication space for many people. Through the use of social media, users have the ability to easily develop their social networks, even including individuals whom they have not personally met. Some people perceive these platforms as opportunities for social interactions, while others leverage them to disseminate their political ideas (Maulana, 2020a, 2020b). Additionally, there are users who utilize social media to develop or maintain relationships with their business partners or customers (Jiménez-Zarco et al., 2021; Sultan & Sharmin, 2020; Vatanasakdakul et al., 2020). Social media has played a role in facilitating both the sharing economy and conventional economic transactions on a smaller scale. However, when interacting with unfamiliar individuals on social media platforms, there are inherent risks that cannot be completely eliminated, as social media was not originally designed for conducting business transactions. Online shopping fraud perpetrated through social media platforms like Facebook or Instagram is occasionally reported in the news. However, there are always individuals who remain unaware of such news and subsequently fall victim to these fraudulent activities (Iskandar, 2020).

E-commerce platforms are designed to prevent fraud by assessing the trustworthiness of both sellers and buyers based on their past behavior information (Frenken & Schor, 2017). In addition to addressing the issue of fraud, these platforms offer consumers the convenience of easily finding desired goods and services. Moreover, these platforms facilitate transactions by integrating online payment systems. They serve as intermediaries as well as data aggregators. To effectively fulfill their role as intermediaries, they need to collect and analyze user data in an efficient and comprehensive manner (Kenney & Zysman, 2016, 2020; Zuboff, 2015). In Indonesia, e-commerce platforms have experienced rapid adoption by individuals and micro, small, and medium-sized enterprises (MSMEs) within a short span of time. This can be attributed to the aggressive marketing campaigns launched by platform companies and, notably, the COVID-19 pandemic. As people's mobility was restricted during the pandemic, sellers recognized e-commerce platforms as the primary channel for conducting business.

For customers, these platforms offer a broader range of choices without the need to physically visit multiple locations. Integration of various services, which include digital payment and shipping, eases both merchants and customers. Platform operators often present themselves as mere intermediaries, but in reality, they exert unprecedented control over the agents interacting on their platforms (Kenney & Zysman, 2020). The platform economy differs from conventional markets in that it involves tripartite interactions between buyers, platforms, and sellers. Unlike traditional markets where buyers and sellers directly interact, platforms serve as intermediaries. These platforms possess an infrastructure comprising hardware and software that enforce rules and provide various services to facilitate transactions (Liang et al., 2022). The process of customers finding their desired products or services is dictated by the algorithms employed by the platforms. What may appear as an invisible hand guiding sellers and buyers is actually a mechanism embedded within the platform companies' algorithms. These algorithms determine the visibility and recommendations of products or services, shaping the overall user experience and influencing purchasing decisions (Darmody & Zwick, 2020; Zuboff, 2015). The algorithm responsible for ensuring convenient and secure transactions is also the mechanism through which platform companies exploit transactions for their own interests. While the algorithm enhances the overall transaction experience, it is designed to serve the platform's goals, which may include maximizing profits, increasing user engagement, or promoting certain products or services. This dual nature of the algorithm highlights the complex dynamics between user convenience, security, and the platform's underlying business motivations.

To draw attention to the growing leverage of platform operators in the ongoing restructuring of the global economy's ecosystem (Kenney & Zysman, 2020), this chapter employs the term "platform capitalism." By raising awareness and highlighting the potential for exploitation, the term serves as a reminder of the significant power wielded by platform operators in shaping the dynamics of the global economy. It is natural for platforms to be guided by profit motives in the long run. In the current phase, where Indonesia has five major e-commerce platforms, they actively compete to attract and retain loyal users. They prioritize providing excellent service to users, even if it means sacrificing immediate profits. However, it is important to acknowledge that this approach may not be sustainable indefinitely, as platforms ultimately need to generate profits to ensure their continued operation and growth.

The primary focus of this chapter is to examine how micro, small, and medium-sized enterprises (MSMEs) are portrayed and perceived within the dominant discourse of platform capitalism, as represented by news articles published on Kontan.co.id, a prominent online business news media outlet in Indonesia. The objective is to gain valuable insights into the media's representation of MSMEs and how their roles are depicted within this specific discourse. Given the substantial number of MSMEs and their often limited organizational capacity, their needs and interests are most often voiced by other stakeholders, including platform companies and the government. Understanding the portrayal of MSMEs within the discourse of platform capitalism is crucial because the claims made about them, regardless of their accuracy, can significantly impact how these businesses are treated or served by platform companies and the government.

5.2 The Nature of Platform Capitalism

Capitalism is renowned for its relentless pursuit of growth and expansion. In light of the extended decline in manufacturing profitability, capitalism has adapted by turning to data as a crucial driver for maintaining economic growth and vitality (Srnicek, 2016). Therefore, the turn to the platform economy is a natural progression of capitalism, as it effectively capitalizes on technological advancements and adapts to evolving consumer preferences. Capitalist economic development is characterized by a process of creative destruction resulting from the constant utilization of innovation (Schumpeter, 2010). This, in turn, occasionally leads to disruptions in technology and industry (Christensen, 2000).

Competition is the defining characteristic of capitalism, making the pursuit of maintaining or enhancing competitiveness an inherent aspect of the capitalist economic system. This drive to remain competitive inevitably fuels technological innovation. The current technological advancements have laid the foundation for the platform economy, seamlessly integrating connectivity, data analytics, and algorithms to establish efficient and expansive marketplaces. E-commerce platforms, functioning on the Internet, possess the technical capacity to connect sellers and buyers globally, with minimal costs for information exchange. The current computing technology also allows the platforms to facilitate efficient matching between individuals and their desired goods or services (Benoit et al., 2017; Kenney & Zysman, 2020), while simultaneously safeguarding them against fraudulent activities or violations. The large-scale matchmaking function is essential for the platforms to capitalize on the network effects, which refers to the increased value derived from a growing number of users transacting through the platform (Acquier et al., 2017). Nevertheless, the extent of their geographical reach is limited by shipping expenses tied to physical goods sold through these platforms. Consequently, although the world may only require one Google Search Engine or one Facebook, which does not require the exchange of tangible goods, it can accommodate diverse e-commerce platforms tailored for different countries. However, e-commerce platforms operating within the same region, and having access to the same shipping services, can engage in fierce competition with one another. Given the capabilities of current technology, these platforms have the ability to process numerous transactions, allowing for the possibility of a single platform dominating the region if it can outcompete its rivals.

Due to the presence of network externalities (Shapiro & Varian, 1999) and operating within a digital network, the platform economy imposes limitations on the number of players. It tends to converge toward a situation where only a few, or even just one, dominant player emerges, often referred to as "the winner takes all." Consequently, intense competition among existing players attracts significant investment, primarily from foreign venture capitalists who are already acquainted with startups operating in industries characterized by network externalities. In contrast, local investors may be less accustomed to making continuous investments over extended periods without a specified deadline for profitability.

However, the investment and the accompanying risks of platform business are justifiable, particularly when taking into account the immense scale of the Indonesian market, boasting a population of approximately 280 million individuals. The platforms' ability to deliver efficient matchmaking between users' needs and offerings is made possible by the transparency of users' digital actions and interactions. However, this transparency also signifies the considerable power that platforms hold over their users (Cutolo & Kenney, 2021; Viljoen et al., 2021). By collecting data using digital surveillance, and automatic computational analyses utilizing statistics and AI, the platforms can algorithmically either better predict or shape customers' choices (Darmody & Zwick, 2020; Maulana, 2019).

The advent of sharing platforms like Uber for car sharing or Airbnb for sharing apartments/houses swiftly enticed individuals who were not necessarily interested in sharing their under-utilized assets but rather saw an opportunity to engage in business by renting out their assets through these platforms. Consequently, the primary function of these platforms has shifted away from facilitating collaborative consumption and transformed into a marketplace where individuals can conduct business by renting out their assets or selling services. In addition, the research presented in this book revolves around the platforms employed by MSMEs for their online transactions. It specifically explores e-commerce platforms that serve as technologically advanced and costly infrastructures requiring significant investments. Thus, to underscore the platforms' significance within the context of capitalism, this chapter prefers to use the term "platform capitalism."

The proponents or companies engaged in platform capitalism may avoid using the term in public discourse due to the negative connotation of "capitalism." However, it is important to recognize that the development of platforms is guided by capitalist principles. The apparent generosity shown toward users, both buyers and sellers, is not driven by social virtues, but rather by the competitive nature of platform businesses. They engage in a race for market dominance, compelled by the principle of network externalities (Shapiro & Varian, 1999). This drive for dominance often entails delaying immediate profits in order to expand their user base and solidify their position in the market.

From the buyer's perspective, the primary value of a platform lies in the abundance of choices it offers in terms of goods and sellers. Similarly, from the seller's perspective, the platform's value is determined by the larger number of potential buyers it can attract. The platform's ability to bring together a diverse range of sellers and a substantial pool of buyers creates a mutually beneficial environment, where buyers have access to a wide selection of products or services, and sellers have a larger market to showcase their offerings. This interdependent relationship between buyers and sellers underscores the significance of a platform's value proposition in terms of choice and market reach. Thus, in the presence of competing platforms within the same market, their paramount goal is to outperform their rivals by attracting a greater number of users. The focus on user acquisition becomes the key driving force for platform growth and success. This network-externalities nature of platform competition fosters a competitive environment where only one company emerges as a winner, resulting in a "winner takes all" scenario. Network effects inherently embed a predisposition toward monopolization within the essence of platforms (Srnicek, 2016). The greater the number of users engaging on a platform, the more valuable the entire platform becomes for each individual user.

The concern arises when the competition concludes and a definitive winner is determined. In such cases, the victorious platform acquires a monopoly and possesses the ability to exert control over users who no longer have alternative channels. This scenario is particularly evident in certain countries, where platform businesses such as Airbnb, Uber, and Amazon have emerged as dominant forces, monopolizing their respective markets and establishing substantial barriers for other players to achieve success and growth. In Indonesia, the ride-hailing service is primarily controlled by two platforms, Gojek and Grab, with ten other platforms, including Uber, facing bankruptcy (Oswaldo, 2023). On the other hand, the e-commerce sector remains highly competitive, with five prominent players—Shopee, Tokopedia, Lazada, Bukalapak, and Blibli—competing for market dominance, while eight other platforms have succumbed to the challenges and ceased their operations (Septiani, 2023).

Platform business models have proven to be disruptive to traditional businesses, as exemplified in Indonesia. The rise of ride-hailing services offered by companies like Gojek and Grab has profoundly undermined the conventional taxi market, giving rise to considerable concerns and disruptions within the industry. In 2016 approximately 6,000 official Jakarta taxi drivers, including those from Bluebird and Express, organized a protest against the presence of those ride-hailing services. The demonstration resulted in the main areas of the capital experiencing heavy congestion and disruption. The protesters prominently displayed banners demanding the cessation of illegal taxi operations (DW, 2016). However, the government seemed to back up this new business model of transportation.

President Joko Widodo of Indonesia has shown his support to the platform businesses. On some occasions he openly expressed admiration and a sense of pride for Indonesia's existing unicorns—privately held startup companies valued at over \$1 billion—and the emerging decacorns, which hold a valuation surpassing \$10 billion. During his first term, President Widodo even brought along the CEOs of four prominent platform companies when he visited the United States, highlighting their importance to Indonesia's economic progress (Panji, 2015).

However, the growth of platform companies cannot be solely attributed to their superior efficiency when compared to traditional businesses. Even today, their operations continue to heavily rely on the financial support provided by mostly their overseas investors. In their early stages, these platforms had to earn the trust of users who were initially unfamiliar with their services. However, as the industry has evolved, these platforms now find themselves engaged in fierce competition with one another, vying for market domination.

5.3 Platform Capitalism and Small Businesses

A few decades ago, the electronic marketplace emerged, transforming online commerce transactions (Stockdale & Standing, 2004). However, at that time, technology, particularly for Indonesian MSMEs, was complex and prohibitively expensive, making it financially inaccessible for them. Today, e-commerce platforms have evolved to become increasingly capable of engaging and facilitating MSMEs in conducting online transactions with ease (Holland & Gutiérrez-Leefmans, 2018). E-commerce platforms operating in Indonesia enable individuals, even those with smartphones at hand, to participate in online shopping as sellers or buyers. During the early stages, major retail companies either underestimated the potential of e-commerce platforms or opted to establish their own online shops. As a consequence, these platforms primarily targeted micro and small businesses.

E-commerce platforms have undeniably played a crucial role in supporting Indonesian MSMEs involved in e-commerce. The ongoing competition among the five e-commerce platforms compels them to provide substantial support to these MSMEs. Both the MSMEs and their customers are valuable assets that these platforms offer to investors, especially when they are still striving to dominate the market and deferring their profit-making goals. The greater the number of users, the more value a platform can provide them, resulting in increased power and influence. However, it is only through competition or the absence of a clear winner that a platform's ability to fully exercise its power is constrained. In the presence of competition, users have options to switch to alternative platforms, which serves as a check on the platform's power.

While platforms may resemble conventional markets on the surface, they possess fundamental differences. What sets platforms apart from conventional markets is their capacity to intervene in the search and interaction between buyers and sellers. The quality and efficiency of these interactions are contingent on the collection of data and the data analytics (Andersson Schwarz, 2017; Srnicek, 2017). Moreover, while a conventional market is a mere arena where economic actors interact and transact, the platforms are distinct entities with their own vested interest in growing their power and influence. Platform technology is specifically designed to shape and influence user interactions, ultimately benefiting the platform companies (Sutherland & Jarrahi, 2018).

Platforms are purposefully structured to extract and harness this data as intermediaries connecting various users. Every interaction a user has with a platform leaves behind a digital trace that can be collected and analyzed (Zuboff, 2015). This transparency in user behavior enables platforms to enhance matchmaking between buyers and sellers. By leveraging this data, platforms can facilitate more effective connections between users for improved outcomes. In addition, the abundance of user data enables platforms to make more accurate predictions about users' future behavior. The extensive data insights help platforms anticipate user preferences, needs, and actions, allowing them to provide tailored experiences and recommendations. Hence, the platform's strength lies in its capacity to collect and analyze user data (Srnicek, 2017).

To be effective, the platform economy should rely on the scale and processing power of computational and network-based systems. It requires a large user population and suitable digital infrastructure for on-demand matchmaking (Sutherland & Jarrahi, 2018). Digital technologies play a crucial role as interfaces for participants and information processors. In the centralized model of sharing economy mediation, extensive automation is used to enhance the convenience, speed, and smoothness of digital interactions. Centralized platforms have a significant presence in facilitating exchanges, assigning matches, handling payments, and providing tools for task completion.

Initially, e-commerce platforms were new to Indonesian MSMEs; however, many of the owners were already familiar with social media platforms. Some of them even utilized social media for specific business purposes, although they encountered limitations as these platforms were primarily designed for social interactions rather than business transactions. Recognizing this, certain platform companies have taken the initiative to actively educate MSMEs and encourage them to conduct transactions through their platforms. Tokopedia, which has recently merged with Gojek to form Goto, and Shopee, two prominent e-commerce platforms, have been actively engaged in educating MSMEs to enhance their effectiveness as online merchants. The dominance of platform companies over their users do not raise concerns among users or policymakers. This is because users perceive value in utilizing the platforms and perceive missed opportunities if they do not engage with them.

The Ministry of Cooperatives and Micro, Small, and Medium Enterprises (MSMEs) is also highly proactive in promoting the adoption of digital technology among MSMEs. The Indonesian government, as exemplified by the President of Indonesia himself, has demonstrated strong support for the utilization of e-commerce platforms. However, the most significant driving force behind the digitalization of MSMEs has been the COVID-19 pandemic. The imposition of mobility restrictions has left traders and buyers with no alternative but to interact through e-commerce platforms.

5.4 Understanding MSMEs in the Discourse of Platform Capitalism

The public is perplexed by a question: Why do the government and certain overseas major venture capitalists provide strong support to platform companies, even when these companies have not demonstrated tangible financial profits? People's actions are often more influenced by ideas than by self-interests, particularly when considering their immediate concerns (Campbell, 2002). Although self-interests do influence policymaking, their influence is framed within the larger context of discourse surrounding the relevant issues. The discourse surrounding the platform economy, which emphasizes the necessity of progress, shapes the aspirations of capitalists and the government's support for these platforms. While the full competitive advantages of these platforms are yet to be realized, the belief in technological and economic progress emboldens capitalists to invest significantly in these businesses, despite the lack of immediate profits. This belief also motivates the government to facilitate the transformation of MSMEs into digital businesses, even though this transformation may have adverse effects on other segments of society. Therefore, the depiction of MSMEs in platform economy discourse will determine how they are and will be treated by platform businesses and targeted by government policies. The depiction may not be accurate, but the discourse is not solely a reflection of reality, it can also be intentionally constructed to shape and influence reality (Foucault, 1978).

The role of MSMEs is crucial in Indonesian and Southeast Asian countries. MSMEs play a significant role in Southeast Asia, comprising 97% of businesses and employing 67% of the working population. Their contribution to the region's gross domestic product averages 40.5% and accounts for 19.2% of total export value (Tan, 2022). MSMEs have long been acknowledged as significant contributors to employment (Ayyagari et al., 2007). Research findings on the impact of SMEs on economic growth vary, ranging from studies suggesting no significant impact (Vijayakumar & Sedláček, 2012) to suggesting they have no impact on the industry sector but demonstrate significance in the service sector (Rotar et al., 2019). Furthermore, there is evidence to suggest that SMEs can serve as a catalyst for economic growth (Cunningham, 2011). Although SMEs, on average, tend to be less innovative than large enterprises, there are exceptional small businesses that exhibit high levels of innovation and achieve productivity levels surpassing those of their larger counterparts (OECD, 2018). Different sectors may have different kinds of SMEs. In the IT sector, there exist small businesses with a relatively small number of employees that exhibit remarkable levels of capitalization.

SMEs display a wide range of roles, capabilities, and levels of innovativeness across countries. In developed nations, governments have a higher level of confidence in the innovation potential of their SMEs. Consequently, they actively foster a supportive business environment, assist in the effective development and utilization of internal strategic resources, and establish an inclusive innovation system that promotes the commercialization of research and caters to the needs of various small and medium-sized enterprises (OECD, 2018). On the other hand, in developing nations, there is a prevailing perception that SMEs lack the capability to innovate. This perception extends to larger domestic corporations as well, as they are also seen as lacking innovation and relying on foreign companies for technological advancements (Lee et al., 2018).

SMEs comprise a broad spectrum of business entities, each with distinct sizes and capabilities, which presents difficulty in formulating equitable policies that treat all SMEs uniformly. Adding to this complexity is the government's incorporation of "Micro Enterprises" into the SME category, leading to the formation of MSMEs. This expansion widens the classification to include businesses operating in the informal sector, often run by individual entrepreneurs.

No matter what literal definitions are contained by the term MSMEs, what the government or business communities understand of MSMEs can be partly sought from how MSMEs are used or positioned in business discourse. The way MSMEs are portrayed in platform capitalism discourse can influence policymaking and implies how big businesses treat them. If MSMEs are consistently marginalized or neglected in public narratives, it can lead to inadequate policy support, limited access to resources, and missed opportunities for growth and development. By examining their depiction, we can identify any biases or gaps in policy discussions and work toward creating a more supportive environment for MSMEs.

5.5 Data and Discussion

This research draws upon news reports published by Kontan (https://www.kontan.co.id/), a prominent Indonesian business media, from January 2020 to April 2023. To gain insights into the position of MSMEs within discourses surrounding platform capitalism, three collections of news reports were compiled using the following Indonesian search keywords: "marketplace," "platform," and "digitalisasi UMKM" (digitalization of MSMEs). The collected results were carefully cleaned to include only news reports, excluding advertisements, press releases, or columns. The dataset for "marketplace" consists of 242 news articles, "platform" has 234 articles, and "digitalization of MSMEs" contains 188 articles. The news reports were selected using the Google search engine, and the desired news articles were collected using the Linkclump Chrome extension. The contents referred to by these links were downloaded using OpenRefine. The resulting dataset, in the form of a CSV file, was uploaded to Google Drive. To facilitate analysis, the news articles were translated into English using the Google Sheet formula "GOOGLETRANSLATE." Each news report, contained in the CSV file, is converted into an abstract of a RIS file. Subsequently, the RIS file is processed using VosViewer, a specialized computer program used for constructing and visualizing bibliometric maps (Van Eck & Waltman, 2010). However, in this particular case, VosViewer is utilized to create a word co-occurrence graph based on the converted news reports in the RIS file. Each important keyword in the VosViewer graph is then further explored in the news reports using LancsBox (Brezina et al., 2021).

5.5.1 Discourses Surrounding "Marketplace"

The dataset related to the "marketplace," consisting of 242 news articles, has been segmented into four clusters using VosViewer, as illustrated in Fig. 5.1. Each cluster is distinguished by different configurations of connected keywords. However, clusters are not separated from each other. As shown in the graphs in the following sections,

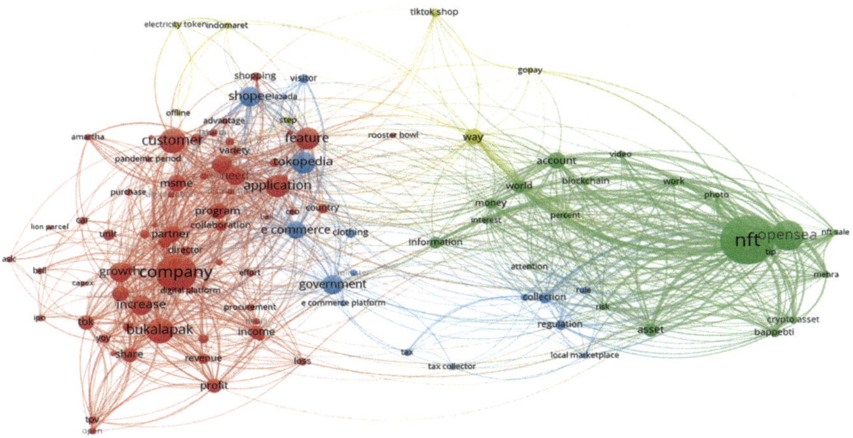

Fig. 5.1 Keyword Co-occurrences in the "Marketplace" dataset

keywords in one cluster are also connected to keywords in other clusters, indicating potential overlap or shared themes.

In the initial cluster (depicted in red), key themes revolve around *company*, *customer*, and *growth*. The term *company* (or *companies*) refers to major corporations, either platform operators or those offering various services, from shipping, delivery, payment systems, and venture capital, with MSMEs as the target market of those companies. The news articles also report various aspects related to a *company*, such as company sales, expansion, investment, and IPO activities. The cluster also highlights the importance of *customers*, the individuals who consume the products. Ultimately, it is the customers who must be served and whose desire must be satisfied. The keyword *growth* refers to the positive impact of e-commerce platforms on businesses, whether on the platform companies themselves or on the businesses that use the platform to reach their markets. The frequent mention of the term *growth* underscores the expansion of e-commerce and the digital economy, as evidenced by the increasing trend in online shopping and the heightened demand for logistics and delivery services. Moreover, there has been a notable surge in digital transactions, encompassing electronic money transfers, digital banking, and online payments, signifying a shift toward a more digitalized economy.

Cluster 2 centers around the rise and subsequent decline of non-fungible tokens (NFTs)—digital certificates that validate ownership of digital assets. Initially capturing considerable attention, NFTs gained popularity due to successful sales by both individuals and celebrities. However, for most people, their potential remains uncertain. This cluster places particular emphasis on OpenSea, a prominent marketplace used by Indonesians for the trading of NFTs.

Cluster 3 (in blue) comprises significant keywords such as "government," "e-commerce," and two platform companies, namely "Shopee" and "Tokopedia." The texts associated with "government" shed light on the government's initiatives and policies aimed at supporting MSMEs and specific sectors. The incorporation of "e-commerce" signifies the swift growth of the Indonesian e-commerce sector. The platform companies employ diverse business innovations to promote e-commerce, which does not solely revolve around digitalization. For instance, they recognize the preferences of certain customers who feel more at ease paying for goods upon delivery. As a result, they offer the convenience of cash-on-delivery (COD) payment options to cater to such demands. "Shopee" and "Tokopedia" are the major e-commerce platforms that offer COD payment services. While these platforms have faced criticism for selling used clothing, they have expressed their commitment to adhere to government regulations. Moreover, they actively cooperate with the government in facilitating tax collection on their transactions.

Cluster 4, highlighted in yellow, demonstrates the recent surge in popularity of "TikTok shop" as an e-commerce channel on the TikTok platform, which was previously only widely known for showing short funny entertainment videos created by its users. This cluster also shows the expansion of "Gopay" as a payment system, which is now not only used for purchasing food and paying for ride-sharing on the Gojek platform but can also be used to pay at major convenience store chains such as "Indomaret," as well as its competitor, Alfamart (which is not shown in the graph but mentioned in the text). Additionally, there have been reports of imported used "clothing" being sold through local marketplaces, despite the practice being prohibited in Indonesia. The Ministry of Trade has emphasized this prohibition, and platforms have committed to eradicating the practice of selling imported used clothing on their respective platforms.

5.5.2 Discourses Surrounding "Platform"

The dataset related to "platform" has been divided into six clusters by VosViewer, as illustrated in Fig. 5.2.

Cluster 1 (depicted in red) features keywords that are closely similar in terms of their frequency. The top three keywords are *e-commerce*, *increase*, and *sale*, indicating the thriving *e-commerce* sector as evidenced by the *rise* in *sales* on e-commerce platforms. The growth of online sales is propelled by the increasing availability of internet access, the rising middle class, and the growing popularity of mobile devices. Moreover, it is noted that online sales positively impact the economy, fostering increased efficiency, productivity, and innovation. While this assertion is generally favorable toward the platform economy, a closer analysis of the news texts reveals concerns about the prevalence of imported products from China being sold online, posing a potential threat to domestic industries.

The primary keywords in Cluster 2 (depicted in green) are digital *platform*, *development*, and *cooperation*, indicating a close interdependence between these factors. This suggests that the evolution of digital platforms and associated services requires collaborative efforts from various entities, including platform companies, technology firms, banking sectors, and other supporting businesses.

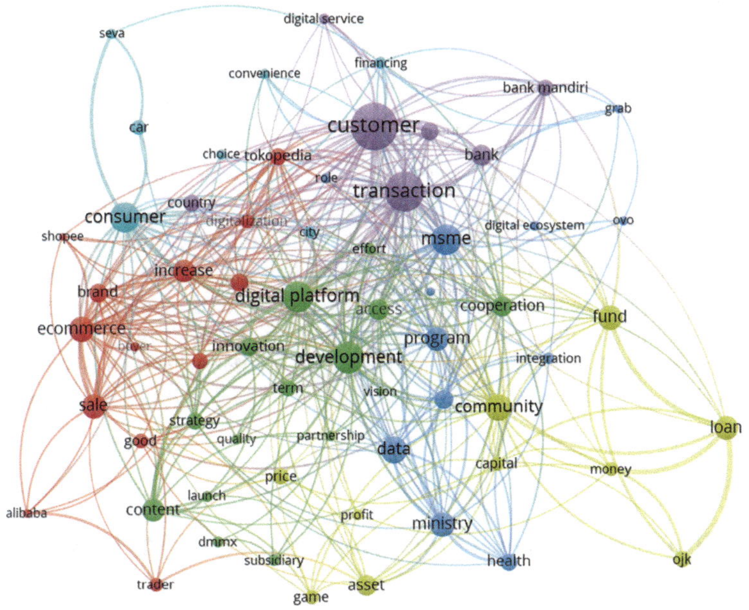

Fig. 5.2 Word Co-occurrences in the "Platform" dataset

The key terms highlighted in cluster 3 (depicted in blue) include *MSMEs*, *program*, *data*, and *ministry*. The term *MSMEs* is referenced in the context of both the challenges faced by these enterprises and the opportunities presented to them through e-commerce. To overcome these challenges and capitalize on the opportunities, the government, through various ministries, implements programs to support MSMEs. The Ministry of Communication and Information is providing support for the development of e-commerce infrastructure, such as the national internet backbone and the electronic system for transactions. The Ministry of Tourism and Creative Economy is promoting e-commerce as a way to boost tourism and the creative industries. The Ministry of Cooperatives and UKM is providing training and support for MSMEs to sell their products online. The Ministry of Health is working with e-commerce platforms to provide telemedicine services to patients. The Ministry of Trade is regulating e-commerce transactions to protect consumers and businesses.

Cluster 4 (depicted in yellow) contains keywords such as *community*, *loan*, and *fund*. This cluster reveals the diverse applications of platform technology that benefit communities by facilitating access to healthcare and education in remote areas, assisting in job searches, connecting individuals, simplifying business operations, and offering financial services. It also highlights various types of *funding* and *loan* options available to individuals and small businesses, including peer-to-peer lending (P2P) platforms, micro-finance services, and government-backed loan programs. Additionally, it discusses the risks associated with illegal loans in Indonesia, which often come with attractive terms but involve hidden fees, high-interest rates, and potential threats or harassment for non-payment.

Cluster 5 (depicted in purple) underscores the significance of meeting *customer* satisfaction and needs, a focal point in the covered news articles. To achieve this, various strategies and technologies have been implemented to create value for customers, leading to increased *transactions*. The cluster also sheds light on the pivotal role of the *banking* sector in facilitating online payments and financial transactions on e-commerce platforms and mobile banking applications. Additionally, it discusses the imposition of transaction fees and its impact on profitability.

Cluster 6 emphasizes the crucial role of the *consumer* as the end-user of goods sold through e-commerce platforms, highlighting their needs as a trigger for innovation. This is exemplified in a news article that mentions the launch of *Seva*, a digital platform that assists consumers in discovering new *cars* and accessing associated financial services.

5.5.3 Discourse Surrounding "Digitalization of MSMEs"

Figure 5.3 illustrates the dataset categorized into four keyword clusters. In cluster 1 (depicted in red), the top three keywords are *platform*, *management*, and *pandemic*. Additionally, the cluster includes the term *digital platform*. A closer reading of the news texts in the dataset reveals the pivotal role of *digital platforms* in supporting the growth of MSMEs in Indonesia. These *platforms* offer access to a broader market, enhance efficiency, and reduce costs by eliminating the need for physical stores, staff, and marketing materials. This, in turn, facilitates the initiation and expansion of MSMEs. Despite the potential benefits, several challenges impede the optimal utilization of platforms, including limited digital literacy, competition from larger enterprises, and the risk of fraud and scams. It is crucial to emphasize that successful technology implementation requires effective *management* practices, as technology alone cannot ensure improved efficiency, growth, and sustainability. The cluster also underscores the impact of the COVID-19 *pandemic* on MSMEs, leading to reduced demand, supply chain disruptions, and financial hardships. Nevertheless, digitalization has provided opportunities for many MSMEs to overcome these challenges and thrive in the current business landscape,

The top three keywords in cluster 2 (depicted in green) are *transaction*, *bank*, and *company*. The COVID-19 pandemic has witnessed a surge in digital *transactions*, marked by a notable increase in the adoption of digital payments, the expansion of e-commerce, and the popularity of contactless payments. This cluster also highlights how *banks* support MSMEs through financial services, offering business advice, facilitating connections with customers, and improving their financial literacy and business management. The term *company* in this context refers to larger enterprises that can assist MSMEs in their business endeavors by providing a range of services or technologies.

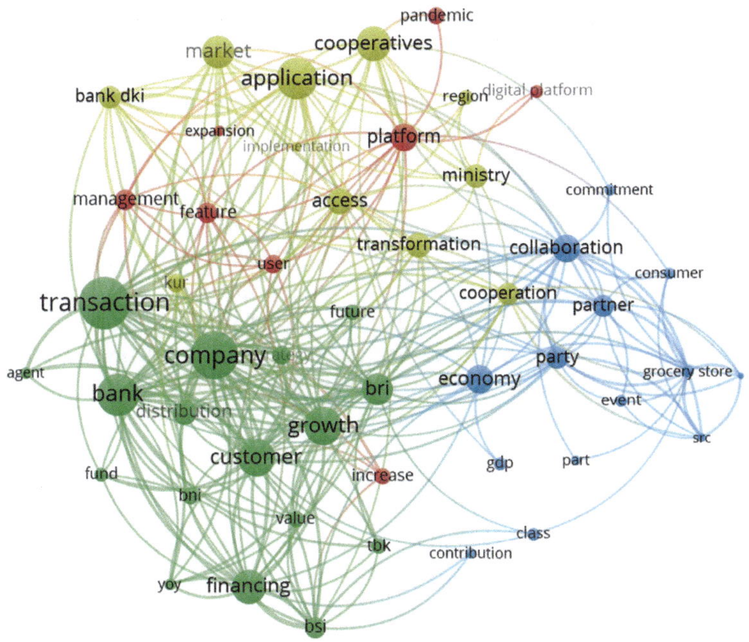

Fig. 5.3 Keyword Co-occurrences in the "Digitalization of MSMEs" dataset

The top keywords in cluster 3 (blue) are *collaboration*, *party*, and *economy*. The texts emphasize government and corporate collaboration to drive digital transformation in MSMEs. Examples include partnerships among financial institutions, government agencies, and tech companies, aiming to advance MSMEs through digital technology. This collaboration underscores the need to combine digitalization efforts to facilitate MSME growth. *Party* refers to entities like government agencies, financial institutions, tech companies, influencers, and local governments collaborating to enhance MSME capabilities, drive digitalization, and promote financial inclusion—the backbone of Indonesia's *economy*.

The primary keywords in cluster 4 (yellow) are *application*, *cooperatives*, and *market*. The texts report *applications* designed to assist MSMEs in various aspects of their operations, from point of sale (POS) systems, inventory management, and customer relationship management (CRM), to marketing and advertising. Since MSMEs and *cooperatives* are both policy targets of the Ministry of Cooperatives and SMEs, news about the Indonesian government's policy on MSMEs occasionally also covers *cooperatives*. The dataset also reveals that the ministry has attempted to promote the digitalization of *cooperatives* by offering financial support, training programs, and technical assistance. The digital transformation of either cooperatives or MSMEs is ultimately aimed at expanding their *market* reach through platforms, fostering their economic growth.

5.5.4 The Position of MSMEs in the Discourse

The datasets on "marketplace" and "platform" do not specifically address MSMEs. For instance, the "marketplace" dataset includes numerous news reports about the NFT marketplace. To comprehend the perception of MSMEs in these reports, LancsBox is utilized to extract collocates related to 'MSMEs'.

Table 5.1 displays the collocates of MSMEs in the dataset of "platform," within the range of five words preceding and following "MSMEs." To the left of the term *MSMEs*, significant keywords such as *empower, help, make*, and *provide* can be observed. These words appear in different statements, indicating that the government, ministries, platform companies, and other relevant large businesses have taken steps to empower, help, and support MSMEs in their online ventures. They accomplish this by providing digital literacy education, and support, and facilitating access to markets, enabling MSMEs to effectively sell their products or services through online channels. This shows that MSMEs are seen as the primary beneficiaries of e-commerce platforms and as the focus of government policies. However, it is worth mentioning that the news mostly relies on statements about MSMEs made by others rather than directly from the MSMEs themselves.

The words having position of left (L) in Table 5.2 illustrate the efforts made by the government, platform companies, and other major corporations to *encourage* and *help* MSMEs in adopting e-commerce, enhancing their digital skills, and sustaining their growth or survival amidst the COVID-19 pandemic. The term *make* is used in a positive sense when the subjects are the government, platform companies, or other corporations. For instance, the government is expected to enact regulations that facilitate the upward mobility of MSMEs. Banks can empower MSMEs with financial expertise, while telecommunications companies can play a significant role in advancing their capabilities. However, it carries a negative connotation when referring to imported products, as they pose challenges for MSMEs.

Table 5.3 has more important keywords related to "MSMEs" because the dataset was collected using the search phrase "digitalisasi UMKM" (digitalization of MSMEs), specifically mentioning MSMEs. The keywords in the left of "MSMEs" are *invite, foster, help, encourage, hope, support, strengthen*, and *make*, which indicate how MSMEs become the target of service, business or policy of others (the government and various corporations). These words also indicate various levels of

Table 5.1 The collocates of MSMEs in datasets of "platform"

Position	Collocate	Stat (MI)	Freq (coll.)	Freq (corpus)
L	empower_v	8.50	5	14
L	help_v	6.07	5	75
L	make_v	5.13	10	289
L	provide_v	4.96	6	195
R	sell_v	3.79	5	365

Table 5.2 The collocates of "MSMEs" in the dataset of "platform"

Position	Collocate	Stat (MI)	Freq (coll.)	Freq (corpus)
L	encourage_v	6.63	7	72
L	help_v	6.13	8	117
L	make_v	4.94	7	233

involvement from other parties with MSMEs. Some express *hope* that MSMEs can weather challenging times or capitalize on the digitalization of business. Others *encourage* and *invite* MSMEs to make use of the technologies or services provided by these parties. There are also more assertive statements that emphasize *support, make and strengthen* MSMEs.

While the words on the right (R) of "MSMEs" indicate what the MSMEs do with respect to digitalization, such as "*move* up the class" or "*enter* the digital ecosystem." Some news reports also state that MSMEs "*need* to have digital business skills," or "*need* to get affordable financing." By using e-commerce or related technologies offered by some big companies, it is expected that MSMEs can *become* an important part of the supply chain, *expand* their market, and *continue* to *grow* and *develop.* Digital innovation also allows them to *grow* faster.

In the above three datasets, the discussions revolve around three main topics related to MSMEs: the benefits of digitalization for MSMEs, the challenges they

Table 5.3 The collocates of MSMEs in datasets of "digitalization of MSMEs"

Position	Collocate	Stat (MI)	Freq (coll.)	Freq (corpus)
L	invite_v	6.17	11	17
L	foster_v	5.74	12	25
R	move_v	5.10	16	52
R	enter_v	4.98	15	53
L	help_v	4.62	39	177
L	encourage_v	4.60	44	203
L	hope_v	4.28	16	92
R	need_v	4.27	18	104
L	support_v	4.22	38	228
L	strengthen_v	4.18	14	86
R	expand_v	3.98	11	78
R	become_v	3.97	16	114
R	grow_v	3.96	17	122
L	make_v	3.91	21	156
R	develop_v	3.86	26	200
R	continue_v	3.75	30	248

encounter when adopting e-commerce, and the roles played by different organizations in supporting MSMEs to overcome these challenges.

The benefits of digital transformation or e-commerce for MSMEs include:

1. **Reaching a Wider Market**: MSMEs can now connect with customers beyond traditional channels, extending their reach to a broader audience. E-commerce platforms, in particular, are recognized for facilitating access to wider markets, including international ones (Jean & Kim, 2020).
2. **Increasing Sales**: Digitalization simplifies the process for customers to discover and purchase products, resulting in a boost in sales.
3. **Becoming More Efficient and Competitive**: Embracing new technologies and tools empowers MSMEs to enhance efficiency, productivity, and customer service, thereby fostering competitiveness in the market.

Despite the earlier advocacy by the government and platform companies for the benefits of the platform economy, not all MSMEs initially embraced these platforms. However, the onset of the pandemic compelled MSMEs to rapidly adopt them, resulting in the realization of the advantages offered by e-commerce platforms, as mentioned above. This was particularly evident during the COVID-19 pandemic when the closure of shopping malls, markets, and stores rendered these platforms indispensable. Furthermore, these platforms not only allowed MSMEs to maintain connections with their existing customers but also facilitated engagement with customers located far away from their physical establishments.

The current technological advancements have lowered the technological barriers to entry for e-commerce ventures. However, it is important to acknowledge that challenges and constraints still exist, preventing the optimal utilization of e-commerce. The challenges in adopting e-commerce include:

1. **Lack of digital skills**: Many MSMEs lack the necessary digital skills for a successful transformation.
2. **Lack of access to finance**: Limited financial resources hinder MSMEs from investing in digital technologies.
3. **Lack of awareness**: Some MSMEs are unaware of the benefits and how to initiate the digital transformation.

In the present day, the technological landscape has undergone significant changes compared to a few decades ago. People have become increasingly familiar with technologies such as social media, e-commerce, and ride-hailing applications. While many individuals can technically adopt e-commerce, it is important to note that to truly leverage its potential for profitability and competitiveness in business ventures, a deeper understanding beyond mere technical usage of applications is required.

To address the aforementioned challenges, several organizations extend support to MSMEs in adopting e-commerce. These organizations include:

1. **The government**: The government offers fiscal incentives, technical assistance, and access to finance to assist MSMEs in their e-commerce endeavors.

2. **Technology companies**: Technology companies provide MSMEs with applications, platforms, and services to enhance various aspects of their businesses in the e-commerce realm.
3. **Financial institutions**: Financial institutions play a crucial role by providing funding opportunities and facilitating access to financial services for MSMEs looking to venture into e-commerce.
4. **Incubators**: Incubators offer MSMEs valuable resources, training, mentoring, and guidance to foster their growth and success in e-commerce.
5. **NGOs**: Non-governmental organizations provide MSMEs with training, mentorship, and financial aid, and facilitate connections with other businesses and government agencies.

Through the collective efforts of these organizations, MSMEs receive the necessary support and resources to navigate the challenges of e-commerce adoption and optimize their chances of success.

Platform companies are at the forefront in supporting the MSMEs to embrace e-commerce, because the high number of MSMEs using their platforms indicates their very success. Some technology companies support MSMEs in various aspects of their businesses, from providing applications that help in managing and optimizing their operations to providing a blockchain platform designed to simplify supply chain management, which can be beneficial for MSMEs involved in the logistics and manufacturing sectors. Another technology company supports MSMEs by providing coaching, education, facilities, payment systems, and marketplace platforms to sell products, promoting digitalization and supporting business growth. The state-owned bank BRI supports MSMEs by providing funding and facilitating access to financial services, especially for businesses that are not yet bankable.

It is essential to emphasize that the promotion of e-commerce aims to enhance connectivity within the business ecosystem, specifically fostering stronger connections between MSMEs and their customers. This connectivity is not solely facilitated by traditional ICT means but also by payment systems, cybersecurity technology, and advanced technologies like big data and AI. These advancements enable seamless matchmaking between customers and the products they require, thereby streamlining the e-commerce experience for both parties.

A rising concern, debated in both social media and conventional outlets, centers on the impact of e-commerce platforms on the sales of imported products, especially from China. The ease of purchasing these imported goods through e-commerce platforms, coupled with their competitive prices, presents challenges for local products in the marketplace. This issue is often overlooked by platform companies and those supporting online businesses, as their primary focus is on facilitating and enabling MSMEs' activities on the platforms, without considering whether the products being sold are locally manufactured or imported.

Addressing this issue requires the implementation of comprehensive manufacturing strategies to effectively tackle production challenges, fostering fair competition and supporting local businesses. Unfortunately, it has not received the necessary attention for a thorough discussion, overshadowed by other pressing issues dominating media coverage. Consequently, finding a viable solution to the challenges posed by e-commerce platforms and competition with imported products has been delayed or neglected.

The news collected in the datasets does not directly reflect the needs or problems faced by MSMEs. They lack a direct voice in these reports, with their issues and interests often communicated by external entities such as the government and large corporations. The latter are expected to present their products or services as valuable offerings that can assist and support MSMEs. Consequently, the discourses surrounding platform capitalism do not originate from the genuine interests expressed by MSMEs but rather from the perspectives formulated by corporations seeking to engage MSMEs either as customers or as entities to be packaged and sold to potential investors.

Moreover, the fragmented nature of MSMEs and their inability to consolidate power may result in their voices being unheard in policymaking, which often favors platform companies. Additionally, the government and policymakers tend to view digital transformation through e-commerce platforms as an indicator of economic and technological advancement that the nation must pursue. However, the touted technological progress has yet to demonstrate clear advantages in terms of business efficiency. In Indonesia, e-commerce platforms are still in pursuit of profitability, relying heavily on capital injections primarily from foreign investors who recognize the untapped prospects they hold. These platforms, akin to the earlier concept of e-marketplaces, pose a potential threat to MSMEs by intensifying competition and leaving non-participating entities vulnerable to the growing dominance of e-commerce-enabled businesses (Stockdale & Standing, 2004).

Articles on Kontan.co.id often present the viewpoints of large corporations that perceive MSMEs primarily as a market segment. Their intended value proposition to MSMEs revolves around providing easy access to the market. However, digital platforms have evolved into markets themselves, guided not by Adam Smith's invisible hand but by an algorithmic hand. Leveraging big data and AI, the behaviors of market participants, namely MSMEs and consumers, on digital platforms become more transparent and potentially manipulable by the platform companies. Considering the multitude of similar products, when a consumer opens the platform app on her mobile phone or searches for a product, what she encounters first is not random but determined by the platform's algorithm. Consequently, the algorithm determines the survival and success of digital merchants, highlighting the power imbalance between platform companies and their users, who often wield limited control over the terms of service and data privacy policies governing their interactions with these platforms (Rahman & Thelen, 2019).

5.6 Conclusions

The platform economy has significantly expanded its presence in numerous sectors, leading to the disruption of traditional business models and practices. Both the government and businesses recognize the inevitability of digital business development or transformation. In order to survive in an increasingly competitive and digitalized economy, businesses, including MSMEs, must embrace this shift.

Although the platform economy initially emerged as a concept known as the sharing economy, which carried a social connotation, platform businesses have now evolved into major enterprises that demand substantial financial resources and highly skilled human capital for their development. This is necessary to create efficient systems that facilitate seamless matchmaking between those in need and those offering goods or services.

In addition, platform businesses operate as network-based enterprises, and their competition is frequently marked by a "winner takes all" scenario. This fuels a race among platforms to dominate the market by offering incentives to users and prioritizing market dominance over immediate profitability. MSMEs are a significant user base targeted by these platforms. They are encouraged and educated to leverage the platform's capabilities to access a wider market without the need for complex technological infrastructure, as was required by older electronic marketplaces.

Prior to generating actual profits, the primary customers of platform companies are investors who inject capital to facilitate the company's dominance in the market. The core product of platform companies is their extensive user base, which consists of merchants and buyers in the case of e-commerce platforms. The attractiveness for investors lies in the large number of users and transactions facilitated by these platforms. The government and investors' conviction in the platform economy as an inevitable progression leads them to support it, even in the absence of immediate profitability. Their belief in the long-term potential and transformative power of platform businesses motivates their ongoing support and investment, recognizing that substantial profits may not materialize immediately. Hence, the engagement of MSMEs by platform companies is intensive due to the high number of MSMEs.

MSMEs play a crucial role in driving the growth of the platform economy. As a result, the government, platform companies, and providers of related technologies and services actively work to convince MSMEs to embrace e-commerce platforms, highlighting the potential to expand their market reach and facilitate more efficient business transactions. MSMEs are encouraged to recognize that adopting e-commerce platforms not only provides them with competitive advantages and new growth opportunities but also serves as a vital factor for their survival in an increasingly digitalized business landscape.

However, it's crucial to highlight that platform business, driven by the goal of expanding user numbers and transactions, may not inherently prioritize the nature of the products being sold. This includes the presence of used or imported goods, which could potentially threaten domestic manufacturing industries. It becomes the responsibility of the government and policymakers to address this concern, ensuring the implementation of appropriate regulations and safeguards to protect domestic manufacturers and maintain a fair marketplace.

References

Acquier, A., Daudigeos, T., & Pinkse, J. (2017). Promises and paradoxes of the sharing economy: An organizing framework. *Technological Forecasting and Social Change, 125*, 1–10. Elsevier Science Inc. https://doi.org/10.1016/j.techfore.2017.07.006

Andersson Schwarz, J. (2017). Platform logic: An interdisciplinary approach to the platform-based economy. *Policy and Internet, 9*(4), 374–394. https://doi.org/10.1002/poi3.159

Ayyagari, M., Beck, T., & Demirguc-Kunt, A. (2007). Small and medium enterprises across the globe. *Small Business Economics*, 29(4), 415–434. https://doi.org/10.1007/s11187-006-9002-5

Benoit, S., Baker, T. L., Bolton, R. N., Gruber, T., & Kandampully, J. (2017). A triadic framework for collaborative consumption (CC): Motives, activities and resources & capabilities of actors. *Journal of Business Research, 79*, 219–227. Elsevier Science Inc. https://doi.org/10.1016/j.jbusres.2017.05.004

Brezina, V., Weill-Tessier, P., & McEnery, A. (2021). *LancsBox (v. 6. X.)[software package]* [Computer software]. Lancaster University.

Campbell, J. L. (2002). Ideas, politics, and public policy. *Annual Review of Sociology, 28*, 21–38. https://doi.org/10.1146/annurev.soc.28.110601.141111

Christensen, C. M. (2000). *The innovator's dilemma.* HarperBusiness.

Cunningham, L. X. (2011). SMEs as motor of growth: A review of China's SMEs development in thirty years (1978–2008). *Human Systems Management, 30*(1–2), 39–54. https://doi.org/10.3233/HSM-2011-0736

Cutolo, D., & Kenney, M. (2021). Platform-dependent entrepreneurs: Power asymmetries, risks, and strategies in the platform economy. *Academy of Management Perspectives, 35*(4), 584–605. ACAD Management. https://doi.org/10.5465/amp.2019.0103

Darmody, A., & Zwick, D. (2020). Manipulate to empower: Hyper-relevance and the contradictions of marketing in the age of surveillance capitalism. *Big Data & Society, 7*(1), 2053951720904112. https://doi.org/10.1177/2053951720904112

DW. (2016). *Demo taxi Lumpuhkan Jakarta.* https://www.dw.com/id/demo-taxi-lumpuhkan-jakarta/a-19132868

Foucault, M. (1978). *The history of sexuality volume 1: An introduction* (R. Hurley, Trans.). Pantheon Books.

Frenken, K., & Schor, J. (2017). Putting the sharing economy into perspective. In *Environmental innovation and societal transitions* (Vol. 23, pp. 3–10). https://doi.org/10.1016/j.eist.2017.01.003

Grabher, G., & Koenig, J. (2020). Disruption, embedded. A Polanyian framing of the platform economy. *Sociologica-International Journal for Sociological Debate, 14*(1), 95–118. Univ. Bologna, Dept. Arts. https://doi.org/10.6092/issn.1971-8853/10443

Holland, C. P., & Gutiérrez-Leefmans, M. (2018). A taxonomy of SME E-Commerce platforms derived from a market-level analysis. *International Journal of Electronic Commerce, 22*(2), 161–201. https://doi.org/10.1080/10864415.2017.1364114

Iskandar. (2020). HEADLINE: Marak Penipuan Online Shop di Medsos, Hati-Hati Modusnya Makin Canggih. *Liputan6*. https://www.liputan6.com/tekno/read/4157301/headline-marak-penipuan-online-shop-di-medsos-hati-hati-modusnya-makin-canggih

Jean, R. J., & Kim, D. (2020). Internet and SMEs' internationalization: The role of platform and website. *Journal of International Management, 26*(1). https://doi.org/10.1016/j.intman.2019.100690

Jiménez-Zarco, A. I., Clemente-Almendros, J. A., González-González, I., & Aracil-Jordà, J. (2021). Female micro-entrepreneurs and social networks: Diagnostic analysis of the influence of social-media marketing strategies on brand financial performance. *Frontiers in Psychology, 12*.https://doi.org/10.3389/fpsyg.2021.630058

Kenney, M., & Zysman, J. (2016). The rise of the platform economy. *Issues in Science and Technology, 32*(3), 61–69.

Kenney, M., & Zysman, J. (2020). The platform economy: Restructuring the space of capitalist accumulation. *Cambridge Journal of Regions, Economy and Society, 13*(1), 55–76. https://doi.org/10.1093/cjres/rsaa001

Lee, K., Szapiro, M., & Mao, Z. (2018). From Global Value Chains (GVC) to innovation systems for local value chains and knowledge creation. *The European Journal of Development Research, 30*(3), 424–441. https://doi.org/10.1057/s41287-017-0111-6

Leong, N., & Belzer, A. (2017). The new public accommodations: Race discrimination in the platform economy. *Georgetown Law Journal, 105*(5), 1271–1322.

Liang, Y., Aroles, J., & Brandl, B. (2022). Charting platform capitalism: Definitions, concepts and ideologies. *New Technology Work and Employment, 37*(2), 308–327. https://doi.org/10.1111/ntwe.12234

Maulana, I. (2019). Big brothers are seducing you: Consumerism, surveillance, and the agency of consumers. In O. Ozgen (Ed.), *Handbook of research on consumption, media, and popular culture in the global age.* IGI Global.

Maulana, I. (2020a). Democracy, technology, and human irresponsibility. In V. Kumar & G. Malhotra (Eds.), *Examining the roles of IT and social media in democratic development and social change.* IGI Global.

Maulana, I. (2020b). Social media as public political instrument. In M. Adria (Ed.), *Using new media for citizen engagement and participation.* IGI Global. https://doi.org/10.4018/978-1-5225-9869-5.ch009

OECD. (2018). *Promoting innovation in established SMEs.* 2018 SME ministerial conference, Mexico City. https://www.oecd.org/cfe/smes/ministerial/documents/2018-SME-Ministerial-Conference-Parallel-Session-4.pdf

Oswaldo, I. G. (2023). Gagal Bertahan, 10 Aplikasi Ojol Ini Bangkrut di RI. *Detik.Com.* https://finance.detik.com/berita-ekonomi-bisnis/d-6664600/gagal-bertahan-10-aplikasi-ojol-ini-bangkrut-di-ri

Panji, A. (2015). Ikut Jokowi ke AS, Ini Misi yang Dibawa CEO Gojek. *CNNIndonesia.Com.* https://www.cnnindonesia.com/teknologi/20151022163406-185-86698/ikut-jokowi-ke-as-ini-misi-yang-dibawa-ceo-gojek

Rahman, K. S., & Thelen, K. (2019). The rise of the platform business model and the transformation of twenty-first-century capitalism. *Politics & Society, 47*(2), 177–204. https://doi.org/10.1177/0032329219838932

Rotar, L. J., Pamić, R. K., & Bojnec, Š. (2019). Contributions of small and medium enterprises to employment in the European Union countries. *Economic Research-Ekonomska Istrazivanja, 32*(1), 3296–3308. https://doi.org/10.1080/1331677X.2019.1658532

Schumpeter, J. A. (2010). Capitalism, socialism and democracy. In *Capitalism, socialism and democracy.* https://doi.org/10.4324/9780203857090

Septiani, L. (2023). Daftar E-Commerce Tutup di Indonesia Selain JD.ID dan Alasannya. *KataData.* https://katadata.co.id/desysetyowati/digital/63d8c9498aca0/daftar-e-commerce-tutup-di-indonesia-selain-jdid-dan-alasannya

Shapiro, C., & Varian, H. R. (1999). *Information rules: A strategic guide to the network economy.* Harvard Business School Press.

Srnicek, N. (2016). *Platform capitalism* (1st ed.). Polity. http://gen.lib.rus.ec/book/index.php?md5=54101e43da5c8a19fa2a6110aee33c78

Srnicek, N. (2017). The challenges of platform capitalism: Understanding the logic of a new business model. *Juncture, 23*(4), 254–257. https://doi.org/10.1111/newe.12023

Stockdale, R., & Standing, C. (2004). Benefits and barriers of electronic marketplace participation: An SME perspective. *Journal of Enterprise Information Management*, *17*(4), 301–311. https://doi.org/10.1108/17410390410548715

Sultan, M. T., & Sharmin, F. (2020). An exploratory investigation of facebook live marketing by women entrepreneurs in Bangladesh. *Lecture notes in computer science (Including subseries lecture notes in artificial intelligence and lecture notes in bioinformatics)*. LNCS (Vol. 12195, pp. 415–430). https://doi.org/10.1007/978-3-030-49576-3_30

Sutherland, W., & Jarrahi, M. H. (2018). The sharing economy and digital platforms: A review and research agenda. *International Journal of Information Management*, *43*, 328–341. Elsevier Sci Ltd. https://doi.org/10.1016/j.ijinfomgt.2018.07.004

Tan, M. (2022). Realizing the potential of over 71 million MSMEs in Southeast Asia. *Asian Development Bank*. https://seads.adb.org/solutions/realizing-potential-over-71-million-msmes-southeast-asia

Van Eck, N., & Waltman, L. (2010). Software survey: VOSviewer, a computer program for bibliometric mapping. *Scientometrics, 84*(2), 523–538.

Vatanasakdakul, S., Aoun, C., & Suyoso Putra, Y. H. (2020). Social media in micro-enterprises: Exploring adoption in the Indonesian retail sector. *Journal of Global Information Management, 28*(3), 184–203. https://doi.org/10.4018/JGIM.2020070110

Vijayakumar, S., & Sedláček, M. (2012). The trend and impact of small and medium enterprises on the economic growth of Sri Lanka. In *Innovation Vision 2020: Sustainable Growth, Entrepreneurship, and Economic Development—Proceedings of the 19th International Business Information Management Association Conference* (Vol. 3, pp. 1426–1437). https://www.scopus.com/inward/record.uri?eid=2-s2.0-84896380915&partnerID=40&md5=1bb413c1667f791a7eac792933f560f9

Viljoen, S., Goldenfein, J., & McGuigan, L. (2021). Design choices: Mechanism design and platform capitalism. *Big Data & Society, 8*(2), 20539517211034310. https://doi.org/10.1177/20539517211034312

Zuboff, S. (2015). Big other: Surveillance capitalism and the prospects of an information civilization. *Journal of Information Technology*, *30*(1), 75–89.

Ikbal Maulana is a researcher at the Research Center of Society and Culture, National Research and Innovation Agency (BRIN). He has master degree in computer engineering and worked as programmer and system analyst before becoming a researcher and pursuing Ph.D. degree in philosophy. His current research interests concern the impact of information technology on society and democracy, philosophy of technology, and social epistemology. His relevant publications in line with the book's topic include chapters titled "Big Brothers Are Seducing You: Consumerism, Surveillance, and the Agency of Consumers," "The Cultural and Institutional Barrier of Knowledge Exchanges in the Development of Open Source Software," and "Challenges of Developing Countries in Imitating Technological Progress." All three chapters are solely authored by the author.

Chapter 6
The Dynamics of Economy in the Regional MSMEs' Digital Ecosystem

Luthfina Ariyani and Adityo Wicaksono

Abstract During the two years of the COVID-19 pandemic, the regional economy of Indonesia has been fluctuating, filled up with sharp fluxes of drop and spike. This situation has been largely influenced by the continuous change of mobility and travel restriction level policies adjusting to the infection rate. Eventually, it has created a new dynamic in the MSMEs ecosystem. This chapter provides a detailed snapshot of the current dynamics in the MSMEs ecosystem. The depiction was developed based on the analysis of several MSME case studies and focus group discussions with multiple actors of the ecosystem within three Indonesian provinces: West Sumatra, West Java, and Yogyakarta. Prior to the pandemic, the development of the digital ecosystem was still in its infancy phase with very limited dominant actors. As the pandemic hit, the digital ecosystem was rapidly expanding and became crowded. In the later phase, several MSMEs were returning to offline mode due to the failure to sustain their digital business mode. Hence, the physical ecosystem started to recover gradually. Meanwhile, the surviving businesses in the digital ecosystem have been growing exponentially as the customers continue to grow. Accordingly, we also categorized three types of MSMEs role, namely dominant, supporting, and passive actors, within the ecosystem according to their network establishment, and how the digital ecosystem has influenced them to survive the pandemic. Furthermore, we identified several influential actors and their roles regarding MSMEs in the regional digital ecosystem.

Keywords Dynamics · MSMEs · Digital ecosystem · COVID-19 pandemic · Actor

L. Ariyani (✉) · A. Wicaksono
National Research and Innovation Agency, Jakarta, Indonesia
e-mail: luth004@brin.go.id

A. Wicaksono
e-mail: adit004@brin.go.id

T. Fizzanty and I. Maulana (eds.), *The Digitalization of Indonesian Small and Medium Enterprises*, Engaging Indonesia, https://doi.org/10.1007/978-981-97-0029-5_6

6.1 Introduction: The Transitioning of Economic Situation in Indonesia

Indonesia has experienced the ups and downs of the economic situation in times before and during the COVID-19 pandemic. This unprecedented phenomenon was significantly influencing the eudaimonia of Micro, Small, and Medium Enterprises (MSMEs) in the country. The sudden drop in the thriving economy has shaped the MSMEs ecosystem, urging them to shift their business model from the physical into the digital ecosystem.

6.1.1 Overview of Pre-COVID-19 Digital Ecosystem in Indonesia

A year before the COVID-19 pandemic hit the Southeast Asia region, the Indonesian macro economy was still growing (5.02%) with a small decrease year on year, namely 2.07% in 2020 (see Fig. 6.1). MSMEs play a vital role in the economic development of Indonesia. They contribute significantly to the country's Gross Domestic Product and are a major source of employment. In 2019, MSMEs contributed IDR 7.034,1 trillion to the nation's GDP and absorbed 119.6 million laborers (Jayani, 2021). Within this period, the majority of MSMEs were conducting their businesses in a conventional way through brick and mortar or offline stores, while several others were starting to learn to adopt digital technology.

Meanwhile, the digital ecosystem in Indonesia was already experiencing growth and evolution, filled with prominent e-commerce, new emerging sellers, and big

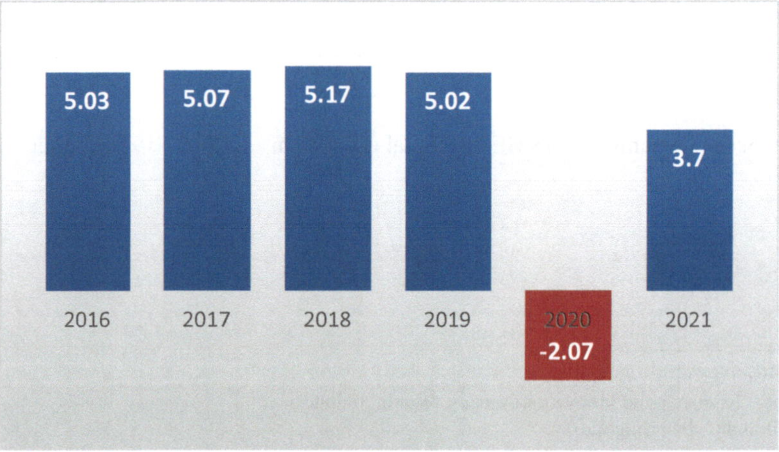

Fig. 6.1 Economic growth of Indonesia from 2017 to 2021. *Source* BPS (2022)

retailers. Prominent e-commerce includes Tokopedia, Bukalapak, Shopee, Lazada, Blibli, and JD.ID. New emerging sellers were businesses that started to sell their products in e-commerce, shifting from the traditional store. Big retailers were supermarkets, which also expanded their marketing channels into e-commerce. According to the data from the Central Bureau of Statistics (BPS) (2019), 15.08% of Indonesian businesses had already been onboarded into e-commerce, while 84.92% were still doing business in conventional ways. Even with this number, the e-commerce industry in Indonesia has been steadily growing, with the government showing commitment to providing ease of investment and protection for MSMEs and businesses venturing into the digital world (Simanjuntak, 2019). This commitment began in 2016 when the Indonesian Government enacted e-commerce policies. The notable policy that supports the development of e-commerce is the XIV Economical Policy Package: e-commerce roadmap. This roadmap covers the enactment of regulations pertaining to funding, tax, consumer protection, education, human resources, logistics, communication infrastructure, and cyber security. The policies create substantial changes that enhance the infrastructure, boost the quality of human capital, attract foreign fundings, and attract foreign actors to conduct business in Indonesia. Since then, the digital ecosystem in Indonesia has experienced significant progress. One of the key driving factors in the growth of the digital ecosystem in Indonesia before the pandemic was the increasing popularity and use of e-commerce platforms.

6.1.2 Digital Economy During the Pandemic in Indonesia 2020–2021

During the COVID-19 pandemic, Indonesia, like many other nations, experienced a huge shock in its economy, including the digital economy. Based on data by the Central Bureau of Statistics, Indonesia's economic growth declined in almost all sectors during the first quarter of 2020 due to the impact of the pandemic (Aisyah et al., 2021). The pandemic presented both opportunities and challenges for Indonesia's digital industry in general. Indonesia's digital economy, which had been experiencing significant growth prior to the pandemic, also faced challenges during this period. The telecommunications industry played a crucial role in facilitating the digitalization process and supporting the continuity of various economic activities during the pandemic (Viargo, 2022). As businesses and society started to adapt themselves to the pandemic conditions, the digital economy was recovering and thriving. There are at least five symptoms that describe this thriving state.

First, digital technology usage increases substantially. The pandemic has expedited digital technology adoption in Indonesia's diverse industries. For the purpose of trade, entertainment, work, and education, people started using online platforms to replace their offline daily activities. During this time, there was a significant increase in demand for digital services, including teleconferencing, internet streaming, food delivery, and e-commerce. Second, e-commerce businesses have expanded exponentially. Due to restrictions on physical storefronts and consumer preference for online buying due to safety concerns, e-commerce saw substantial expansion during the pandemic. Significant Indonesian e-commerce players, like Tokopedia, Shopee, and Bukalapak, have been reported rising. Along with the three giants, other smaller firms, such as Lazada, Blibli, Zalora, and Bhinneka, also have been growing. Third, digital payment adoption has been accelerated, being endorsed by the government and central bank (Bank Indonesia). To minimize physical contact and cash handling, there was a surge in digital payment usage. E-wallets (such as GoPay, OVO, and Dana) gained popularity as people embraced contactless payments for online and offline transactions. The government also promoted digital payment adoption to support financial inclusion and reduce the use of cash. Fourth, online services are rising and expanding. Various online services, including food delivery, ride-hailing, and online entertainment platforms, witnessed increased demand. Companies like Gojek and Grab expanded their services to include grocery deliveries and partnered with local businesses to support them during the pandemic. Fifth, almost all levels of learning have been adopting digital education. As schools and universities transitioned to online learning, there was a surge in digital education platforms and tools. Online learning platforms, such as Ruang Guru and Quipper, experienced an increase in user engagement. The government collaborated with private sector entities to provide online learning access for students across the country. Meanwhile, several digital start-ups faced challenges, especially those dependent on sectors severely affected by the pandemic (e.g., travel and tourism), and the others identified new opportunities. Start-ups involved in health tech, remote work solutions, and digital infrastructure development witnessed growth and investment interest.

6.1.3 The Digital Transformation of Indonesia's MSMEs in 2020–2021

One area that is severely affected by the pandemic is the digital ecosystem of MSMEs in Indonesia. Since the outbreak of COVID-19 in 2020, the growth of e-commerce in Indonesia has significantly increased. This increase in e-commerce transactions reflects the rapid digitalization of MSMEs as they adapt themselves to the changing circumstances brought by the pandemic and the need for social distancing measures. Studies conducted on digitalization and MSMEs in Indonesia have shown that digitalization plays a crucial role in the sustainability of these businesses (Marsdenia et al., 2022). Several studies' findings also indicate that prior to the COVID-19 pandemic, MSMEs in Indonesia had already embraced digitalization, leveraging technologies such as social media for marketing to reach a wider audience at a lower cost.

However, the COVID-19 pandemic has exacerbated the importance of digitalization for MSMEs as they face various challenges and changes in market demand and supply. The pandemic has caused MSMEs in Indonesia to experience a decrease in revenue by 84% of, as reported by the Central Bureau of Statistics (Primadana et al., 2021). This decrease in revenue can be attributed to several factors, such as changes in consumer behavior, knowledge gaps in managerial and technology skills necessary for digitalization, reduced operational hours, and delays in the supply chain. Furthermore, MSMEs need to enhance their management skills, strategic planning capabilities, and innovation knowledge in order to formulate new business models that can meet the new market demands and survive in the post-pandemic era. The shift into a digital economy has become imperative for MSMEs in Indonesia to stay afloat during these challenging times. The COVID-19 pandemic has necessitated the adoption of digital technology by MSMEs as a means of enduring and prospering in ever-changing circumstances. The integration of digital technology has become ubiquitous across various facets of business operations, encompassing various functions, such as marketing, sales, supply chain management, and customer service. Digital platforms, remote work assistance, automation, data analytics, and artificial intelligence are widely utilized by MSMEs as key technological tools.

Despite the progress in digital adoption, Indonesia also faced challenges related to the large disparity in digital literacy and inadequate digital infrastructure. Not all Indonesian citizens had access to reliable internet connectivity and devices, thereby limiting their participation in the digital economy. Efforts were made to improve digital infrastructure and expand internet access to underdeveloped areas. The Indonesian Government recognized the importance of the digital economy during the pandemic and implemented various measures to support its growth. These included tax incentives for digital businesses, regulatory reforms to facilitate digital transactions, and initiatives to improve digital infrastructure and internet connectivity. In a nutshell, the COVID-19 pandemic accelerated the digital transformation in Indonesia, with increased adoption of digital technologies across various sectors. The digital economy played a crucial role in sustaining economic activities during the challenging period, and efforts were made to address the existing challenges and promote digital inclusion.

Under the concept of ecosystem, MSMEs digitalization cannot be separated from interdependencies through complex and dynamic interactions of multiple stakeholders (Lenkenhoff et al., 2018). This might affect how far digitalization fosters MSMEs resilience during the pandemic, or even in the later phase of the pandemic. Therefore, we want to explain the dynamism of MSMEs digital ecosystem before, during, and after the pandemic within three Indonesian provinces, namely West Sumatra, Yogyakarta, and West Java. Specifically, this chapter aims to explain the actors, their roles, and interactions, as well as the dynamism and challenges within MSMEs digital ecosystem.

6.2 Existing Relevant Views of Ecosystems

Comprehending existing views of ecosystems in the field of business and economics is necessary to properly depict and understand the current dynamics of digital ecosystems. Hence, this article highlights several important views of the ecosystems. Previously, there were at least three major views, including (1) Business Ecosystem, (2) Entrepreneurial Ecosystem, and (3) Digital Ecosystem.

6.2.1 *Business Ecosystem*

The notion of a business ecosystem has gained considerable attention in the contemporary and interrelated commercial environment. The concept of business ecosystem was first introduced by Moore (1993), which refers to a set of interconnected organizations, institutions, and individuals that build their capabilities and roles and rely on each other as they pursue overall performance and survival (Iansiti & Levien, 2004; Moore, 1993). According to Moore (1996), the business ecosystem consists of a wide variety of agents, which are categorized into three levels: core business, extended enterprises, and business environment. The first two pertain to those actors interacting within the supply chain domain, in which the former denotes the direct supply chain partners, whereas the latter denotes partners with indirect supply chain partners. Meanwhile, the business environment refers to those that do not directly interact as supply chain partners, but greatly influence the ecosystem, such as government, quasi-government, industry associations, standards bodies, and competitors. Rong and Shi (2015) added that the business environment can be associated with the opportunity space, in which the interdependent actors exchange their ideas and visions for future growth.

Certain scholarly works also emphasize the dynamic nature of the business ecosystem. The perspective put forth by Moore (1996) posited that the business ecosystem undergoes four S-curved phases as follows: the birth phase, during which companies identify opportunities to generate value for customers; the expansion phase, wherein the company achieves scalability; the authority phase, in which the company establishes a stable leadership position; and finally, the renewal phase, marked by the emergence of new ecosystems along with the introduction of novel ideas and innovations. Meanwhile, Rong and Shi (2015) also posited that a business ecosystem progresses through five distinct stages in its lifecycle, namely emergence, diversification, convergence, consolidation, and renewal. In general, the emergence of a business ecosystem has been driven by market forces (Rong, 2011). However, in a study conducted by Lu et al. (2014) on the electric vehicle business ecosystem, it was observed that the ecosystem initiatives may also originate from governmental bodies. Furthermore, Makinen and Dedehayir (2012) posited that the dynamism of the ecosystem may occur due to internal and external forces, such as the co-evolution of capabilities and roles among actors, the transformations of governance within the ecosystem, fluctuation of socio-economic conditions, or advancements in technology.

6.2.2 Entrepreneurial Ecosystem

The large body of literature explored various meanings of entrepreneurial ecosystem (EE), from the biological perspective to the artificial ecosystem concept. The earliest conceptualization of EE was proposed by Spilling (1996), which explained the EE as a system comprised of actors and environmental elements that exist in a particular geographical territory. Then, Cohen brought up the concept of sustainable EE from the root of the biological ecosystem: "An interconnected group of actors in a local geographic community committed to sustainable development through the support and facilitation of new sustainable ventures" (Cohen, 2006, p. 3). In a more recent development, the definition had expanded in a more complex way, describing EE as "a self-organized, adaptive, and geographically bounded community of complex agents operating at multiple, aggregated levels, whose non-linear interactions result in the patterns of activities through which new ventures form and dissolve over time." (Roundy et al., 2018, p. 5) These definitions are derived from the natural ecosystem characteristics, which do not require intervention. The authors highlighted the geographical boundaries and actors' interactions.

In its progression, previous studies have acknowledged several advantages of EE formation. First, EEs can stimulate the creation of new ventures that shapes the industry and foster economic growth (Fritsch, 2008). Second, the establishment of new ventures significantly contributed to the emergence of various types of employment (Haltiwanger et al., 2013). Third, the density of firms within geographical boundaries can act as a catalyst for interactions among entrepreneurs (Motoyama & Knowlton, 2016). Lastly, Cohen (2006) argued that a sustainable EE can enhance environmental conditions and reduce poverty. These benefits provide additional motivation to the knowledge generation effort for replicating EEs and fully exploiting its potency.

Existing literature covered two different views of EE evolution, namely bottom-up and top-down approach (Colombo et al., 2019). The bottom-up approach describes that EE emerges and evolves naturally, like the formation of the ecosystem in biology. Actors in the ecosystem show self-interest behaviors that are governed by an "invisible hand." This description is suitable for ecosystem such as Silicon Valley; the ecosystem emerged and evolved naturally, governed by a unique culture as an "invisible hand" (Colombo et al., 2019).

On the other hand, the top-down approach describes that EE can be formed and governed intentionally by a Chandlerian "visible hand." Based on this concept, the government provides the necessary resources to facilitate the growth of the ecosystem (Stam, 2015). The actors' interaction is institutionally organized by public policies (Audretsch & Belitski, 2017; Lehmann & Menter, 2018). Each EE has its distinctive path of evolution (Cukier & Kon, 2018), in which several ecosystems show the characteristics of bottom-up evolution, while others go with top-down. Several of them thrive, while not a few of them stunt.

Colombelli et al. (2019) argued that the governance and actors' interaction with the ecosystem will change as they adapt themselves to the life cycle phase of the ecosystem and other external factors. In the emerging stage, the governance model is hierarchical, while interaction among actors is unlikely structural. As it evolves, the governance model becomes less hierarchical and shifts into a more relational model. In this phase, the actors' interactions are interconnected and become self-reinforcing. Then, in the consolidation phase, the governance model is relational, while interactions are systemic pursuing common purposes.

The EE development does not only need business establishments; it requires infrastructures, formal institutions, and support that strengthen each other. Spigel (2017) described that the ecosystem is shaped by the interactions among elements, rather than merely the availability of elements. Trust among members of EE will enhance the actors' cooperation and knowledge transfer (Tötterman & Sten, 2005). For instance, Motoyama and Knowlton (2016) described that the industries and common processes would drive start-ups to collaborate. In contrast, a lack of trust can trigger opportunistic behaviors and escalate unhealthy competition in the ecosystem (Inkpen & Tsang, 2005; Lado et al., 2008).

Overall, existing literature largely covered micro and medium-level unit analysis by examining individual actors and interactions of actors. Many previous studies overlooked the holistic view of actors' interactions that influence the EE development. Employing a macro-level unit of analysis is necessary to expand the current perspective towards the ecosystem. The macro level unit of analysis examines the whole interactions within the ecosystem and its connections to external elements.

6.2.3 Digital Ecosystem

In recent years, this concept has evolved, considering the aspects of the development of digital technologies. The integration of business and digital ecosystems has led to the emergence of novel collaborative organizational networks known as Digital Business Ecosystems (DBE) (Stanley & Briscoe, 2010). The DBE can be viewed as a continuation of Moore's (1993) business ecosystem, wherein digital platforms hold a predominant position. According to previous studies, digital platforms are defined as technological structures that enable participating organizations to efficiently create, customize, and provide sophisticated services on an unparalleled level.

6.3 Depiction of Indonesia's MSMEs Digital Ecosystem

For depicting MSMEs digital ecosystems in Indonesia before and during the pandemic, focus group discussions and thorough observations were conducted in three provinces (Yogyakarta, West Sumatra, and West Java). These three provinces were chosen as they have thriving MSMEs ecosystems. A detailed depiction and explanation of the digital ecosystem, including the actors, interactions, roles, dynamism, and challenges, will be provided in this chapter.

The three provinces have similar characteristics, as they are rich in cultures, blessed with many tourist destinations, complemented by universities existence, and have abundance of culinary treats. The local economy was benefiting from tourism, and tertiary education bloomed. The three regions are also famous for their nature landscapes and cultural tourist destinations, which can attract many domestic and foreign tourists. Domestic tourists and temporary college students are the main customers of local MSMEs in these three provinces.

Before the pandemic, Yogyakarta was visited by 338,858 foreign tourists and 3,384,134 domestic tourists (Agency of Tourism Yogyakarta Special Region, 2019). The amount of tourists is almost as big as the residences of this province (3.8 million people). In addition, there were 368,066 college students, of which 30% of them (110,419 students) were visitors or temporary residents (Bappeda DIY, 2020). Meanwhile, West Sumatra has been visited by 19,412,170 tourists and 207,552 college students (BPS, 2019; Ministry of Research, Technology, and Higher Education, 2019). For comparison, West Java had a far higher number of tourist visits in 2019, which reached 68,256,265 people (jabarprov.go.id, 2020). This province also had a significantly large number of college students in 2019, which reached 878,512 students (Ministry of Research, Technology, and Higher Education, 2019). Along their journeys, tourists and visitors purchased many of MSMEs' products as mementos or souvenirs. When the mobility was restricted during the pandemic, the visits were slumped and MSMEs sales were plummeting.

In three FGDs, participants explained that there were only a few MSMEs that conducted business through digital channels (or both physical and digital) before the pandemic. Several MSMEs that were already onboarded into the digital ecosystem have survived the economic downturns during the pandemic and become regional champions, while the other MSMEs were dimming into bankruptcy.

> I was starting to sell my product through online channels way before the pandemic happened and way before e-commerce was blooming. Previously, my fellow MSMEs were focusing on their offline shops rather than spending their time building an online store. When the pandemic emerged, their shops started to close. In contrast, my online sales went up from June 2020 until January 2021. This shows that my business was thriving during the pandemic. ST-business owner

> The pandemic caused gudeg businesses in Yogyakarta to drop for about 60–70%, as the businesses rely heavily on the tourism sector. When the tourists stopped visiting this region, they were unable to purchase our products through offline channels. Meanwhile, only 30% of us were adopting digital technology and selling through online channels. We were becoming role models to those who haven't conducted online selling. CH-gudeg business owner

> The majority of fashion MSMEs relies on offline stores. During the pandemic, their sales decreased by about 60%. To tackle this issue, we built synergic collaboration among MSME's community, local government agencies, and the ministries. By early 2021, we adopted several digital technologies and onboarded into social media marketing. By doing this, we can survive through the pandemic. EW-batik fashion business owner

When the pandemic hit this region, a large number of MSMEs that relied on their offline business went bankrupt. The survivors shifted their business mode into the digital ecosystem; selling their products through e-commerce and social media. Meanwhile, people who lost their jobs were trying to make money in the digital ecosystem, namely by creating new businesses and new products, reselling other people's products, becoming freelancers, and selling their digital assets. They became the emerging MSMEs in Yogyakarta digital economy. Hence, the digital ecosystem was growing rapidly, becoming dense and crowded, while the physical ecosystem was abandoned. However, it was less structured or organized in nature.

> ... as they see the value of doing the business online, then they started to flock in the digital ecosystem trying to earn profit just like their existing peers. EK-consultant

> During the pandemic, unemployed people were desperate trying to get back on their feet by starting businesses online or become resellers for other people products. WS-government official

> We even built our own government-made e-commerce platform called Sibakul to help the MSMEs in Yogyakarta to onboard into the digital ecosystem and conducting business online. It was quite successful, as plenty of them were joining the platform, actively selling their products, and obtaining revenues from it. WK-government official

In the later phase of the pandemic, several MSMEs and new entrepreneurs who tried to conduct their businesses online were failing due to fierce competition, imitation, and incapability to cope with the unpredictable situation in the digital ecosystem. Several of them were returning to offline mode. As a result, the digital ecosystem became less crowded than before, and the physical ecosystem started to recover at a slow pace. Meanwhile, as the pandemic situation was still forcing people to stay at home, customers kept buying their daily needs online. This situation has made the surviving businesses in the digital ecosystem grow exponentially. Furthermore, based on the FGD result and observations, the situation of MSME's physical and digital ecosystem before and during the pandemic can be depicted in Fig. 6.2. Before the pandemic, only a few central government agencies and prominent e-commerce platforms actively engaged in the digital ecosystem and became the dominant actors, which attracted several MSMEs and big retailers to participate in the ecosystem. Then, during the pandemic, the central government became less dominant and was replaced by local governments, which understand more deeply the MSMEs' condition in their regions. Then, MSMEs as the regional champions emerged and acted as the main economic power in the ecosystem. They became role models and attracted other MSMEs to participate in the digital ecosystem.

The existence and role of local government agencies and e-commerce were crucial in accelerating the capability of MSMEs to shift their business mode into the digital ecosystem. A wide range of training was provided by the governments

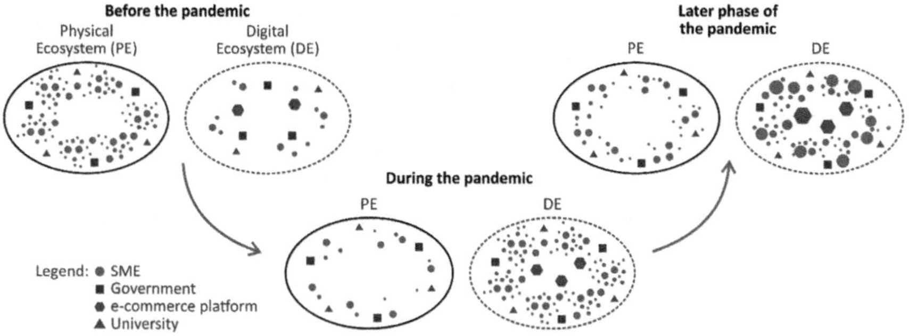

Fig. 6.2 Depiction of MSMEs' physical and digital ecosystem in Indonesia

and e-commerce, such as digital literacy, financial literacy, digital marketing, social marketing, and content production. Big e-commerce platform players became the central actors that provide the digital place for MSMEs to sell their products, while local platforms gained temporary popularity.

6.3.1 Peculiar Actors and Interactions

6.3.1.1 Case Studies Descriptions

There were several actors involved with unique interactions among them. They act according to the dynamics of the situation during and in the later phase of the pandemic. Successful MSMEs actors became champions or role models to those who were late in transitioning into the digital ecosystem. Fast learning and adaptation were essential to cope with the market fluctuation. The descriptions of MSMEs cases and how their network influences their business during the pandemic are presented as follows.

(1) **ZS** maintains a favorable relationship with the craftswomen who supply their products to ZS. This relationship is informal in nature. However, it concerns not only the manner of supply partnership but also the form of sharing information and expertise. ZS encourages the growth of craftswomen by helping them acquire the skills required to create superior products. ZS's positive relationships with local authorities allow it to attend several internships and exhibitions that boost its professional development and increase the business' visibility. Unfortunately, since the business relies heavily on tourism activities, its continuity has been significantly impeded due to the COVID-19 pandemic. The level of government-organized assistance was also decreased significantly due to the pandemic. On the other hand, ZS had tried to penetrate the e-marketplace, but the environment was considered unsuitable for crafts businesses, especially those

with higher prices and that tend to be easily imitated. Nevertheless, ZS has yet to ascertain the optimal digital business model to deliver its product value.

(2) **CH** is a food MSME. It is highly committed to nurturing partnerships with smaller business partners that serve as its product suppliers. CH maintains quality standards for its partners in order to guarantee the taste quality of the products. Its relationship with the government has opened the opportunity for CH to attend several trainings and seminars for professional development, as well as for export opportunities. However, CH was unable to fulfill this export opportunity due to the high standards and volume of inquiries. Customer needs are evaluated and addressed by CH through the introduction of new products. The digital business has undeniably played a significant role in mitigating the impact of the pandemic. However, the proportion of market share derived from digital initiatives remains relatively small due to its revenue that still predominantly relies on tourism activities.

(3) **WK** is an MSME that operates in the health and green sectors, and engages in positive relationships with farmers and its partners. It equips farmers with information and knowledge about organic farming techniques. WK also consistently fosters relationships with its customers and potential customers by holding several community activities related to health and the environment, such as education, environmental preservation activities, bazaars, and others. This community network turns into a knowledge network that encourages knowledge sharing and education. WK also establishes network with media to support their business' visibility. The digital business model has been an integral component of WK for quite a long time, contributing significantly to its resilience amidst the pandemic. Notably, the business has exhibited an upward trend due to the alignment of its product value with health-related concerns.

(4) **GJ** maintains the network with local farmers as a hub for them to market their agricultural products. GJ also provides cultivation techniques for farmers and encourages its continuous application. Despite the ongoing pandemic, GJ demonstrates a commitment to supporting farmers by accommodating or purchasing their harvested product, thereby aiding in their financial stability. In addition to maintaining relationships with end customers, the network with resellers is also highly favorable. The maintained network with the government has given GJ several opportunities to participate in overseas training for skill development. GJ also engaged in collaborative efforts with researchers at Public Research Institute (PRI) to facilitate the development of various health products derived from mushrooms. GJ's business model, which previously had a narrow focus on providing the end product, is currently undergoing expansion to encompass various activities, both upstream and downstream. This includes the incorporation of training, cultivation of products and services, and several variants of end products. This, and supported by digital business, had allowed GJ to survive during the pandemic.

(5) **BB** empowers artisans, particularly women in its region, and educates them on the proper application of batik techniques to supply the products to BB. The owner of BB is an active individual who occupies a strategic position within the

MSME association. BB also maintains a positive relationship with the government and becomes a fostered partner of a state-owned enterprise. This network provides opportunities for BB to participate in several trainings and seminars, exhibitions, and overseas trade promotions. This also brings opportunities for BB to rapidly shift its business model into the production of personal protective equipment (PPE) during the pandemic for local government and large businesses. BB was also given opportunities to participate in digital exhibitions held by the local government. Through all of this, its business can survive during the pandemic and even empower other artisans.

(6) **OR** enables producers to cultivate formerly low-value arrowroot tubers and transform them into local sustenance. Its relationship with resellers and agents provides opportunities for OR to increase its market share. To increase the capability of its agents and resellers, OR equip itself with product knowledge and enhance its digital marketing skills. Becoming an MSME supported by a district government is the first step towards expanding the OR network with local and national governments and gaining access to many seminars, exhibitions, mentoring, licensing, capital, and export opportunities. Moreover, networking with universities assists OR with production assistance, product testing, and development, as well as product promotion. Its business visibility and product branding are supported by its network with media partners. During the pandemic, the value of its healthy products and digital marketing strategy has actually been a boon. Its business model innovation is not only focused on developing new products but also on creating new revenue streams by providing other brands with toll manufacturing services.

6.3.1.2 The Role of MSMEs Within the Business Ecosystem

Based on the above case and according to its network establishment within the core business and business (B&B) environment level, we identified three categories of MSMEs role within the business ecosystem: dominant, supporting, and passive. The depiction of the six MSMEs cases within the ecosystem is shown in Table 6.1.

(1) **The dominant MSMEs**. Within the core business level, this category of actors typically has extensive and strong relationships with their suppliers or distributors. MSMEs also cultivate collaborative relationships with their suppliers or distributors. This is commonly not a simple buy-and-go relationship in the context of the supply chain. Instead, it is a deeper relationship developed through coaching, training, or knowledge sharing. This type of relationship not only ensures the availability of basic materials and the flow of finished products but also ensures that the MSMEs' values are effectively communicated to customers. Generally, they also take the initiative to develop relationships with customers or potential customers, either through direct interactions, such as hosting gatherings or visiting specific communities, or by actively participating in social media. MSMEs were also extensively involved with government agencies, associations, academic institutions, media, and other organizations at the

Table 6.1 MSMEs Network and Its Role Within the Business Ecosystem

MSME	Network		Role in ecosystem
	Core business level	Business environment level	
ZS	Encourage craftswomen by equipping them with knowledge about embroidery techniques in order to meet ZS quality standards	During the business initiation, an embroidery foundation provided ZS with production materials Before the pandemic, ZS received production equipment and had many opportunities through the local government to participate in training and exhibitions	Supporting
CH	Encourage smaller business partners by equipping them with knowledge and quality standards to ensure product quality. CH purchased the products in cash, thus increasing trust between CH and its partners Established saving-and-loan cooperative for partners	Before the pandemic, CH received an invitation from the local government to attend training and seminars. CH had experience with export opportunities but was unable to fulfill them due to the high required standard and volume	Supporting
LE	The relationships with suppliers are primarily in the form of the procurement of raw materials and tend to be relatively informal	Once participate in government-organized training	Passive
WK	Maintain the relationship with farmers and supply partners. Empower farmers by enhancing their capacity to cultivate healthy and sustainable agricultural commodities Nurture relationships with customers through post-purchase service	Maintain relationships with local communities through various environmental care activities Maintain relationships with the media for branding and promotion	Dominant
GJ	Empower farmers with mushroom cultivation techniques Become a hub for farmers to market their products Maintain relationships with resellers and direct customers	Received opportunities through the local government to participate eight times in overseas training for mushroom cultivation Become a PRI-assisted business for the development of mushroom-based health products Hold a strategic position in a mushroom farming group	Dominant

(continued)

Table 6.1 (continued)

MSME	Network		Role in ecosystem
	Core business level	Business environment level	
IP	The relationships with suppliers are primarily in the form of a supply chain of raw materials and products with suppliers and resellers	Had participated in an exhibition held by the local government	Passive
BB	Enhance the capabilities and autonomy of artisans through the acquisition of batik skills, thereby enabling them to generate higher income by supplying quality products to BB	Received training, online and offline exhibitions, as well as overseas trade promotions from the local government Holds an important position in the Batik Association Obtain product procurement from the local government and private companies Become an assisted business of a state-owned enterprise Maintain relationships with the media to increase business visibility	Dominant
OR	Empower farmers to grow products with high economic value Foster agents and resellers with product knowledge and digital marketing techniques	Receive assistance from the local government in submitting permits, attending training and seminars, access to capital, and exhibitions Receive support from universities for product testing and development, production, and promotion Maintain relationship with the media to increase business visibility	Dominant

business environment level. During the COVID-19 pandemic, these MSMEs were typically still able to maintain their network well, and in several cases, this network was becoming stronger and more beneficial to their long-term resilience. According to Iansiti and Levien (2004), actors in this category are commonly known as "Keystones" in the business ecosystem. They are the focal firms in the ecosystem, playing a pivotal role and exerting significant influence, as well as networking closely with other actors. This category of actors tends to play a dominant role with a substantial market share. This category of MSMEs typically has an established business model supported by intensive digital technology utilization. They can generate value for their consumers by employing a method to ensure that their value is well-communicated and well-delivered to consumers, as well as able to generate new revenue streams alongside the development of their value. Regarding the COVID-19 pandemic, they are aided by the offered value that meets the consumers' requirements during the pandemic, or they can adjust promptly to establish the value that consumers require. MSMEs value delivery will be aided by digital utilization patterns that have been established since before the pandemic, or by rapid catch-up of digital capabilities.

This is aligned with Ariyani et al. (2021), which posited that a longer experience in digital technology might boost business resilience during the pandemic.

(2) **The supporting MSMEs**. This category of MSMEs commonly has a relatively robust network at its core business level. The relationship with the distributors and suppliers is well-established, both in the supply chain and knowledge relationship. Although their relationship with customers is not as intense as it is in the dominant category, it is typically maintained through informal communication or social media. Usually, the supporting MSMEs have already fostered networks with other parties at the business environment levels. However, these networks are maintained at a minimal level; for instance, they only collaborate with the local government. Moreover, during the COVID-19 pandemic, this network was less intensified or even hampered, preventing MSMEs from reaping their benefits to sustain their business. Since the outbreak of the COVID-19 pandemic, the business models of these actors tend to be somewhat unstable, despite generally being more stable before the pandemic occurred. The ability to support MSMEs to create value in order to meet the consumers' dynamic needs, or reap benefits from digital technology, is still considered minimal.

(3) **The passive MSMEs**. This category of MSMEs tends to be more passive within the ecosystem. Networks within core business levels are minimally maintained or they even must establish relationships with suppliers or distributors. They typically find themselves not compelled to conduct this kind of network because the primary materials are typically readily accessible and extensively available on the market, and because their production capacity is relatively low. Nevertheless, when the pandemic hit, they tended to be more susceptible as the raw materials became scarce, while they had no allied suppliers at the same time.

Due to their weak competitive positions, the majority of them tend to overlook the customer network. Consequently, they may overlook market trends or opportunities. In addition, relationships with professionals, academics, or other organizations have yet to be established. Accordingly, they tend to be less informed about the available support or assistance from other parties, particularly during the pandemic.

Regarding the value creation, this group of MSMEs typically lacks enthusiasm to routinely upgrade their capabilities. Generally, these MSMEs are very small, so it is impractical to invest in training and qualified professional development. This also applies to their investments in cutting-edge technology for business purposes. Therefore, the process of value creation is not emphasized within this group. This typically occurs as a result of the scarcity of resources. In several cases, we discovered that very small businesses—typically household-based enterprises, in which the operational and managerial roles are handled directly by the owner—may confront this issue as if they are already overwhelmed with the operational process; not to mention their responsibility towards household affairs, especially if the owner is a woman. In terms of value delivery, MSMEs tend not to keep up with the progress of competitors and consequently are not constantly improving their products or services. They are generally consistent—even tend to be complacent—with their current business processes, with minimal modifications. Likewise, with regard to value capture, they also adhere to current business conditions and tend to disregard production process advancements for streamlining production. This category of MSMEs has also been severely affected by the COVID-19 pandemic. They are typically unprepared for changes in business models, which affects their ability to thrive in their business.

6.3.1.3 The Role of Complementary Actors Within the Ecosystem

We have identified a minimum of six more actors within the ecosystem who engage with MSMEs and fulfill distinct responsibilities. The classification of the roles of these actors is shown in Table 6.2.

(1) **Association**. The association is essential in facilitating the connection between MSMEs and a diverse range of stakeholders. This organization typically serves as an intermediary between different government assistance initiatives and

Table 6.2 Roles of Actors within MSMEs Business Ecosystem

Actors	Task and functions in the ecosystem	Roles in ecosystem
Local government	• Provide access to competency development, promotion, foreign market, infrastructure, and financing • Provide regulatory framework • Provide government procurement • Provide regional digital platform	Dominant
Central government	• Provide regulatory framework	Supporting
Large enterprise	• Provide competency development and procurement as a part of the company CSR program	Supporting
MSMEs association	• Provide access to competency development • Provide access to governments' support • Bridge networks to other stakeholders	Supporting
Universities and research institutes	• Provide talent, competency development, technology, product testing and development	Supporting
Distributors	• Provide access to potential customers, • Provide access to digital technology and value delivery to customer	Supporting
Solution provider	• Provide competency to fully exploit digital platforms and maximize value delivery to customer	Supporting
E-commerce platform provider	• Provide access to digital platform • Provide competency development especially with regard to its platform • Provide reliable services and payment gateway	Dominant
Media	• Provide access to promotion	Supporting

its MSME members. HW, a business association in Yogyakarta, had taken the initiative to collaborate with the local government for the procurement of PPE and masks, which contribute significantly to the resilience of its MSME members during the COVID-19 pandemic. Associations commonly offer routine programs, including training and mentoring initiatives, to cater to the needs of their members. Associations also play a crucial role as a platform for MSMEs to foster networking opportunities, including facilitating their access to business mentoring. An MSME association in West Java, AP, has partnered with the local government to offer digital marketing training programs. It also provides knowledge-sharing support through a WhatsApp group for members seeking in-depth discussions and the chance to exchange their digital marketing experiences. HW offers a quite comprehensive approach to social media marketing, encompassing the use of various applications and platforms. Additionally, it provides guidance to enhance the digital marketing abilities of its members, specifically in relation to copywriting and marketing content design.

(2) **Universities and Research Institutes**. These organizations are essential in establishing a digital ecosystem, especially for talent development, as well as creating new technologies or ideas for product development. Universities are typically equipped with community service directorate with a mission of empowering MSMEs. This directorate oversees a range of initiatives designed to directly engage with MSMEs, such as training programs, mentoring opportunities, and facilitating marketing access. This is similar to what Jones and Corral de Zubielqui (2016) mentioned, where an interaction between the university and MSME could occur in the form of knowledge transfer. However, this still falls under the category of low engagement interaction. The above case of OR networking with universities in terms of product development and testing is perhaps what Jones and Corral de Zubielqui (2016) refer to as strong relational involvement, in which both actors collaborate on a certain project, such as research partnerships or research facilities utilization. Furthermore, one of Yogyakarta's universities created a web-based marketplace to assist MSMEs in marketing their products during the pandemic. Moreover, the current curriculum implemented in tertiary institutions has been specifically tailored to cultivate a conducive learning atmosphere for students with an aim to nurture their entrepreneurial skills and capabilities. Likewise, a university in West Sumatra, UN, has taken steps to foster the development of new entrepreneurs by implementing business incubation and business matchmaking programs. This campus also has a creative economy committee that focuses on fostering partnerships between small businesses and production partners. The institution also provides a student community service program that aims to support MSMEs in adopting social media platforms.

(3) **Distributor**. Distributors or resellers play a crucial role in the digital ecosystem, especially in assisting other businesses to deliver value through the digital environment. Typically, MSMEs that are incapable of optimizing their use of digital platforms but wish to expand their market access will rely on digital platform

expertise for distributing their products or services. By doing this, MSMEs can expedite market penetration and maximize resource efficiency compared to when they conduct it independently. In the meantime, MSMEs could even concentrate on developing new products and gaining customer feedback and insight from their distributors. During the FGD, the chairman of the AP association highlighted the existence of a generation gap within MSMEs. This gap poses challenges for MSMEs when it comes to entering the digital market, particularly among older owners. One possible solution to address this issue is to utilize the expertise of younger distributors who are more knowledgeable about digital platforms. By doing this, MSMEs can maintain the opportunity to concentrate on their production process while relying on the expertise of younger distributors to effectively deliver products to end customers. In general, in such circumstances, MSMEs will cultivate collaborative relationships with distributors. MSMEs provide distributors with product knowledge, while distributors deliver value to customers by utilizing digital platforms.

(4) **Solution provider**. Generally, these solution providers see opportunities in the inability of non-digital MSMEs to completely exploit the advantages of digital platforms. Usually, they offer their services as consultants and intermediaries to assist MSMEs in the development of digital strategies and digital business models. In our cases, these MSMEs assist other MSMEs with digital marketing strategy via digital platforms, such as Instagram. They usually develop collaborative networks with each other. They cooperate with other MSMEs for a period of time to assist them in digital business strategy. In addition to enhancing their capabilities, these MSMEs are also involved in a knowledge-sharing network. According to a solution provider in Yogyakarta, they typically provide MSMEs with several services, such as marketing content design, product design, as well as strategies to target specific customers and to optimize the use of search engines for social media platform. When MSMEs decide to join digital services, it is important for them to acquire a comprehensive understanding about the various aspects of digital business. This includes learning how to present their products in a professional manner to attract potential buyers, learning digital marketing strategies, and exploring ways to expand their business in order to reach a wider network of potential customers. In West Java, AP, an MSME association that offers digital solution services, plays a dual role. It also has a digital marketing team that offers services to assist MSMEs in digitalizing their operations. These services include product photography and marketing content design.

(5) **Digital Platform Provider**. The ongoing rise in the development of digital platforms has resulted in a competitive landscape among providers, as they strive to offer platforms that more effectively serve the users' needs, which in this case is MSMEs. Not only providing the platform, such as marketplaces, digital financing entities, or operational management supports, providers typically also offer a range of program initiatives, including training and mentoring, to facilitate their platform penetration to MSMEs. Despite their minimum activities in the local areas, these providers have a central role in building and maintaining a sustainable or reliable digital ecosystem. One of the digital providers

in Yogyakarta offers training support to MSME partners in order to help them boost their sales. This support includes raising awareness among partners about the importance of timely responses towards customer orders, ensuring neat and safe packaging, and maintaining effective communication with customers. Meanwhile, platform providers in West Sumatra and West Java take part in conducting training sessions for their MSME partners. The aim of these training programs is to enhance the digital literacy skills of the MSMEs, enabling them to effectively utilize the digital platforms provided by these providers.

(6) **Media**. The increasing accessibility of information has led to a significant role for the media in enhancing the business visibility of MSMEs. The promotion of public knowledge, particularly in relation to MSMEs' brand recognition, and the range of products and services they provide, can be facilitated through diverse forms of media coverage.

6.3.2 The Dynamism of the Ecosystem

As previously noted in extant literature, ecosystems possess dynamic attributes and are influenced by external factors. In the present context, the COVID-19 pandemic serves as an exogenous factor that propels the dynamism of ecosystems, particularly in relation to the roles and networks of actors within MSMEs ecosystems. The government's role has undergone expansion, particularly in relation to institutions, as it has assumed the additional responsibility of serving as a digital platform provider for MSMEs in response to the COVID-19 pandemic. In addition, it is worth noting that the prevailing pandemic circumstances have the potential to alter the MSMEs level within the ecosystem. For instance, those that previously held a dominant role may shift themselves into a supporting role. However, the adverse effects of the pandemic hindered their sustainability. The prominence of a particular actor, or a keystone actor, is diminished or altered due to the presence of other keystone actors. This is also relevant to the transformation of keystone actors within a business ecosystem due to the expansion of digital platform utilization (Geurts & Cepa, 2023).

Nevertheless, it is worth noting that certain actors possess the ability to uphold their position as pivotal players within a given context due to the virtue of their continued dominance. This can be attributed to their proactive efforts in ensuring the sustainability of the network or their adaptability to evolving business models. At the onset of the global pandemic, there was already a notable emergence of novel actors within the digital subsystem, characterized by an increase in the diversity of their business level.

6.3.3 Challenges to Sustain the Digital Ecosystem Growth

We identified a number of obstacles and challenges confronted by MSMEs during the onset of the pandemic. In general, it was an unprecedented event to which no one was acclimated, causing dread and panic, also causing a significant shift in demand and commerce sector. Immediately, consumers' needs shifted to focus more on meeting primary and health needs. Several MSMEs that succeeded in adapting themselves to these market changes will tend to endure longer than others, while those that adapt too slowly or fail to adapt to this condition will merely become followers.

6.3.3.1 Disordered Supply Chain

The pandemic has impeded nearly all MSME activities. Due to their limited availability on the market because of pathogen transmission and transportation restrictions, the procurement of raw materials is insufficiently supplied. On the one hand, the production process was unable to run smoothly and caused unfulfilled customer demands due to the physical activities' restriction. On the other hand, the demand had also decreased due to the broad economic decline.

6.3.3.2 Financial Capital

Even though MSMEs, particularly those in the retail industry, can utilize basic technology to access the digital market (e.g., by using smartphones for e-commerce), maximizing digital business in MSMEs is not as simple as it seems. In addition to investing in hardware and subscribing to various software requirements that are advantageous for MSME businesses, they must also spend a substantial amount of money to meet digital marketing needs. In the throes of the pandemic, it would be extremely difficult to accomplish this due to the financial limitations of MSMEs.

6.3.3.3 Limited Access and Skill

MSMEs that are not accustomed to the significant shift in value distribution patterns from a reliance on physical stores to online platforms will, of course, get confused. Even the most fundamental requirements for accessing the digital market will be difficult for several smaller scale businesses, particularly in terms of device availability and stable internet connection. It was also difficult for them to invest in digital devices due to a lack of capital and unfavorable financial conditions due to declining demand during the pandemic.

Even if they could access the technology, they may encounter additional challenges in comprehending the technology required to enter the market, particularly if they only focused on offline channels prior to the pandemic. Obviously, skills that have started to be mastered when the pandemic strikes are unlikely to bring a major impact on business resilience in the later phase of the pandemic or long after that. In addition, they might also be unaware of the threats of cyber security and piracy constituted in the digital market.

The use of overly technical language during training is considered ineffective in assisting MSME in comprehending digital usage, particularly if the MSME proprietor is an elderly person. In addition, the training typically provides only the fundamentals know-how, while proactive exploration by MSMEs is also required. Meanwhile, the production process has already consumed MSMEs' time, leaving them with insufficient resources to better explore the necessary technology for their business strategies. Pandemic conditions necessitate MSMEs to swiftly transition to keep up with the precursor MSMEs. Accessing a marketing consultant may be extremely beneficial for those with sufficient capital. While for others, digital skill development will be tougher.

6.3.3.4 Business Model Adjustments

Transitioning business mode into the digital ecosystem requires not only technical expertise, but also the need to impose the digital strategy into MSMEs business strategy. For example, in the use of a marketplace, many businesses failed to reap the benefit of it because they believe that using a marketplace is merely about subscribing and product posting, then the customers will automatically be captivated. Nevertheless, numerous strategies need to be considered, especially on how to develop a business model towards digital direction. For example, to make sure that their products have a competitive advantage over other products, MSMEs can provide excellent photo displays, complete product descriptions, and timely service to ensure that digital customers have the same shopping experience as when they visit physical stores. Not to mention the need for frequent updates on the digital platform as the communication channels between MSMEs and the customers. Unfortunately, not all MSMEs are aware of the need to modify these business models. In several cases we encountered, they did not reap the benefits of adopting e-commerce because they presented less informative products with less appealing photos and media content, yet gave slow responses towards consumers' requests.

In addition, several things also need to be considered when MSMEs are transitioning their business mode into the digital ecosystem. MSMEs need to sense business opportunities and innovative concepts to provide customers with a superior value proposition. The proliferation of business entities in the digital realm has led to an excessive level of unhealthy competition, especially regarding product prices. Therefore, innovative and superior products will certainly be an added value for MSMEs. In addition, the rapid development of technology also occurs in digital business. Therefore, relying solely on one digital platform may not be advantageous. MSMEs will maintain a competitive advantage by enhancing their mastery of digital platforms. Utilizing national or international digital platforms, such as marketplaces or social media, may be quite effective in increasing the market share of an MSME.

However, for MSMEs with more qualified capabilities and resources, developing their own digital platforms, such as personal web commerce, will provide the benefit of being able to monitor traffic and use it to determine future business strategies.

6.4 Conclusions

The regional MSMEs digital ecosystem was experiencing dynamic changes in the time before, during, and in the later phase of the COVID-19 pandemic. Before the pandemic, the physical ecosystem was growing gradually due to the people's mobility in the tourism sector. Meanwhile, the development of the digital ecosystem was still in its infancy phase, with few dominant actors. Then, as the pandemic hit, people's mobility was restricted, and the physical ecosystems were abandoned by the customers and MSMEs. They were transitioning into the digital ecosystem. The new ecosystem was growing fast and became crowded, although it was less organized in nature. In the later phase, several MSMEs were failing due to fierce competition, imitation, and incapability to sustain their existence in the digital ecosystem. Several of them were returning to offline mode. Hence, the digital ecosystem became less crowded than before, and the physical ecosystem started to recover gradually. Meanwhile, the surviving businesses in the digital ecosystem were growing exponentially as the customers continued to grow.

At first, the central government and prominent e-commerce platforms were dominant in the development of the regional digital ecosystem. Then, during and in the later phase of the pandemic, local governments became more dominant than the central government in supporting the digital transition of MSMEs. Prominent e-commerce platforms consistently acted as dominant actors that sustain the ecosystem by providing their services. MSMEs as local champions emerged during this transition, and they became role models that attract other MSMEs in onboarding into the digital ecosystem.

References

Agency of Tourism Yogyakarta Special Region. (2019). *Tourism statistics (statistik kepariwisataan)*. Agency of Tourism Yogyakarta Special Region.

Aisyah, E., Zuraidah, Z., & Maulayati, R. (2021). Risk mitigation of COVID-19 pandemic in Baitul Maal Wat Tamwil. *Advances in Social Science, Education and Humanities Research*. https://doi.org/10.2991/assehr.k.210421.100

Ariyani, L., Hermawati, W., Helmi, R. L., Rosaira, I., & Budiansyah, A. (2021). MSME perceptions towards internet use: A comparison of before and during the COVID-19 outbreak in Indonesia. *Asian Journal of Business and Accounting, 14*(2). https://doi.org/10.22452/ajba.vol14no2.7

Audretsch, D. B., & Belitski, M. (2017). Entrepreneurial ecosystems in cities: Establishing the framework conditions. *Journal of Technology Transfer, 42*(5), 1030–1051. https://doi.org/10.1007/s10961-016-9473-8

BAPPEDA DIY. (2020). *Data peserta didik 2019*. Bappeda DIY.

BPS. (2019). *Jumlah perjalanan wisatawan nusantara menurut provinsi asal.* BPS.
BPS. (2022). *PDB Indonesia Triwulanan 2017–2021.* BPS Indonesia.
Cohen, B. (2006). Sustainable valley entrepreneurial ecosystems. *Business Strategy and the Environment, 15*(1), 1–14. https://doi.org/10.1002/bse.428
Colombelli, A., Paolucci, E., & Ughetto, E. (2019). Hierarchical and relational governance and the life cycle of entrepreneurial ecosystems. *Small Business Eonomics, 52*, 505–521. https://doi.org/10.1007/s11187-017-9957-4
Colombo, M. G., Dagnino, G. B., Lehmann, E. E., & Salmador, M. P. (2019). The governance of entrepreneurial ecosystems. *Small Business Economics, 52*(2), 419–428. https://doi.org/10.1007/s11187-017-9952-9
Cukier, D., & Kon, F. (2018). A maturity model for software startup ecosystems. *Journal of Innovation and Entrepreneurship, 7*(1), 1–32. https://doi.org/10.1186/s13731-018-0091-6
Fritsch, M. (2008). How does new business formation affect regional development? Introduction to the special issue. *Small Business Economics, 30*(1), 1–14. https://doi.org/10.1007/s11187-007-9057-y
Geurts, A., & Cepa, K. (2023). Transforming the music industry: How platformization drives business ecosystem envelopment. *Long Range Planning.* https://doi.org/10.1016/j.lrp.2023.102327
Haltiwanger, J., Ron, S. J., & Miranda, J. (2013). Who creates jobs? Small versus large versus young. *Review of Economics and Statistics, 95*(2), 347–361.
Iansiti, M., & Levien, R. (2004). *The keystone advantage: What the new dynamics of business ecosystems mean for strategy.* Harvard Business School Press.
Inkpen, A. C., & Tsang, E. W. (2005). Social capital, networks, and knowledge transfer. *Academy of Management Review, 30*(1), 146–165.
jabarprov.go.id. (2020). https://opendata.jabarprov.go.id/id/infografik/wisatawan-di-jawa-barat. Retrieved from /opendata.jabarprov.go.id: https://opendata.jabarprov.go.id/id/infografik/wisatawan-di-jawa-barat
Jayani, D. (2021, August 13). Kontribusi UMKM terhadap Ekonomi Terus Meningkat. Retrieved from databoks.katadata.co.id: https://databoks.katadata.co.id/datapublish/2021/08/13/kontribusi-umkm-terhadap-ekonomi-terus-meningkat
Jones, J., & Corral de Zubielqui, G. (2016). Doing well by doing good: A study of university-industry interactions, innovationess and firm performance in sustainability-oriented Australian MSMEs. *Technological Forecasting & Social Change, 123*, 262–270. https://doi.org/10.1016/j.techfore.2016.07.036
Lado, A. A., Dant, R. R., & Tekleab, A. G. (2008). Trust opportunism paradox, relationalism, and performance in interfirm relationships: Evidence from retail industry. *Strategic Management Journal, 29*(4), 401–423. https://doi.org/10.1002/smj.667
Lehmann, E. E., & Menter, M. (2018). Public cluster policy and performance. *Journal of Technology Transfer, 43*(3), 558–592. https://doi.org/10.1007/s10961-017-9626-4
Lenkenhoff, K., Wilkens, U., Zheng, M., Süße, T., Kuhlenkötter, B., & Ming, X. (2018). Key challenges of digital business ecosystem development and how to cope with them. *Procedia CIRP, 73*, 167–172. https://doi.org/10.1016/j.procir.2018.04.082
Lu, C., Rong, K., You, J., & Shi, Y. (2014). Business ecosystem and stakeholders' role transformation: Evidence from Chinese emerging electric vehicle industry. *Expert Systems with Applications, 41*(10), 4579–4595. https://doi.org/10.1016/j.eswa.2014.01.026
Makinen, S. J., & Dedehayir, O. (2012). Business ecosystem evolution and strategic considerations: A literature review. In B. Katzy, T. Holzmann, K. Sailer, & K. D. Thoben (Eds.), *Proceedings of the 18th International Conference on Engineering, Technology and Innovation* (pp. 1–10). IEEE. https://doi.org/10.1109/ICE.2012.6297653
Marsdenia, N., Diaz, P., & Deni, K. (2022). The effectiveness of digitalization of SMEs' sustainability during the COVID-19 pandemic. *Advances in Social Sciences, Education and Humanities Research.* https://doi.org/10.2991/978-2-494069-07-7_60

Ministry of Research, Technology, and Higher Education. (2019). *Higher education statistics*. Ministry of Research, Technology, and Higher Education.
Moore, J. F. (1993). Predators and prey: A new ecology of competition. *Harvard Business Review, 71*(3), 75–86.
Moore, J. F. (1996). *The death of competition: Leadership and strategy in the age of business ecosystems* (1st ed.). Harper Business.
Motoyama, Y., & Knowlton, K. (2016). Examining the connections within startup ecosystem: A case study of St. Louis. *Entrepreneurship Research Journal, 7*(1), 1–32. https://doi.org/10.1515/erj-2016-0011
Primadana, L., Ramdani, M., Sahara, S., & Aprianingsih, A. (2021). Redefining transformation drivers in SMEs toward business performance with COVID-19 situation in Indonesia. *Jurnal Sains Pemasaran Indonesia, 3*(20), 212–240. https://doi.org/10.14710/jspi.v20i3.212-240
Rong, K. (2011). *Nurturing business ecosystem from firm perspectives: Lifecycle, nurturing process, constructs, and configuration pattern* [Ph.D. thesis]. University of Cambridge.
Rong, K., & Shi, Y. (2015). Business ecosystems: Constructs, configurations, and the nurturing process. In *Business ecosystems: Constructs, configurations, and the nurturing process*. Palgrave Macmillan. https://doi.org/10.1057/9781137405920
Roundy, T. P., Bradshaw, M., & Brockman, B. K. (2018). The emergence of entrepreneurial ecosystems: A complex adaptive systems approach. *Journal of Business Research, 86*(May 2018) 1–10. https://doi.org/10.1016/j.jbusres.2018.01.032
Simanjuntak, P. (2019). Indonesia's policy on e-commerce regulation and its challenges. *Bulletin of Social Informatics Theory and Application, 3*(2), 69–74. https://doi.org/10.31763/businta.v3i2.176
Spigel, B. (2017). The relational organization of entrepreneurial ecosystems. *Entrepreneurship Theory and Practice, 41*(1), 49–72. https://doi.org/10.1111/etap.12167
Spilling, O. R. (1996). The entrepreneurial system: On entrepreneurship in the context of a mega-event. *Journal of Business Research, 36*(1), 91–103. https://doi.org/10.1016/0148-2963(95)00166-2
Stam, E. (2015). Entrepreneurial ecosystem and regional policy: A sympathetic critique. *European Planning Studies, 23*(9), 1759–1769. https://doi.org/10.1080/09654313.2015.1061484
Stanley, J., & Briscoe, G. (2010). The ABC of digital business ecosystems. ArXiv, abs/1005.1899
Tötterman, H., & Sten, J. (2005). Start-ups: Business incubation and social capital. *International Small Business Journal, 23*(5), 487–511. https://doi.org/10.1177/0266242605055909
Viargo, A. (2022). Prediction of the telecommunication service providers' stock prices in Indonesia to support the digital economy. *International Journal of Mathematics and Computer Research, 10*(7), 2726–2730. https://doi.org/10.47191/ijmcr/v10i7.01

Luthfina Ariyani works as a junior researcher at the Indonesian National Research and Innovation Agency. She holds a Master Degree (M.Sc) of Industrial Engineering from Gadjah Mada University. She is particularly interested in Micro, Small, and Medium Enterprises (MSMEs) sector through her research in the discipline of management of technology and innovation. Some of her latest international publications are entitled Interactive Components of Digital MSMEs Ecosystem for Inclusive Digital Economy in Indonesia (Journal of The Knowledge Economy, 2022) and MSME Perceptions towards Internet Use: A Comparison of before and during the COVID-19 outbreak in Indonesia (Asian Journal of Business and Accounting, 2021). Currently, she is involved in the research focusing on innovative entrepreneurship and digitalization in Batik MSMEs.

Adityo Wicaksono works as a researcher at the Indonesia's National Research and Innovation Agency. He holds a Master of Business Degree from The University of Queensland, Australia. Previously, he has extensive experience working in the technology transfer and business development field. Currently, he focuses on researching technology transfer and startup or SME development. One of his notable publication is "Understanding Technological Knowledge Spillover in a STP Ecosystem: An Ethnographic Study" in the Asian Journal of Technology Innovation.

Chapter 7
The Role of Government in Facilitating Digital Economy for Micro, Small, and Medium Enterprises

Nyimas Latifah Letty Aziz and Aisah Putri Budiatri

Abstract Micro, small, and medium enterprises (MSMEs) play a significant part in boosting economic growth and raising the standard of living in Indonesia, particularly during and after the COVID-19 pandemic. Moreover, these MSME roles are increasingly strengthened using digital technology and through partnerships between local governments and private digital platforms. Thus, both the central and local governments have made progressive efforts to emphasize strengthening MSMEs, especially the digitalization of MSMEs. Despite the government's high attention to MSMEs, based on quantitative and qualitative research, it was found that the government's program to strengthen the role of MSMEs in the digital world does not appear to be running optimally. There are three main problems with the program: government programs for business actors have not been accessed evenly, data on national MSMEs has not been integrated, and the MSME digitalization program between the central and regional governments has not been optimally coordinated. Therefore, a comprehensive plan and coordination run by the governments must be created to solve these issues.

Keywords National Government · Local Government · MSMEs · Digital Platforms

7.1 Introduction

The Indonesian Government believes that the digital economy is a new source of economic growth and has the potential to overcome the middle-income trap, create new jobs, promote inclusiveness, and enhance economic efficiency (Hartarto, 2023). This expectation is quite reasonable because Indonesia's digital economy value in

N. L. L. Aziz (✉) · A. P. Budiatri
National Research and Innovation Agency, Jakarta, Indonesia
e-mail: nyim002@brin.go.id

A. P. Budiatri
e-mail: aisa001@brin.go.id

T. Fizzanty and I. Maulana (eds.), *The Digitalization of Indonesian Small and Medium Enterprises*, Engaging Indonesia, https://doi.org/10.1007/978-981-97-0029-5_7

2022 is USD 77 billion, growing by 22% (yoy), and is predicted to almost double to USD 130 billion in 2025 (Google Temasek, Bain, & Company, 2022). In 2022, around 40% of the transaction value of ASEAN's digital economy comes from Indonesia. Moreover, with more than 2400 startup companies, Indonesia becomes the sixth ranked country with the most startup companies in the world. Furthermore, the majority of the eight unicorn companies in Indonesia are currently engaged in e-commerce and fintech (MPR, 2023).

The roles of the digital economy in strengthening Micro, Small, and Medium Enterprises (MSMEs) are strategic amidst the future situation of Indonesia's population. In the period 2020–2035, Indonesia is predicted to experience a demographic bonus, where the number of the productive age population (aged 15–64 years) is greater than the non-productive age population (under 15 years and above 64 years). During this period, the productive age population is predicted to reach 64% of the total projected population of 297 million (Bappenas, 2017). In a condition where the population is dominated by young people, the new growth strategy adopted by the Indonesian government must involve young people as the main actors.

To obtain the maximum benefit from the demographic bonus, it is important to strengthen the capacity and competence of the productive age human resources. The young population has the characteristics of being easy to accept change, adapting quickly, and possessing high knowledge and capabilities related to digital technology (Bencsik et al., 2016). With these characteristics, digital technology can be used to empower the productive age population to compete and seize economic opportunities. Thus, the demographic bonus should be utilized as momentum to support the national economy through the elaboration of the digital economy in two transmissions, namely potential market expansion (increasing consumption for the growing population) and increasing national productivity through the quality of human resources in productive sectors such as MSMEs. If this momentum is not properly prepared and implemented, what Indonesia will face will not be economic gains (the window of opportunity), but instead increasing economic burdens, potential unemployment, social conflict, and various other socio-economic problems (the door to disaster).

Moreover, the digital economy has the potential to overcome, or at least minimize, problems faced by MSMEs in Indonesia. As has been described in many previous studies, MSMEs in Indonesia face four main problems in optimizing added value and contributing to the national economy, such as (1) the personal quality of SME entrepreneurs, (2) innovation and quality of SME products (including mastery of technology), (3) access to capital and financing, (4) poor infrastructure (Global Business Guide Indonesia, 2016; Hermawan, 2022; OECD, 2002; Tambunan, 2008). Meanwhile, the digital economy is seen as a potential alternative for innovative solutions in increasing access to productive resources for the development of MSMEs in Indonesia. The digital economy offers ease and flexibility of access, which has the potential to reduce problems in the MSME area.

Though digital technology has potential roles in strengthening MSMEs, there are still challenges and obstacles. One of the challenges is internet availability to support the business processes of MSME entrepreneurs. The challenge is that currently, the internet network has only covered 85% of Indonesia's territory with difficulties to reach the outermost, foremost, and lagging areas (Kominfo, 2020). Until 2019, only 13% of the total population of Indonesian MSMEs had access to digital technology (Ministry of Cooperatives and SMEs). Another challenge is the regulations faced by MSMEs entrepreneurs. Local e-commerce platform owners in Indonesia must comply with domestic regulations, while these regulations are unlikely to apply to global e-commerce platform owners (Rumata & Sastrosubroto, 2020). This unbalanced condition can create an uneven basis of competitiveness between local and global entrepreneurs.

Facing the great opportunity of the digital economy to stimulate MSMEs but at the same time, facing difficult challenges raises further questions about what strategies have been taken by the government to build a supportive digital economy ecosystem for MSMEs entrepreneurs. The government, moreover, plays various important roles in developing the digital economy, including setting policies, investing in human and organizational complements, supporting R&D and innovation, and improving telecommunications infrastructure and the internet to ensure digital economy inclusivity (Aminullah et al., 2022). Thus, it is important to see what obstacles, related to the government's regulations and programs, are faced by MSMEs entrepreneurs in expanding their businesses using digital technology. Moreover, it is important to discuss this topic since the existing literature discussed the specific roles of the government in the digital economy but not specifically related to the digitalization of MSMEs (Michael Spence, 2021). In addition, the digital economy ecosystem approach and its relation to the local context have not been revealed much, especially when discussing government support for the ecosystem. In fact, it is essential to discuss it because Indonesia implements a decentralized government system in which autonomous regions have a large role and authority in development. Therefore, this chapter will discuss all these important and interesting questions and aspects by examining the governance of the development of the digitalization of MSMEs in Indonesia based on cases that occurred in West Java, West Sumatra, and Yogyakarta in 2020, in the middle of Covid-19 outbreak.

7.2 State Policies and Programs on MSMEs Digitalization in Indonesia

7.2.1 State Policies on MSMEs Digitalization

Indonesia is a country that has been open to technological developments since the 1960s, when computerized technology became known, leading to the development of today's digital world. The government opens access to technology, encourages the development of technological science, and expands the use of technology across various aspects of life, including the economy and industrial sectors. In the latest developments in digital technology, the Indonesian state, including the government and parliament, has enacted two policies: Law No. 19 of 2016 on Information Technology (ITE Law) and Government Regulation No. 71 of 2019 on the operation of electronic systems and transactions (PP 71/2019). These basic rules govern the development, utilization, and various aspects related to digital technology, including endeavors in the digital economy.

The basic rules related to economic business transactions through the internet network, termed as e-commerce, are part of what is regulated in the ITE Law. The ITE Law discusses consumer protection, trade contracts for online transactions, legal processes for trade contract violations (for example, if there is a loss), and others. The rules in the ITE Law are also discussed, in more detail, in PP 71/2019 as its derivative regulations. It shows that the applicable legal regulations regarding information technology have accommodated the needs of the development of the digital economy in Indonesia.

Since before the issuance of the ITE Law and PP 71/2019, the government has realized the importance of developing the digital economy, specifically in the MSME business. Therefore, the government has five directives which were then translated into government regulations and programs to develop digital MSME businesses: improving broadband access, providing support and assistance to MSME entrepreneurs, expanding electronic payments or e-payments, expanding access to investment both from domestic and global investors, and expanding government services electronically (e-government) (Savithri, 2015). These five directives play an important role because previously, there were no formal legal regulations, such as laws, that specifically discussed economic digitalization for MSMEs. The Law No. 20 of 2008 on Micro, Small, and Medium Enterprises, which became the initial legal basis for MSMEs, did not particularly regulate e-commerce. This law indeed regulated the importance of efforts to encourage the application of technology for MSMEs, but it does not explicitly refer to the digital economy.

The absence of specific rules that regulate details regarding economic digitalization for MSMEs has urged the government to promote regulatory reforms. This is important due to the rapid development of e-commerce in the Indonesian economy, especially in the last five years. The increase in the number of online shop members, many of whom are contributed by MSME entrepreneurs, has led to the increasing value of e-commerce transactions in Indonesia. In 2018, the transactions reached 77.766 trillion Rupiah. This number is significantly improved compared to the previous year, which only reached 30.942 trillion Rupiah (Karyati, 2019). Thus, the government then released various economic policies that regulate the digital economy, which also includes e-commerce for MSMEs.

The government provides an electronic-based national trade system by releasing Presidential Regulation No. 74 of 2017 on the Road Map E-Commerce 2017–2019. This grand design becomes a reference for government agencies, both at the national and local levels, to develop work programs related to e-commerce, including programs for MSMEs. In this roadmap, the programs that will be run by the government include providing funding support, tax incentives, and tax management improvement, ensuring consumer protection, strengthening human resources (business actors), improving communication infrastructure by expanding broadband networks, developing logistics systems, strengthening cybersecurity, and forming a special committee to implement this grand design. The roadmap that should have continued after 2019 had to stop after Indonesia, as well as other countries around the world were hit by the COVID-19 pandemic. This regulation was repealed and replaced by a new regulation that focuses on national economic recovery following the pandemic. In line with the revocation of this regulation, the special committee formed to oversee the implementation of this roadmap was disbanded.

Though the roadmap for strengthening e-commerce (2017–2019) has stopped running, efforts to strengthen the digital economy, especially those carried out by MSME entrepreneurs, are still being pursued by the government through the creation of new regulations. These new regulations are important since MSMEs are the pillar of economic growth in Indonesia during the pandemic, and most of them can conduct their activities through e-commerce transactions. Therefore, the government produced Law No. 11 of 2020 on Job Creation (UU Cipta Kerja), 48 implementing regulations of The Law of Job Creation, and Government Regulation No. 7 of 2021 on the Convenience, Protection and Empowerment of Cooperatives and MSMEs (PP 7/2021). This regulation is currently the government's guide for implementing work programs to strengthen MSMEs in the digital arena.

The Law of Job Creation, though controversial in the production process, is believed to provide many business development opportunities for MSME entrepreneurs. This regulation not only simplifies and addresses various regulations that previously overlapped but also aims to build an ecosystem to support the digitalization of MSMEs. This law, for example, contributes to the development of the digital economy for MSMEs by promoting the acceleration of internet broadband expansion and setting upper and/or lower price rates for the Internet in the context of organizing communications. The goal is to protect the consumers and to ensure fair business competition in the local and global e-commerce world. This law is considered to help MSMEs adopt digital technology in developing their businesses (Clinten, 2020).

Efforts to encourage digitalization of MSMEs, especially by the government, are re-strengthened by Government Regulation (PP) 7/2021 on the Convenience, Protection and Empowerment of Cooperatives and MSMEs. This regulation controls various aspects of empowering and protecting MSMEs, not only in conventional trading practices but also in the e-commerce platform. Several rules in PP 7/2021 are specifically related to the government's efforts to strengthen the digitalization of MSMEs: granting business licenses that are integrated electronically; supporting product marketing through e-commerce; strengthening the digital literacy of business actors; improving product, packaging, and store design showing displayed in online trading; and encouraging the development of online business aggregators to assist in online marketing and sales.

7.2.2 Government Programs on MSMEs Digitalization

Based on the existing policies and regulations, since 2017, various ministries in the central government have created various work programs aimed at supporting the role of MSMEs in the digital economy. These programs are executed under a jargon called "UMKM go online." The ministries that mainly focus on the programs are the Ministry of Cooperatives and SMEs and the Ministry of Communication and Informatics. They have generated many programs, including encouraging the Indonesian e-commerce (idEA) to provide greater opportunities for local MSMEs, creating an application called the UMKM Digital Market (PaDi UMKM) to optimize spending for State-Owned Enterprises (BUMN) on MSMEs, providing aid funds for MSMEs, offering training and assistance on digital literacy for MSMEs, increasing MSME entrepreneurs' capacity through eduKUKM, webinar series, smart campus, digital heroes, promoting MSME products through local communities and applications, providing UMKM Integrated Business Service Center (PLUT), expanding internet access, and others. These steps were taken not only to ensure MSME business actors have sufficient understanding and capacity to digitalize their business but also to develop products that are ready to be marketed through digital methods.

The Go-Online program has been running since 2017 and was further strengthened after 2019, when the COVID-19 pandemic hit Indonesia. At the time of Covid-19, Micro, Small and Medium Enterprises (MSMEs) were one of the sectors that were adversely affected. Based on data from the Ministry of Cooperatives and Small and Medium Enterprises, the contribution of MSMEs to GDP fell by 37.3% during the pandemic. Several problems contributed to the decline: a change in habits in consuming public goods and services from offline to online and the imposition of Large-Scale Social Restrictions (PSBB) has limited production and distribution of the products (Sulastri, 2022). However, digital technology has supported MSMEs to survive and even develop in carrying out their economic activities during the pandemic. Therefore, government programs to encourage the digitalization of MSMEs are very important. Activities that have been carried out by the government to encourage MSMEs to go digital during the pandemic include providing free credit, promotional support on digital platforms, digital marketing, and English language training (Yolandha, 2020).

To realize the government's work priorities to accelerate the digitalization of MSMEs, the central government allocates a large budget for the protection and development of MSMEs. In 2022, the figure reached IDR 123.46 trillion, ranking second in the APBN list after social protection, and this cost is higher than corporate financing. The government stated that this fund allocation is one of its main targets to be used for the development of the digitalization of MSMEs. As part of accelerating national economic recovery after the COVID-19 pandemic, in 2022, the government is also implementing a digital technology adoption program 4.0. for MSMEs that are not yet connected to the digital world. This program targeted 30 thousand MSMEs to scale up the adoption of digital technology 4.0 in 13 regions, namely North Sumatra, Bangka Belitung, Banten, DKI Jakarta, East Java, DI Yogyakarta & Central Java,

North Maluku, West Nusa Tenggara, East Nusa Tenggara, Southeast Sulawesi, West Kalimantan, Papua, and West Papua (Rahmawati, 2022).

The central government also encourages the use of digital technology for MSMEs, which are considered ready for export but still face several challenges: a lack of knowledge of foreign markets, consistency of product quality and capacity, certification, and logistical problems. To overcome these problems, the government is trying through the Law of Job Creation to encourage SME actors to take advantage of partnership opportunities with large businesses. The government facilitates partnerships for Medium and Large Enterprises (UMB) with Micro and Small Enterprises (UMK) including Cooperatives, aiming to increase the competence and business level of UMK and Cooperative actors. In addition, the government also launched the National Proud Movement for Indonesia (Gernas BBI) program, which aims to encourage digitalization (onboarding) for offline MSMEs and promote the national branding of superior MSME products on various marketplaces.

The government also supports for MSMEs in penetrating the global market by facilitating the sale of local products abroad, such as to Malaysia and Singapore through "Kreasi Nusantara, From Local to Global," which facilitates the purchase of local products by customers from Malaysia, Singapore, Brunei, Hong Kong, and Taiwan through "BukaGlobal," and helps to increase cross-border e-commerce transactions in the Southeast Asian region through "ASEAN Online Sale Day (AOSD)." AOSD is a shopping event held simultaneously by e-commerce platforms in ten ASEAN countries. AOSD coincides with ASEAN's anniversary which falls on August 8, 2020. AOSD participants are traders from the ASEAN region who offer goods and services through Trading Through Electronic Systems (PMSE). AOSD is an opportunity for Indonesia to promote and build the image of local archipelago products in the ASEAN arena, as well as encourage and increase exports of Indonesian products.

The AOSD program is effective enough to encourage exports, promotion, and branding of local brands, as well as bring an export nuance to startups that are still focused on domestic inward looking. This program invites business actors, including startups and SMEs, to open and target larger foreign markets (Kominfo, 2021). The government's push through the AOSD program has effectively opened wide opportunities for business actors to participate in AOSD 2021. It was recorded that during the registration period, there were 313 potential participants. From there, 97 business actors were curated who were deemed worthy of representing Indonesia as participants. Participating Indonesian business actors or platforms can choose to participate in Tier 1, namely the Indonesian market (domestic transaction), Tier 2, namely ASEAN countries other than Indonesia (cross-border purchasing) or participate in both. The participants get access to free promotions and branding for both domestic consumers and consumers in the Southeast Asian market, including targeting the Indonesian diaspora, in the e-commerce shopping arena (Kominfo, 2021).

Programs to strengthen MSMEs in the digital economy are also implemented by the local governments. Like the central government, they carry out various programs ranging from providing training and funding to building internet infrastructure (see Table 7.1). However, in contrast to the central government, which runs the same program for each province, the local government is better able to develop programs that are adjusted to the needs and conditions of each province. Referring to case studies in three provinces, namely Yogyakarta, West Java, and West Sumatra as examples, they developed MSME development programs based on their superior products and MSME conditions. In the context of the COVID-19 pandemic, local governments launched local initiatives to support MSMEs in securing the market.

7.2.3 Partnerships of Local Governments-Digital Business for MSMEs Digitalization

The Yogyakarta Government has established its own local e-market hub called Si Bakul Jogja as a place for MSMEs in this province to transact. This market hub also features MSME products in popular markets in the province, such as in Malioboro and Kota Gede. In this case, local government staff served as operators to operate Si Bakul Jogja. Similar paths are also taken by the West Java Government with the borongdong.id application and West Sumatra Government through an application called bajojo.id. In West Sumatra, local businessmen act as operators of this market hub.

The Regional Government of West Java has a Champion MSME program aimed at various things, including strengthening business actors' databases, enhancing the way of thinking of business actors to survive, strengthening business actors' understanding of business digitalization opportunities, and others. The West Java government has also collaborated with several marketplaces, such as Shopee, Blibli, Tokopedia and Bukalapak, to provide training, offer special promos to MSME players, and/or increase MSME involvement in the marketplace business. Furthermore, the West Java Provincial Government has created its own marketplace called borongdong.id, which is a special digital space for MSME businesses. Borongdong.id is considered strategic as a step to restore the economy during a pandemic because it targets hundreds of thousands of local government state civil servants (ASN) as consumers. Not only that, the West Java Provincial Government is also collaborating with Mbiz, an e-commerce service provider, regarding the use of mbizmarket.co.id as an e-marketplace platform for shopping or procuring goods and services within the West Java Provincial Government agencies and empowering MSMEs in the Province of West Java. The regional government has also developed the Mesra West Java Bank (BJB) application, aimed at facilitating the provision of loans to MSMEs, as well as creating Kabayan as an online consulting application on access to finance for MSMEs. BJB and the provincial government is also working with BRI, Bank Mandiri, and Link Aja to provide working capital assistance to MSMEs in West Java.

In addition to collaborating and establishing a digital platform for MSMEs, the West Java regional government also provides technical training to MSMEs, so they understand more about the digital market ecosystem, as well as aiding MSME entrepreneurs. The Regional Government of West Java specifically targets the development of MSMEs at the village level so that they are more easily accessible to business actors and can be spread widely. Training for digital literacy is carried out through various partners and communities, including ICT Volunteers and Village Patriots. There is also a Mobile Internet Training Car for the Successful Independent Work Business, abbreviated as Bi Imas Keramas, as a mobile training program aimed at making it easier for MSME players to receive training and consult on business development and business digitalization. Assistance is also carried out through managing the potential of MSME aquaculture in collaboration with eFishery and managing the potential of agricultural MSME in collaboration with Habibi Garden. The West Java Provincial Government is also trying to continue providing and strengthening internet infrastructure, which is the basis for developing MSME digitalization through collaboration with BAKTI in the free wi-fi procurement program with VSAT.

Various regional government innovations were carried out not only by the West Java Provincial Government but also by West Sumatra. Innovations aimed at increasing the digital literacy of MSME business actors and developing MSME digitalization have been carried out by the local government, both through internal programs of local government agencies and through collaboration with other parties. There are several programs that have been implemented by the Regional Government of West Sumatra, including: developing local start-ups to strengthen MSME digitalization, collaborating with national marketplaces, collaborating with local banks and national banks, and providing training to MSME entrepreneurs.

Bajojo.id is a local e-commerce platform owned by West Sumatra because of collaboration between the local government and the young people of West Sumatra. Bajojo.id is a place for marketing MSME products fostered by the government, as well as a place to provide education about the development of business digitalization and as a data collection portal for MSME units in West Sumatra. Not only local marketplaces but there is also a Jojo rider as a local application that provides goods delivery services in the city of Padang. It is hoped that the presence of the Jojo rider will work closely with West Sumatra MSME business actors to facilitate access to their sales. Not only developing local start-ups, but the local government has also collaborated with JNE, Gojek, and PT Pos to develop local MSMEs.

The Regional Government of West Sumatra, since 2016, has been working with entrepreneurs, practitioners, and academics in the fields of business and economics to establish and develop the Minangkabau Business School—Entrepreneurship Center (MBS-EC). Through the MBS-EC, MSME actors are prepared to become entrepreneurs, traders, and distributors who have good business knowledge. One of the things being encouraged in the MBS-EC is strengthening the capacity and ability to utilize digital technology in doing business. Regarding training for digitalizing MSMEs, the Padang Job Training Center also has several programs for MSME businessmen, including Simpul Talenta Padang (Talent Hub) which provides online mentoring-based training classes for one month and Competency-Based Training (PBK).

Like West Sumatra, the Special Region of Yogyakarta is also developing a local marketplace as an effort to expand the digitalization of its MSMEs. The DIY Regional Government pioneered and developed the Yogya Cooperative and Business Actor Development Information System (SiBakul), which, as of March 2021, has had more than 1,500 MSMEs joining it. To attract businesses and consumers to use this application, and differentiate it from other online marketplaces, SiBakul Jogja has become a free shipping market hub. The Regional Government has allocated a significant amount of funds as a substitute for postage which, in other marketplaces, is borne by consumers. In 2020, the Regional Government allocated a total of 350 million Rupiah to finance free shipping. This figure is insignificant when compared to the benefits for MSMEs whose transaction value in this program reaches 2.25 billion Rupiah. The size of this profit means that the free shipping program will be continued and even with a bigger allocation in the following year.

The Sibakul Jogja program is not only used to develop MSME businesses through digital technology, but also as a centralized data recording center for business actors by the DIY Regional Government. Data collection for business actors who are not integrated is changed through Sibakul Jogja which helps the local government carry out an MSME data collection scheme based on the National Identity Number (NIK). Thus, the regional government will have a more structured collection of data on who are the individual business actors in Yogya, and in more detail than that, it will be possible to determine the type of business, the completeness of its certification, and whether it is competitive or not. This is important as the basis for the government to create empowerment programs and policies for MSMEs.

Sibakul Jogja is also a portal for businesspeople to get education about business and business development. Through this application, MSME businessmen can consult on how to run proper business governance. MSME actors in the Sibakul Yogya network also receive training in developing business, applying for certification, and utilizing digital media for business. MSME actors in Sibakul Yogya can also take part in offline exhibitions to market their products.

Sibakul Yogya is the epicenter of the MSME digital development program in DIY. Not only that, based on the free shipping program earlier, the DIY Regional Government has also collaborated with various parties, including Gojek, PT Pos Indonesia, and Sendinaja. Regarding data collection for business actors through Sibakul Jogja, the DIY regional government is also collaborating with Jogja Economic Resilience for COVID-19 (Jercovid) to see how the COVID-19 pandemic has impacted MSME businesses in the Yogya region, including in Gunung Kidul, Sleman, Bantul, Kulon Progo, and the City of Yogyakarta. Simultaneously with this data collection, the Regional Government has also provided services and assistance to MSMEs during this pandemic in collaboration with the DIY Association of Indonesian Economic Scholars (ISEI) and the DIY Indonesian Advocates Association (Peradi) and is supported by the DIY Indonesian Chamber of Commerce and Industry (Kadin).

Apart from training through the Sibakul Yogya program, the DIY Communication and Information Office also conducts special training for business actors to carry out digital marketing. The training materials provided include content production training, social media training, and website training. This is done so that businesses can make maximum use of digital media to develop their profits and business. Diskominfo DIY has fostered more than 60 MSMEs between 2019 and 2020. Apart from this program, Diskominfo DIY is also working to improve internet facilities and infrastructure to facilitate businesses' efforts to access and utilize digital technology. Diskominfo does this by expanding the provision of free wi-fi access points with a minimum bandwidth of 10 Mbps. From only 21 points in 2014, access points have grown to 126 points, including 71 MSME points and 55 points in public facilities in 2019.

From the various local government work programs that have been described, local government programs for digitalization MSMEs can be categorized into four forms: (1) application development, marketplace, and local digital media for MSME development; (2) training and assistance to increase the digital capacity of MSME actors; (3) cooperation with national marketplaces, banks, companies, entrepreneurs, practitioners, and academics to provide easy access and services for developing MSME digitalization; and (4) improving internet and digital infrastructure and facilities for MSMEs. These four programs are run in parallel and even synergize between programs.

7.2.4 MSME's Views on the Government Policies in West Java, West Sumatra, and Yogyakarta

The government regulations and programs to increase the involvement and activities of MSMEs in the digital space have made significant progress in the last five years. What is interesting to look at further is how MSME entrepreneurs know and evaluate the programs offered by the government. This is important to know to find out how far these programs reach business actors and whether this program is really needed and answers the problems faced by MSME entrepreneurs. A survey conducted of 718 MSME business actors in West Java, West Sumatra, and Yogyakarta in 2020 will show how the entrepreneurs view the government policies. In this survey, the assessment of government work is divided into an assessment of regulations and work programs.

Related to government regulations or policies regarding efforts to digitalize MSMEs, the level of satisfaction of business actors appears to vary among the three regions. Yogyakarta is the area with respondents who have the highest satisfaction regarding the existence of regulations and policies regarding the digitalization of MSMEs. There were 65.26% of MSME entrepreneurs surveyed stated that existing government regulations and policies had been optimal and very optimal in encouraging the digitalization of MSMEs, while the rest or around 30% stated otherwise. The second highest satisfaction rate of the three research areas is West Java. In West Java, although not as high as in Yogyakarta, there were 59.93% of respondents who stated that regulations were optimal and very optimal, with the majority, or 57.05% stating that regulations were optimal. Unlike the other two regions, where most respondents were satisfied with existing government regulations and policies, respondents in West Sumatra considered the opposite. More than half, namely 58.55% of respondents stated that the regulations owned by the government were lacking and did not work optimally to develop the digitalization of MSMEs. Only 34.72% of respondents in West Sumatra stated that the regulations had been optimal. West Sumatra shows higher dissatisfaction than satisfaction with government regulations, and this contrasts with the situation in West Java and Yogyakarta (Figs. 7.1, 7.2 and 7.3).

In your opinion, how optimal are the current government regulations/regulations supporting digitalization (internet/online use/digital solutions) for SMEs?

(Yogyakarta: 213 respondents, West Java: 312 respondents, West Sumatera: 193 respondents).

Like the assessment pattern on questions about government regulations, of the three areas surveyed, the level of entrepreneur satisfaction with the MSME digitalization programs is highest in Yogyakarta. A total of 65.26% of respondents state that the government's digitalization programs had been optimal and very optimal, while only 34.74% state that it was not optimal and not optimal. West Java is the

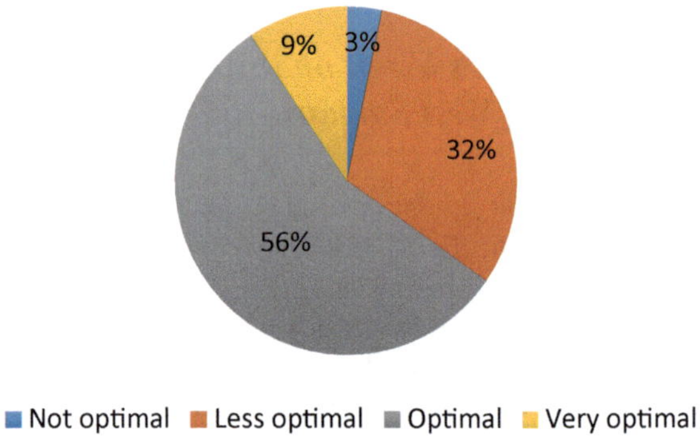

Fig. 7.1 MSMEs's perception of Yogyakarta's government regulations or policies in SME digitalization. *Source* Fizzanty et al. (2021)

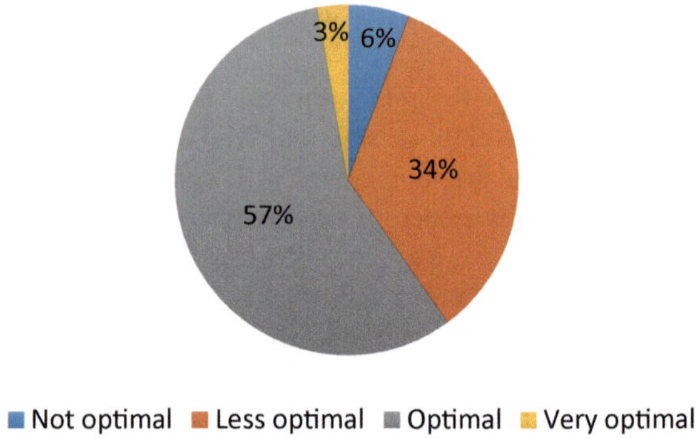

Fig. 7.2 MSMEs's perception of West Java's government regulations or policies in SME digitalization. *Source* Fizzanty et al. (2021)

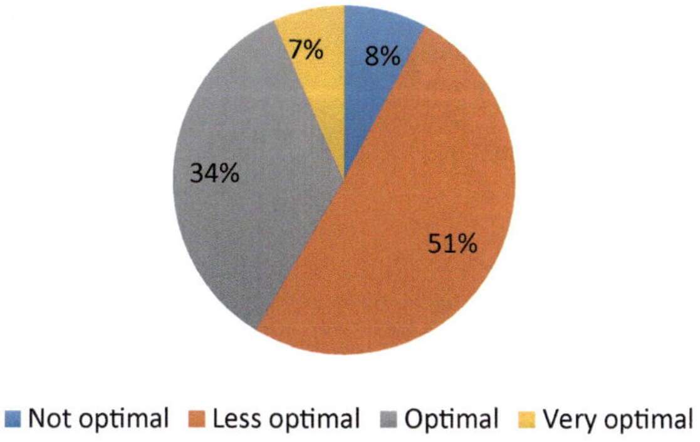

Fig. 7.3 MSMEs's perception of West Sumatra's government regulations or policies in SME digitalization. *Source* Fizzanty et al. (2021)

area with the second highest level of satisfaction after Yogyakarta, where 57.69% of respondents state that the program had been optimal and very optimal. Even though the level of satisfaction is quite high in West Java, there are still 37.18% who think the program is not optimal and 5.13% is not optimal. Among the three research areas, West Sumatra respondents have the lowest level of satisfaction, namely only 32.64% who state that the program had been optimal followed by 5.18% who acknowledge that it had been very optimal. Meanwhile, most respondents, or more than 50% of respondents stated that the MSME digitalization program is not optimally carried out by the government (Figs. 7.4, 7.5 and 7.6).

In your opinion, how are the current government programs supporting digitalization (internet/online use/digital solutions) for SMEs?

(West Java: 193 respondents, West Sumatra: 193 respondents, Yogyakarta: 213 respondents)

This survey, an assessment of government programs for digitalizing MSMEs, moreover, is divided into several forms of the program, including (1) capacity building programs, for example, training, business consulting, business assistance, and others; (2) provision of business and digital equipment; (3) provision of working

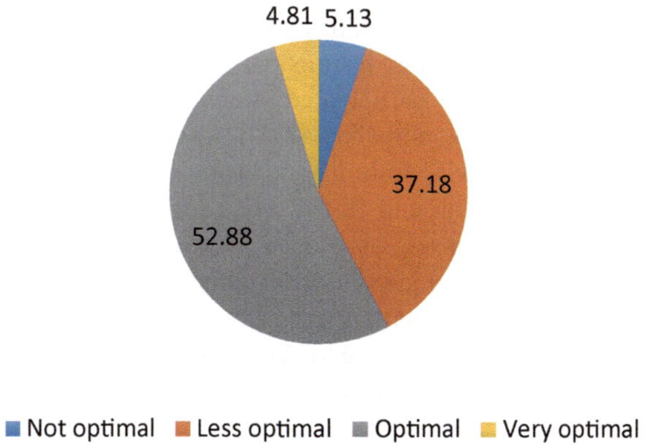

Fig. 7.4 MSMEs's perception of West Java's government programs in SME digitalization. *Source* Fizzanty et al. (2021)

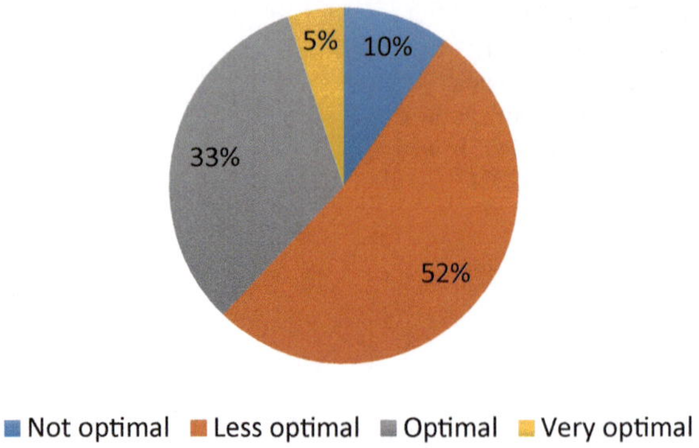

Fig. 7.5 MSMEs's perception of West Sumatra's government programs in SME digitalization. *Source* Fizzanty et al. (2021)

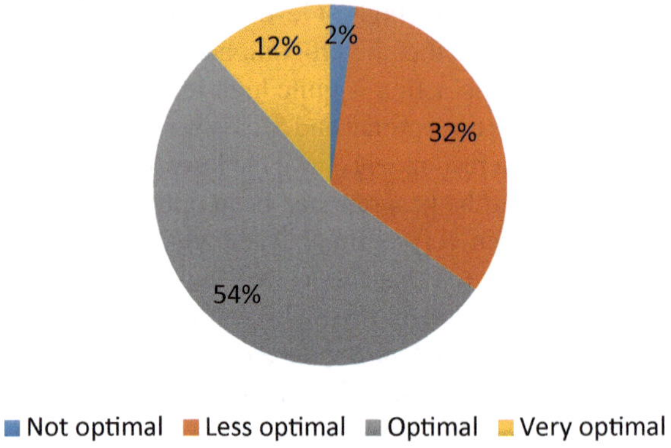

Fig. 7.6 MSMEs's perception of Yogyakarta's government programs in SME digitalization. *Source* Fizzanty et al. (2021)

capital; (4) licensing assistance program, for example for halal certification, BPOM permit certification, and others. The survey then attempts to capture the extent to which respondents have participated in and/or received the government program. It is interesting to examine further whether the level of satisfaction with the program, in general, discussed earlier is in line with their level of involvement in this program.

In Yogyakarta, which has the highest level of satisfaction with government regulations and programs, it turns out that almost half, or 46.47% of respondents have never received or participated in government programs to develop MSME digitalization. Even so, more than 44% of respondents admit that they have received or are currently receiving training and business assistance. A small portion of the respondents, namely around 8–10%, had received assistance with equipment, business capital and licensing assistance. Not much different from Yogyakarta, West Java, which has a fairly good level of satisfaction with the program, it turns out that not many respondents have ever participated in the program. More than 58% stated that they had never received and participated in the MSME digitalization program organized by the government. This figure is the highest compared to Yogyakarta and West Sumatra. Lower than Yogyakarta, only about 25% of respondents in West Java stated that they had attended training and mentoring programs. However, the number of respondents in West Java who had received licensing assistance was higher than the number of respondents in Yogyakarta, which was 20.83%. Meanwhile, only less than 10% of respondents in West Java received equipment and business capital assistance.

Like respondents in Yogyakarta and West Java, many of the MSME business actors surveyed stated that they had never received and participated in government programs. Half of the respondents stated that they did, and this figure was almost even with those who said they had attended. As in the two previous regions, most respondents who stated that they had participated in the digitalization development program by the government were those who attended training and business assistance. There were 36.78% of respondents who said they had participated in the program. Meanwhile, only a few respondents participated in the equipment and licensing assistance program, namely only 4.66% had received business equipment assistance and only 8.29% had received licensing assistance (Tables 7.1, 7.2 and 7.3).

Have you received any assistance/support for digital SME development as below?

(Yogyakarta: 213 respondents, West Java: 312 respondents; West Sumatra: 193 respondents)

Based on the survey, the involvement of MSME business actors in government programs for the development of MSME digitalization is still not optimal; the programs are only able to reach about half of the respondents. However, compared to other actors giving assistance programs, the government is considered as an actor that

Table 7.1 Participants received assistance programs for digital SME development in Yogyakarta

No	Assistance programs	Answer yes (participated)	%
1	Capacity building (training, business assistance, etc.)	94	44.13
2	Equipment	18	8.45
3	Working capital	19	8.92
4	Licensing assistance (halal certificate, BPOM certificate, etc.)	23	10.79
5	Never	99	46.47

Source Fizzanty et al. (2021)

Table 7.2 Participants received assistance programs for digital SME development in West Java

No	Assistance programs	Answer yes (participated)	%
1	Capacity building (training, business assistance, etc.)	79	25.32
2	Equipment	24	7.69
3	Working capital	31	9.93
4	Licensing assistance (halal certificate, BPOM certificate, etc.)	65	20.83
5	Never	181	58.01

Source Fizzanty et al. (2021)

Table 7.3 Participants received assistance programs for digital SME development in West Sumatra

No	Assistance programs	Answer yes (participated)	%
1	Capacity building (training, business assistance, etc.)	71	36.78
2	Equipment	9	4.66
3	Working capital	16	8.29
4	Licensing assistance (halal certificate, BPOM certificate, etc.)	28	14.50
5	Never	97	50.25

Source Fizzanty et al. (2021)

provides the greatest assistance to them. In Yogyakarta, 41.31% of respondents stated that it was the government that had provided the greatest assistance to them, in terms of digitalizing MSMEs. Not much different from Yogyakarta, there are more than 38% of respondents in West Sumatra saying the same thing. However, only around 25% of respondents in West Java admit that the biggest assistance they receive comes from the government. Even though it is low, compared to the contributions made by other actors, including banks, work partners, marketplace companies, and others, this 25% figure is still higher. However, there is an important note in this aspect, namely the large number of respondents who answered they did not know. In Yogyakarta, those who answered that they did not know reached more than 28%, while in West Sumatra, it was 34.72% and in West Java, it was even higher at 48.72%.

From the survey results, it appears that the government is the central actor in the process of developing the digitalization of MSMEs. This is because the government is not only recognized as the largest provider of assistance programs but also because quite a few business actors, above 40% of respondents, receive business digitalization development programs from the government. However, an important note that deserves further attention is the optimization of regulations and programs, as well as the range of programs provided by the government. Generally, in the three survey areas, more than 30% of respondents argued that the government's programs are not optimal and/or less optimal. Moreover, not all assistance programs are equally accepted by all MSME entrepreneurs. Training and mentoring programs are more evenly received by many MSME entrepreneurs, while programs for financial assistance, equipment support, and licensing assistance are only received by a few entrepreneurs.

7.2.5 Governance Problems in the Digitalization of MSMEs in Indonesia

Based on the previous explanation, it is known that the Indonesian government, both at the central and local levels, has made various policies and programs to digitalize

MSMEs. However, from the survey results, it is also found that according to business actors, the government's efforts, especially in implementing their programs, are still not running optimally. The views of the survey respondents indicate that there are still problems with the implementation of policies and programs related to strengthening the digitalization of MSMEs in Indonesia. There are at least three problems related to how the government manages its policies to strengthen MSMEs in the digital world.

First, the government has attempted to run various programs to digitalize MSMEs, but in the implementation, these programs are still not equitable to be accessed and utilized by entrepreneurs. As previously explained, from the results of the survey, respondents stated that it was more difficult to access programs for financial assistance, equipment support, and licensing assistance, compared to training and mentoring programs. It indicates that programs for financial credits, licensing arrangements, and equipment support are still not evenly accessible to entrepreneurs, though they need this kind of support.

Another example of the problem of retrieving government programs can also be seen from the ability of the Indonesian population to access the internet. Based on data from the Central Statistics Agency (BPS), the level of internet penetration is not evenly distributed nationally. In 2022, the highest number of internet users will be in DKI Jakarta, reaching 84.65%, and the lowest will be in Papua, only 26.32%. Spatially, there is inequality in internet use due to the uneven support of digital infrastructure and ecosystems in Indonesia. This also indirectly shows that the ability of MSME entrepreneurs to connect with the digital world is also uneven, depending on the availability of existing infrastructure in their area. MSMEs in Jakarta, for example, have better access to involvement in e-commerce than those in Papua. Moreover, data specifically discussing the use of digital technology for MSMEs in 2022 shows that there are only 21 million or around 32% of the total 64 million MSMEs in Indonesia. This means that there are still 68% of MSMEs that have not utilized digital technology (Kominfo, 2023).

Secondly, the central and regional governments do not have comprehensive integrated data on existing MSMEs along with their actual conditions, including their capabilities and roles in the digital economy. Each ministry has MSME data which may be different from that owned by regional government agencies. In addition, local governments also have different levels of data ownership between one another; for example, the Governments of West Java and Yogyakarta already have updated MSME data that can be accessed online, while many other regions do not have it. The absence of this data will be a problem for the government to develop programs and involve MSMEs in the program in an appropriate manner. For example, the government has generalized a training program on the use of e-commerce and how to open trading accounts in e-commerce for all MSMEs in one region. This training will be useful for MSME entrepreneurs who are not yet active in e-commerce, but for those who have been in e-commerce for a long time, this training is not required. Those who are already active in e-commerce need advanced training, such as how to increase their competitiveness and market their products in e-commerce.

This absence of data at least makes it difficult to optimize government programs to strengthen MSMEs, including in the world of the digital economy, which has been increasingly being carried out in the last five years. However, this weakness is not unnoticed by the government. Since 2021, the idea of a single data requirement has emerged in central government discussions and was even emphasized by President Joko Widodo in 2022 (Handayani, 2022). The Ministry of Cooperatives and SMEs then coordinate efforts to integrate this data, and it is hoped that it will be fulfilled soon in 2023. An important step if data is integrated what has been done is to ensure that this data will become the basis for the central and regional governments in any program preparation and become a source for determining business targets that will receive the program. If this is done, government programs will be more in line with the conditions and needs of MSMEs. With this situation, the sectoral ego that often arises between government institutions and programming that is not based on data will no longer exist. Thus, the program will be more optimal in achieving the goals of MSMEs that are getting stronger and more productive.

Thirdly, the MSME digitalization strengthening programs run by the central government and local government are not integrated. It should be recognized that the central and local governments have paid great attention to MSMEs, marked by the numerous programs emphasizing the strengthening and digitalization MSMEs. However, these programs tend to be structured and administered by ministries and local government agencies with weak coordination between them. This has resulted in many programs with the same or similar activities and assistance being held by different institutions at the central and local government levels. Ultimately, the same MSME entrepreneurs are involved in similar programs from different government institutions, rendering government programs ineffective. For example, it is recorded that in 2023, at least the Ministry of Education, the Ministry of Finance, the Ministry of Cooperatives and SMEs, and the Ministry of Communication and Informatics had the same training program on digitalizing MSMEs (Digitalent Kominfo, 2023; Hidayat, 2023; Khairunnisa, 2023; Prasetya, 2023; Zia & Somantri, 2023). Outside of these ministries, agencies at the local government level also conducted training with similar content, such as those held in West Java, Central Kalimantan, and Bali (Brilyana, 2023; Diskominfo Kobar, 2023; Diskopukmp Badung, 2023).

There are three key governance issues for government programs to strengthen MSMEs, especially regarding their role in the world of digital economy, which have been explained. These three problems are the root of why, although many government programs have been provided for MSMEs, they have not been able to reach their maximum effectiveness. Facing this problem, one of the important steps that can be taken by the central government as the main coordinator of programs and policies in Indonesia at this time is to create a grand design for MSME development, including the digitalization of MSMEs. This grand design is not new and was initiated in 2017 but had to stop due to the government changing its work focus to address economic problems due to the pandemic. This grand design should have been compiled and re-implemented for the implementation of comprehensive and long-term government program work. As a supporter of this grand design, the government has also prepared factual integrated data on MSMEs and their conditions. The preparation of a grand design regarding long-term directions and specific work programs is then based on this integrated data. This grand design was prepared based on discussions and coordination between various central and local government agencies, and even the private institutions involved. This coordination will reduce the potential for overlapping work programs, suppress agency sectoral ego, make effective use of program budgets, and optimize the work of each institution according to its capacity. Therefore, the preparation and implementation of a grand design for SMEs is something that is urgent at this time.

7.3 Conclusion

MSMEs have enormous potential to strengthen economic growth and create opportunities to improve people's welfare in Indonesia. The role of MSMEs has strengthened after the COVID-19 pandemic, as they have proven to have managed to survive and become key actors for economic growth during that time. This effort is further strengthened by partnerships between local governments and private digital platforms, such as Shopee, Blibli, Tokopedia, Bukalapak, etc. The significant economic contribution of MSMEs is inseparable from their activities in the digital economy. Therefore, both the central and regional governments have made progressive efforts in the last five years to formulate policies and implement programs that emphasize strengthening MSMEs, especially in digitalizing MSMEs.

Amid the government's strong attention to MSMEs, based on survey results, it was found that government programs to strengthen the role of MSMEs in the digital space did not seem to be running optimally. There are three key governance issues for these government programs: the programs are still not equitable to be accessed and utilized by the entrepreneurs, the central and regional governments do not have comprehensive integrated data on existing MSMEs along with their actual conditions, and the MSME digitalization strengthening programs run by the central government and local government are not integrated. Facing this problem, the government needs a fast and strategic breakthrough, namely by compiling a grand design to strengthen MSMEs accompanied by the preparation of integrated data related to MSMEs and their factual conditions.

References

"Asean Online Sale Day 2021, Peluang Tunjukkan Kekuatan Indonesia". (2021). https://m.kominfo.go.id/content/detail/36172/asean-online-sale-day-2021-peluang-tunjukkan-kekuatan-indonesia/0/berita. Accessed 1 July 2023.

Aminullah, E., et al. (2022). Interactive components of digital MSMEs ecosystem for inclusive digital economy in Indonesia. *Journal of Knowledge Economy*. https://doi.org/10.1007/s13132-022-01086-8

Bappenas. (2017). Bonus Demografi 2030-2040: Strategi Indonesia Terkait Ketenagakerjaan dan Pendidikan. Siaran Pers. Retrieved from file:///D:/Downloadku/156%20Siaran_Pers_-_Peer_Learning_and_Knowledge_Sharing_Workshop.pdf

Bencsik, A., Juhasz, T., & Horvath-Csikos, G. D. (2016). Y and Z Generations at Workplaces. *Journal of Competitiveness*. https://doi.org/10.7441/joc.2016.03.06

Brilyana, Y. A. (2023, Oktober 30). bandung.go.id. Retrieved from bandung.go.id: https://www.bandung.go.id/news/read/8647/umkm-awards-2023-bantu-tingkatkan-daya-saing-pelaku-usahamikro-kota-b

Clinten, B. (2020). *tekno.kompas.com*. Retrieved from tekno.kompas.com: https://tekno.kompas.com/read/2020/10/22/11100027/kominfo-uu-cipta-kerja-bikin-tarif-internet-di-indonesia-makin-murah

Digitalent Kominfo. (2023). Wirausaha & UMKM: Digital entrepreneurship academy. Digitalent Kominfo. https://digitalent.kominfo.go.id/program?akademi=DEA

Diskominfor Kobar. (2023). Disperindagkop UKM Kobar Adakan Pelatihan Keriwausahaan Membangun Transformasi Digital Bisnis bagi Pelaku UMKM. Diskominfo Kalteng. https://mmc.kalteng.go.id/berita/read/41324/disperindagkop-ukm-kobar-adakan-pelatihan-kewirausahaan-membangun-transformasi-digital-bisnis-bagi-pelaku-umkm

Diskopukmp Kabupaten Badung. (2023). Materi Pelatihan UKM. Diskopukmp Kabupaten Badung. https://diskopukmp.badungkab.go.id/materi-pelatihan-ukm

Fizzanty, T., Aminullah, E., Nawawi, Maulana, I., Suryanto, J., Aziz, N. L., Pranata, N., Budiatri, A. P., Suardi, I., Ariyani, L., & Wicaksono, A. (2021). Pengembangan Ekosistem Ekonomi Digital UKM Indonesia. Prioritas Riset Nasional Pengembangan Ekonomi Digital Indonesia Tahun 2020. Laporan Akhir Kegiatan (No.199/E1/PRN/2020). Organisasi Riset Ilmu Pengetahuan Sosial Humaniora, Badan Riset dan Inovasi Nasional (Indonesia).

Global Business Guide Indonesia. (2016). Indonesia SMEs: Increased government support to overcome challenges. Global Business Guide Indonesia. http://www.gbgindonesia.com/en/main/why_indonesia/2016/indonesia_smes_increased_government_support_to_overcome_challenges_11603.php#:~:text=Experts%20have%20identified%20factors%20such,compete%20against%20their%20regional%20counterparts

Handayani, R. (2022). Basis data Tunggal Penting untuk Kembangkan UMKM. Pajak.com. https://www.pajak.com/ekonomi/basis-data-tunggal-penting-untuk-kembangkan-umkm/

Hartarto, A. (2023). Public statement of the coodinating ministry of economic affairs, Indonesia. Optimalkan Potensi Pertumbuhan Ekonomi Digital, Pemerintah Dorong Penciptaan Ekosistem Digital yang Kondusif (Optimizing the growth potential of the digital economy, the government encourages the creation of a conducive digital ecosystem).

Hermawan, D. (2022). Challenge of culture-based SMES digitalization. BI Institute. https://www.bi.go.id/en/bi-institute/BI-Epsilon/Pages/Tantangan-Digitalisasi-UMKM-Berbasis-Budaya.aspx

Hidayat, A. N. (2023, Januari 31). djkn.kemenkeu.go.id. Retrieved from djkn.kemenkeu.go.id: https://www.djkn.kemenkeu.go.id/kpknl-medan/baca-artikel/15879/Mengenal-Program-Pembinaan-UMKM-Kemenkeu-Satu-Tahun-2023.html

Humas Kota Bandung. (2023). Kominfo Gelar Pelatigan Digital Wirausaha, Gratis dan Ada Pendampingan. Humas Kota Bandung. https://www.bandung.go.id/news/read/7764/kominfo-gelar-pelatihan-digital-wirausaha-gratis-dan-ada-pendampingan

Karyati, I. P. (2019). E-Commerce untuk UMKM dan Pertumbuhan Ekonomi Indonesia (E-Commerce for MSMEs and Indonesia's Economic Growth). *Kementerian Keuangan*. https://bppk.kemenkeu.go.id/pusdiklat-keuangan-umum/berita/e-commerce-untuk-umkm-dan-pertumbuhan-ekonomi-indonesia-237095

Kementerian Perindustrian Republik Indonesia. (2021). ASEAN online sale day 2021: Mendorong cross border E-Commerce Di Asean. Accessed 1 July 2023.

Kominfo. (2020, Juni 15). kominfo.go.id. Retrieved from kominfo.go.id: https://www.kominfo.go.id/content/detail/27128/kominfo-gandeng-operator-seluler-bangun-jaringan-4g-di-wilayah-3t/0/sorotan_media

Khairunnisa. (2023). UMKM level up Tahun 2023, program Pelatihan Wirausaha Gratis dari Kominfo. UKMIndonesia.id. https://www.ukmindonesia.id/baca-deskripsi-posts/umkm-level-up-tahun-2023-program-pelatihan-wirausaha-gratis-dari-kominfo

MPR. (2023, Juni 22). mpr.go.id. Retrieved from mpr.go.id: https://www.mpr.go.id/berita/Manfaatkan-Ekonomi-Digital-untuk-Topang-Pertumbuhan-Perekonomian-Nasional
OECD. (2002). *Financing SMEs and entrepreneurs 2022: An OECD scoreboard*. OECD Publishing.
Prasetya, A. (2023). Mengenal program Pembinaan UMKM Kemenkeu Satu Tahun 2023. *DKJN Kemenkeu*. https://www.djkn.kemenkeu.go.id/artikel/baca/15879/Mengenal-Program-Pembinaan-UMKM-Kemenkeu-Satu-Tahun-2023.html
Rahmawati, F. (2022). Bangkitkan Ekonomi Nasional Pasca Pandemi, Kominfo Luncurkan Program Adopsi Teknologi Digital 4.0 Bagi UMKM. *Kominfo*. https://aptika.kominfo.go.id/2022/05/bangkitkan-ekonomi-nasional-pasca-pandemi-kominfo-luncurkan-program-adopsi-teknologi-digital-4-0-bagi-umkm/
Rumata, V. M., & Sastrosubroto, A. S. (2020). The paradox of Indonesian digital. Retrieved from Web of Science: https://pdfs.semanticscholar.org/f1f3/7775b94415c459d8bc7dcf9bbcb80d4fc7cb.pdf?_gl=1*okl1os*_ga*MTczOTcxNDM2NS4xNjkzODA0OTA4*_ga_H7P4ZT52H5*MTY5MzgwNDkwNy4xLjAuMTY5MzgwNDkwOS41OC4wLjA
Savithri, A. (2015). Ini 5 Arahan Kebijakan untuk UKM Digital di Indonesia (these are 5 policy directions for digital SMEs in Indonesia). *Bisnis.com*. https://ekonomi.bisnis.com/read/20150822/87/464631/ini-5-arahan-kebijakan-untuk-ukm-digital-di-indonesia
Spence, M. (2021). Government and economics in the digital economy. *Journal of Government and Economics*. https://doi.org/10.1016/j.jge.2021.100020
Sulastri. (2022). Peran Penting UMKM dalam Ancaman Isu Resesi. https://www.djkn.kemenkeu.go.id/kpknl-balikpapan/baca-artikel/15677/Peran-Penting-UMKM-dalam-Ancaman-Isu-Resesi.html. Accessed 1 July 2023.
Tambunan, T. T. H. (2008). *Development of SMEs in ASEAN*. Readworthy Publications Ltd.
Temasek, G., & Company, B. &. (2022). e-Conomy Sea 2023. https://services.google.com/fh/files/misc/e_conomy_sea_2023_report.pdf
Yolandha, F. (2020). Kominfo Dorong UMKM Manfaatkan platform digital. *Republika*. https://republika.co.id/berita/qgsl8l370/kominfo-dorong-umkm-manfaatkan-platform-digital
Zia & Somantri, C. (2023). Gandeng Kementerian Koperasi dan UKM, Direktorat Kursus dan Pelatihan Sempurnakan Program PKW. Kementerian Pendidikan Kebudataan, Riset dan Teknologi. https://kursus.kemdikbud.go.id/detail-artikel/136

Nyimas Latifah Letty Aziz is a researcher in the Research Center for Political Studies, National Research and Innovation Agency (BRIN). Her research interests focus on political economy and regional development planning. She achieved her bachelor's degree from the Faculty of Economy, Jambi University-Indonesia in 1999 and her master's degree from the Erasmus University of Rotterdam majoring in Urban Management and Development (2012) linkage Urban and Regional Planning in Gadjah Mada University (2013). Her research focuses on Decentralization and Regional Autonomy. Some of her latest academic works are Village Funds Management: A Study from the Democracy Side and the Capacity of Village Government (LIPI Press, 2019), Actors in Special Autonomy Demand: A Case Study of Bali and North Maluku (Yayasan Obor Indonesia, 2020), Asymmetrical Decentralization Management Model in the Republic of Indonesia (Yayasan Obor Indonesia, 2020).

Aisah Putri Budiatri is a researcher in the Research Center for Political Studies, National Research and Innovation Agency (BRIN). She graduated with a master's degree in political science from the State University of New York at Albany and is currently a Ph.D. candidate in the Graduate School of Asian and African Area Studies at Kyoto University. Prior to her current position at BRIN, Ms Budiatri worked with the Research Development Media Group Metro TV and Women Research Institute. Her key research interest focuses mainly on Indonesian democracy, looking at political parties, elections, parliamentary works, civil society, the Papuan conflict, and on gender issues.

Chapter 8
Epilogue: Lessons Learned and Future Directions

Ikbal Maulana and Trina Fizzanty

Generally, the digital transformation of MSMEs in Indonesia has been primarily driven by two key actors: platform companies with a vested interest in onboarding as many MSMEs as possible to attract investors and the government, which views digital transformation as a necessary economic advancement. This progress has led to the emergence of complementary services, which further bolster the digital transformation of MSMEs, with a specific focus on digital payment systems and delivery services. Notably, among the startups that have reached Unicorn status, one is dedicated to electronic payments (OVO), while the other excels in the field of shipping services (J&T).

Presently, at least five active e-commerce platforms are actively competing and striving to acquire users, including MSMEs. These platforms are actively engaging with MSMEs, extending support to enhance their technological capabilities for customer attraction. The COVID-19 pandemic has greatly expedited digitalization, with e-commerce platforms emerging as the primary sales channels for numerous MSMEs. Even after the pandemic, both buyers and sellers have continued to benefit from the convenience of online shopping, contributing to the sustained growth of digitalization. The ongoing competition among digital platforms proves advantageous for MSMEs, ensuring they are not burdened with excessive fees.

While entrepreneurship and innovation from MSMEs are crucial, certain challenges cannot be resolved solely by individual businesses and require government intervention. These challenges include ensuring equitable access to a reliable digital

I. Maulana (✉)
Research Center for Society and Culture, National Research and Innovation Agency (BRIN), Jakarta, Indonesia
e-mail: ikba002@brin.go.id

T. Fizzanty
National Research and Innovation Agency (BRIN), Jakarta, Indonesia
e-mail: trin003@brin.go.id

T. Fizzanty and I. Maulana (eds.), *The Digitalization of Indonesian Small and Medium Enterprises*, Engaging Indonesia, https://doi.org/10.1007/978-981-97-0029-5_8

network, fostering the availability of digital talents and knowledge, and providing financial support for initiating and expanding new business endeavors.

The development of the digitalization of MSMEs cannot be separated from the development of startups offering the platforms. Platform companies still rely on investment funds to operate and keep attracting users even after years of operation. This type of investment is beyond the business logic of most local investors, and, hence, they mostly rely on foreign investors. Therefore, the transformation of MSMEs' businesses is influenced not only by their local environment but also indirectly by global capitalism. Global capitalism provides capital and technologies to Indonesian platform companies, which, in turn, actively engage local MSMEs in e-commerce endeavors.

Indonesia is not the only country experiencing the digital transformation of its economy; numerous nations are undergoing similar changes. Just like in Indonesia, the global pandemic of COVID-19 has accelerated the spread of e-commerce in countries affected by the pandemic. Nevertheless, Indonesia's distinct conditions provide valuable insights and lessons, which can be highly beneficial for others to learn from. Indonesia's vast geography and large population offer a unique combination of strengths and weaknesses, presenting a blend of challenges and opportunities. With over 270 million people spread across thousands of islands, Indonesia faces unique challenges in implementing digital technologies and bridging the digital divide (Puspitasari & Ishii, 2016; Sujarwoto & Tampubolon, 2016).

Indonesia is currently entering the demographic bonus era, which takes place when the working-age population, typically aged 15–64, exceeds the number of those outside this range, including those who are 15 years or younger or 65 years and older. This demographic advantage can significantly boost economic growth, and it is expected to reach its peak in 2037 (Kompas, 2020). In terms of the digital economy, the large young population implies a significant number of individuals familiar with digital technology. While their use for productive activities may be a subject of consideration, their engagement in digital consumption is undoubtedly high.

The success of digital transformation relies on much more than merely technology infusion. Fostering technology development and innovation is still a great challenge for Indonesia because it prevents further development. In the mid-1990s, Indonesia presented itself to the global community as a thriving and rapidly progressing economy, confidently positioning itself alongside other industrial powers in the dynamic Asia–Pacific region (Booth, 1998). Indonesia's economic growth has been praised as one of the East Asian Miracles (The World Bank, 1993). However, since then and up to the present day, Indonesia has grappled with the persistent challenge of the middle-income trap, which has hindered its path toward achieving higher levels of economic prosperity. To escape this trap, the country still needs to develop its industrial sector, increasing the industries' technological capabilities and innovativeness (Basri & Putra, 2016). Optimal and innovative utilization of technology requires entrepreneurial acumen.

Despite the relatively low level of entrepreneurship in Indonesia compared to its neighboring countries, number of entrepreneurs in Indonesia yet lesser than South

East Asia (Amin, 2020) and low level of technological capability Indonesia has high growth of e-commerce (Chap. 2), which can be partly attributed to its large population. This strategy increased local consumption of various products from local and global markets and also exposed Indonesia's MSMEs to global competition. Meanwhile, MSMEs are lacking in digital talents, which are a key to digital transformation. The competitive digital economy becomes a high risk to the Indonesian MSMEs' lack of industry and innovation capacity and entrepreneurship.

The large size of its market attracts either other e-commerce companies from overseas or foreign venture capitalists to support local startups. A number of indigenous platform companies, such as Gojek, Tokopedia, and Traveloka, have developed into big companies, successfully attracting foreign investments, thus enabling them to sustain their expansion. The injection of foreign capital, technology, and local entrepreneurship has been instrumental in catalyzing significant disruptions and transformations across various sectors in Indonesia. Furthermore, the digitalization of the economy has been accelerated by the impact of the COVID-19 pandemic.

8.1 What Drives the Growth of the Platform Economy?

8.1.1 Harnessing Global Technology to Seize Local Opportunities

In contrast to industry-leading platform companies such as Amazon and Alibaba, renowned for their advanced information technology development in the retail sector (Klinge et al., 2023), Indonesian platform companies have not achieved a comparable reputation, even at the national level. However, their business operations demand a high-skilled workforce in information technology, a requirement that local talent alone cannot fulfill.

As a result, some platforms are actively seeking to recruit IT engineers from locations like Singapore and Bengaluru, India (Akbar & Hardiyati, 2021). The advancement of information technology, coupled with the seamless integration of various technology services through the Internet, enables the establishment of an e-commerce platform even in countries lacking a robust technological ecosystem. This integration encompasses services such as Google Maps and digital payment systems, making it feasible to set up and operate an e-commerce platform in such environments.

In its early stages, the ride-hailing company Gojek relied on phone calls as a means of interaction with its customers, which proved to be inconvenient and impractical. However, with the advancement of Internet technologies, Gojek was able to offer its customers more convenient methods of interaction and transactions. In the past, marketplaces were only used as a sales platform for one company, while other companies had to entrust their goods to that company if they wanted to sell through the marketplace. In the past, interconnection methods such as electronic data interchange (EDI) were excessively complex and expensive for the majority of MSMEs.

However, in today's context, anyone with a smartphone can easily sell goods through e-commerce without the need to invest in additional hardware. With its vast market potential, Indonesia has positioned itself as a significant destination for the global expansion efforts of technology companies, empowering the country to leverage cutting-edge technologies and capitalize on its expansive market.

8.1.2 Indonesia is Part of Global Capitalism

The development of e-commerce platforms is intricately linked to the progression of global capitalism. Capitalism is renowned for its relentless drive for growth and expansion, and in light of the extended decline in manufacturing profitability, it has adapted by prioritizing data as a crucial driver for maintaining economic growth and vitality (Srnicek, 2016). The globalization of capitalism is strengthened by interconnected networks of technological infrastructure and businesses. This phenomenon is evident not only from a global standpoint but also from the perspective of Indonesia, where market integration enables Indonesian companies to access foreign markets and allows foreign companies to enter the Indonesian market.

The substantial population of Indonesia reflects the immense size of its markets, which in turn attracts sellers and investors eager to capitalize on the opportunities offered by Indonesian platform companies. However, the concept of the platform economy is relatively unfamiliar to local investors, who have traditionally focused on conventional sectors. As a result, the platforms established by Indonesian young entrepreneurs gain strength through the financial support provided by foreign investors.

One prominent example that contradicts the rationale of local investors is the fact that platform companies have not yet generated profits. Nevertheless, investors continue to invest in these companies, providing the necessary funding for them to achieve market dominance, expand their user base, and increase transactions on their platforms.

At present, numerous e-commerce platforms are in competition with each other, and it is highly unlikely that all of them would survive without significant financial support from strong investors. The dynamics of network externalities within the platform economy make it challenging for multiple similar platforms to coexist and thrive simultaneously (Shapiro & Varian, 1999). As a result, these platforms engage in competitive strategies to outperform one another, prioritizing market dominance and delaying immediate financial gains. While local investors may struggle to fully comprehend the dynamics of the platform economy, foreign investors are actively entering the Indonesian market and injecting capital to fuel the growth and intensify the race for market dominance among Indonesian platform companies.

8.1.3 Political Legitimation of Platform Economy

Platform companies have received substantial support from the government (Chap. 7), including from the Indonesian president himself. Through various ministries, the government has implemented policies and programs aimed at fostering the adoption of the platform economy, particularly among MSMEs. Although the effectiveness of these initiatives may vary, the government's backing provides institutional legitimacy, which has significantly contributed to the growth of the platform economy. For instance, in the face of past violent protests against ride-hailing companies in several major cities, the government has consistently stood in support of these platform companies. The president has demonstrated his pride in the remarkable growth of certain platform companies, commonly referred to as unicorns and decacorns.

8.1.4 Culture, Infrastructure, and Ecosystem

The progress of digitalization among MSMEs in Indonesia varies, particularly among provinces outside Java. The country, being vast in size, grapples with the issue of infrastructure inequality across its diverse regions. As discussed in Chap. 2 by Fizzanty, there is unequal access to the Internet among provinces in Indonesia. However, it is suspected that culture, in the sense of inherited habits and values, is not the determining factor of this inequality. Since most people access the Internet through their mobile phones, and mobile phones are innovations with high observability, popular applications on mobile phones can easily spread because users can easily teach each other about them. While culture does play a role in explaining varying technology adoption, the difference is not so much among regions but more between different generations. Young generations, regardless of location, tend to be more receptive to digital technology (Chap. 3). They are more ready than their predecessors to adopt a digital innovation culture, which requires digital literacy, innovativeness, adaptability, and agility to flourish in the digital era.

The low adoption of technology appears to be more influenced by the limited reach of digital infrastructure and technological and business ecosystems. For complex technology utilization where individuals cannot solely rely on their own knowledge and skills, those residing in larger cities are more inclined. Therefore, being part of a comprehensive technological and business ecosystem is more conducive to the adoption and sophisticated utilization of technology, such as becoming content creators or engaging in e-commerce activities.

8.2 Challenges

8.2.1 From Local Competition to Global Competition

The digital integration of businesses not only drives market expansion but also nurtures thriving business ecosystems (Chap. 6). Through cooperation or competition links, various types of business entities are interconnected, benefiting customers and ultimately boosting customer spending. However, the massive sales of imported goods through these platforms have raised concerns among some individuals, prompting them to question whether these platforms are actually opening the local market to foreign products, rather than fostering opportunities for local businesses to expand internationally.

The digitalization-driven growth of the retail sector undeniably brings about positive impacts. One notable benefit is the creation of employment opportunities, as a robust retail industry can generate significant job prospects. In addition, a vibrant retail sector encourages consumer spending, which is a major driver of economic activity. When consumers have access to a wide range of products, they are more likely to spend money, thus stimulating demand and supporting other sectors of the economy. Retail businesses generate tax revenue for governments through sales taxes and corporate taxes. This revenue can be used to fund public services and infrastructure development, thus benefiting the overall economy.

Even if the retail sector is dominated by imported goods, it still presents opportunities for domestic producers to exhibit and sell their products alongside the imports. This arrangement can effectively support local businesses and foster innovation and competitiveness within the domestic market. However, market forces do not necessarily trigger local innovativeness and competitiveness, and government intervention is needed when the market mechanism falls short of enhancing local competitiveness (Lall, 1996; Lall & Teubal, 1998). The presence of overwhelmingly strong competitors, who leave little room for victory, can potentially discourage innovation.

8.2.2 The Issue of Productivity

E-commerce platforms are designed to enhance connectivity and streamline interactions and transactions among entities connected to the platforms. Basic technology is sufficient for mere participation in e-commerce platforms, enabling a large number of micro-enterprises to become users. Consequently, the challenge of inclusivity primarily lies in access to digital infrastructure, especially internet connectivity, rather than the capabilities of digital platforms themselves.

Platform companies primarily concentrate on facilitating interactions and transactions rather than engaging directly in production or manufacturing. Their main aim is to promote and streamline interaction and transactions on their platforms, rather than enhancing the production and innovative capabilities of their users. What the platform companies do for MSMEs is also supported by the government. The government's initiatives regarding the platform economy are intended to encourage the widespread adoption and utilization of e-commerce platforms.

As part of its efforts to enhance national productivity, the Ministry of Industry introduced the policy "Making Indonesia 4.0," which focuses on revitalizing the manufacturing sector through the extensive and intensive utilization of information and communication technologies (ICT). However, the progress and outcomes of these initiatives may not be readily apparent to the public. To achieve its objectives, the successful implementation of the policy requires addressing the challenge of enhancing the technological capabilities of individual manufacturing companies. The endeavor to enhance technological capabilities within the manufacturing sector poses a greater challenge compared to promoting the growth of the platform economy. In the platform economy, technological sophistication is centralized within the platform itself, allowing users, including MSMEs, to utilize relatively simple tools and interfaces. However, in the manufacturing sector, the task of upgrading technological capabilities across various entities is more complex and demanding.

8.2.3 The Loss of Tangibility on Digital Platforms

The transition to online business presents a formidable challenge for MSMEs due to their limited visibility within the market. While these enterprises may possess commendable reputations, such recognition often remains confined to a narrow segment of the market. This challenge is particularly pronounced when dealing with tangible products where competition hinges on product quality. The intricacy arises from the fact that product quality evaluation typically necessitates in-person inspection, involving the sensory experience of seeing and touching the items. Only standardized products of big corporations can easily be sold at high prices because customers are already familiar with them. For unknown MSMEs, customers often hesitate to take the risk of buying their expensive products. This situation leads many MSMEs to sell low-cost products and engage in cost competition rather than quality competition.

8.2.4 Human Resource Development

If the sole concern is the adoption of e-commerce, MSMEs as users do not face any significant human resource development issues. However, when it comes to enhancing national competitiveness, Indonesia encounters a substantial problem that demands attention. It is crucial to address and solve the issues in the production or manufacturing sectors. Otherwise, e-commerce platforms would merely function as markets connecting buyers and sellers, without contributing to the sustainability of the country's productive sectors. Additionally, Indonesia must prioritize the sustenance of its productive sectors, since they are the primary providers of employment opportunities in the country.

8.2.5 *Technological Development*

The development of human resources in innovative sectors is inherently intertwined with the advancement and innovation of technology. Unless the sole objective of human resource development is limited to utilizing technologies created by others, it cannot be divorced from technological development and innovation. The ongoing technological advancements, including platform development, have caused significant disruptions to various industries and the corresponding job market associated with them (Scully-Russ & Torraco, 2020). When a nation actively participates in technological development, it gains the ability to anticipate and prepare for the remarkable progress made in technology beyond its borders. This proactive engagement allows the nation to avoid surprises and shocks, enabling it to make the necessary preparations and stay at the forefront of technological advancements.

8.2.6 *Financing Digital Transformation*

The successful digital transformation of MSMEs necessitates a harmonious blend of technology and technological capabilities, hinging on a skilled and qualified workforce. This undertaking calls for substantial investment to acquire the necessary technology and either hire technologically skilled staff or enhance the capabilities of existing personnel. Many MSMEs struggle to obtain funding and identify the right technologies for their digital transformation (*Chap. 4*). To address this issue effectively, a solution necessitates not only funding but also knowledge acquisition through training and hands-on learning.

8.3 Future Directions

In the final section of this chapter, and indeed the entire book, we put forward our recommendations on how policies should be directed to bolster the national economy, with a particular focus on empowering MSMEs, which play a crucial role.

Boosting e-commerce platforms is essential for connecting MSMEs with their business ecosystem. A strong digital presence allows these enterprises to reach a broader audience, access new markets, and streamline their operations. However, we must recognize that connectivity alone will not suffice to overcome the economic challenges that the country faces, notably the middle-income trap. It demands a multifaceted approach that addresses various aspects of economic growth.

While e-commerce platforms are vital, we also need to direct attention to improving the productivity and innovativeness of the manufacturing sectors. MSMEs contribute significantly to the manufacturing landscape, and enhancing their capabilities will have a ripple effect on the entire industry. By investing in research, development, and technology adoption, we can fuel greater productivity and foster a culture of innovation among these businesses.

The revitalization of the industry, as pursued by "Making Indonesia 4.0," is a step in the right direction. However, we must intensify these efforts to drive sustainable growth and competitiveness in the global market. Policies that incentivize technological advancements, promote collaborations between MSMEs and large enterprises, and provide targeted financial support can further accelerate the revitalization process.

Moreover, it is crucial to recognize that improving the productivity and innovativeness of MSMEs cannot be achieved in isolation. To maximize their potential, we must focus on transforming their relationship with their ecosystems. This entails fostering partnerships and collaborations with business entities in their value chains, enabling access to financial sectors for upskilling support, and leveraging the education system to ensure a steady supply of skilled human resources. However, business initiatives and innovative utilization of technology require entrepreneurship.

Education and training play a vital role in equipping the workforce with the necessary skills to thrive in the digital era. By investing in relevant training programs, we can upskill the workforce and empower them to adapt to evolving technological trends. Additionally, facilitating access to financing and financial literacy education will enable MSMEs to invest in their growth and modernization.

In conclusion, bolstering the national economy and overcoming economic challenges requires a comprehensive approach that empowers MSMEs and strengthens their ties with the broader business ecosystem. By fostering innovation, revitalizing the manufacturing sector, investing in human capital, and fostering entrepreneurship, we can create a thriving environment for MSMEs to prosper, thus driving sustainable economic growth and prosperity for the entire nation.

References

Akbar, M., & Hardiyati, R. (2021). The absorpotion of HRST from technology-based companies of Indonesia. *STI Policy and Management, 6*(1), 67–75.

Basri, F., & Putra, G. A. (2016). *Escaping the middle income trap in Indonesia: An analysis of risks, remedies and national characteristics*. Friedrich-Ebert-Stiftung Indonesia Office.

Booth, A. (1998). *The Indonesian economy in the nineteenth and twentieth centuries: A history of missed opportunities*. Macmillan.

Klinge, T. J., Hendrikse, R., Fernandez, R., & Adriaans, I. (2023). Augmenting digital monopolies: A corporate financialization perspective on the rise of Big Tech. In *Competition and Change* (Vol. 27, Issue 2, pp. 332–353). https://doi.org/10.1177/10245294221105573

Kompas. (2020). *Indonesia's demographic bonus to peak in 2037*. https://go.kompas.com/read/2020/11/24/194547174/indonesias-demographic-bonus-to-peak-in-2037

Lall, S., & Teubal, M. (1998). "Market-stimulating" technology policies in developing countries: A framework with examples from East Asia. *World Development, 26*(8), 1369–1385.

Lall, S. (1996). *Learning from the Asian tigers: Studies in technology and industrial policy*. Macmillan.

Puspitasari, L., & Ishii, K. (2016). Digital divides and mobile Internet in Indonesia: Impact of smartphones. In *Telematics and Informatics* (Vol. 33, Issue 2, pp. 472–483). https://doi.org/10.1016/j.tele.2015.11.001

Scully-Russ, E., & Torraco, R. (2020). The changing nature and organization of work: An integrative review of the literature. In *Human resource development review* (Vol. 19, Issue 1, pp. 66–93). Sage Publications INC. https://doi.org/10.1177/1534484319886394

Shapiro, C., & Varian, H. R. (1999). *Information Rules: A Strategic Guide to the Network Economy*. Harvard Business School Press.

Srnicek, N. (2016). *Platform capitalism* (1st ed.). Polity. http://gen.lib.rus.ec/book/index.php?md5=54101e43da5c8a19fa2a6110aee33c78

Sujarwoto, S., & Tampubolon, G. (2016). Spatial inequality and the Internet divide in Indonesia 2010–2012. In Telecommunications Policy (Vol. 40, Issue 7, pp. 602–616). https://doi.org/10.1016/j.telpol.2015.08.008

The World Bank. (1993). *The East Asian miracle: Economic growth and public policy*. Oxford University Press.

Ikbal Maulana is a researcher at the Research Center of Society and Culture, National Research and Innovation Agency (BRIN). He has master degree in computer engineering and worked as programmer and system analyst before becoming a researcher and pursuing Ph.D degree in philosophy. His current research interests concern the impact of information technology on society and democracy, philosophy of technology, and social epistemology. His relevant publications in line with the book's topic include chapters titled "Big Brothers Are Seducing You: Consumerism, Surveillance, and the Agency of Consumers," "The Cultural and Institutional Barrier of Knowledge Exchanges in the Development of Open Source Software," and "Challenges of Developing Countries in Imitating Technological Progress." All three chapters are solely authored by the author.

Trina Fizzanty is Head of the Research Center for Education at Indonesia's National Research and Innovation Agency (BRIN) in Jakarta. She was the former Director of Research Center for Science and Technology Development, Indonesian Institute of Sciences (LIPI). She was the principal investigator for the research project "The Development of Digital Economy Ecosystem of SMEs in Indonesia" (2020–2021). She holds Ph.D degree from The University of Queensland, Australia in Integrative System. Her research area is on management of innovation and R&D. She has published her research in international journal and books. She worked collaboratively with other scholars in several international research projects and also works as a reviewer for international journals and she was as the Editorial Board of LIPI Press. Her current publication in international journal with a title "Interactive Components of Digital MSMEs Ecosystem for Inclusive Digital Economy in Indonesia" in Journal of The Knowledge Economy, November 2022.

GPSR Compliance

The European Union's (EU) General Product Safety Regulation (GPSR) is a set of rules that requires consumer products to be safe and our obligations to ensure this.

If you have any concerns about our products, you can contact us on ProductSafety@springernature.com

In case Publisher is established outside the EU, the EU authorized representative is:

Springer Nature Customer Service Center GmbH
Europaplatz 3
69115 Heidelberg, Germany

Batch number: 10725825

Printed by Printforce, the Netherlands